Counsellor Competencies

Bernd-Joachim Ertelt • William E. Schulz •
Andreas Frey

Counsellor Competencies

Developing Counselling Skills for Education, Career and Occupation

Springer

Bernd-Joachim Ertelt
University of Applied Labour Studies
Mannheim, Germany

William E. Schulz
University of Manitoba
Winnipeg, MB, Canada

Andreas Frey
University of Applied Labour Studies
Mannheim, Germany

ISBN 978-3-030-87412-4 ISBN 978-3-030-87413-1 (eBook)
https://doi.org/10.1007/978-3-030-87413-1

This Springer imprint is published by the registered company Springer Nature Switzerland AG.
The registered company address is: Gewerbestrasse 11, 6330 Cham, Switzerland

Preface

This book by ERTELT, SCHULZ and FREY provides an opportunity to reflect in depth on counselling competencies in view of the current challenges and the emerging changes in the counselling landscape.

It is not only about the description of counsellor competencies, but mainly about the linkage of competencies to well-researched counselling theories for the various fields of counselling. It is our hope that these counselling competencies will be absorbed and implemented in research studies and in active counsellor practice.

Looking at the competence profiles for counsellors and the many characteristics for good counselling that have emerged on a national and international level in the last decade alone, the critical question thus becomes the transfer of differing counselling orientations and counsellor qualifications with counsellor practice. It also seems to us that the expanding experiential knowledge and the "personal theories" of counsellors have not been sufficiently included in professional discussions and writings.

Against this background, publications on guidance competencies are to be evaluated by the extent to which they result in neither an unsystematic eclecticism nor an orientation towards newly-formulated, unresearched fashionable concepts and models.

The authors of this work have decades of experience on the importance of counsellor qualifications and on application-oriented counselling research at both national and international levels.

This focus on application-oriented counselling is evident both in the exemplary selection of operational counselling approaches and in the comprehensible presentation of even complex counselling issues. We would like to emphasise that the theoretical backgrounds to the development of the selected theories (which are explained briefly for each model), contribute significantly to their transferability into individual counsellor practice, be it in education, career or vocational counselling. To help develop individual counsellor competencies, carefully elaborated, specific exercises have been developed for each counselling model.

We are aware, however, that the choice of approaches discussed in this book is not entirely free from the selectivity of perception and subjectivity of evaluation.

Allen E. IVEY's Microcounselling model has not lost any of its importance for the cross-methodological foundation of counselling and is currently gaining in importance in its multicultural formulation. The conflict-free combination of non-directive and directive counselling methods is remarkable.

The popularity of Gerard EGAN's approach to Problem Management, which has continued unabated for over 35 years, is reflected in the latest edition of The Skilled Helper (2018), which has been revised specifically for Europe, South Africa, and the Middle East. It should be noted, however, that the procedures and skills described therein refer to both therapeutic and non-therapeutic counselling settings. These factors should always be considered critically when transferred to educational and vocational counselling. The present volume by ERTELT, SCHULZ and FREY also offers excellent support for making appropriate adjustments for education and career counselling.

This critical view of the transferability of methods is also appropriate with regard to Solution-Oriented Brief counselling. In this approach, it is important to avoid some misunderstandings, such as the possibility of saving time and increasing efficiency, but possibly losing effectiveness.

The Information Structural Methodology (ISM) developed by ERTELT and SCHULZ in close connection with the study programme for vocational guidance at the University of Applied Labour Studies of the Federal Employment Agency in Germany (HdBA)—including international approaches and independent research—deserves special attention.

In the characteristics of this behaviourist-oriented approach, which include the analysis of cognitive-emotional information structures in heuristic decision-making behaviour, we see innovative application possibilities both in information management and in individual counselling in education, career choice, career development, further education, and job placement. Increasing digitalisation tends to strengthen supply-oriented information and guidance services with a potential oversupply of data. It seems, therefore, very appropriate to focus on the phenomenon of bounded rationality (in the sense of Herbert SIMON) in individual decision-making and problem-solving processes.

We have further strengthened the application reference to education, career and occupation with the concluding chapter on Competence-Oriented counselling. The focus is on the concept of transferable competences according to FREY, which is of particular importance for career guidance and guidance-based placement. We see opportunities and challenges in the inclusion of Artificial Intelligence (AI) to support the guidance and counselling process.

From the perspective of university didactics, the extensive exercise sections should also contribute effectively to the development of counselling competencies because the exercises are derived directly from the respective theoretical backgrounds. These exercises designed to build counsellor competencies can also lead to expanded self-reflection and further development of subjective, action-relevant theories.

As in our previous books, the intention is to select and present counselling approaches and practices in such a way that they can contribute to an independent professional understanding of counselling that meets recognised standards. That is why we have included many additional exercises. However, we know very well that methods must never become an end in themselves but must always be measured by the contribution they can make to problem-solving in the counselling process. Counselling must bring progress!

We understand the respective framework conditions and target groups differ in counselling practice and therefore require situation-specific adaptations. We see particular challenges here in the multicultural field. Also, the boundaries between therapeutic and non-therapeutic areas of application are not always clear-cut, as we can see from the many differences among those coming from a career or education perspective.

Therefore, we see counselling competence as a constant process of research-based examination of our own counselling practice. Collegial interaction with other counselling professionals and ongoing studies in research and teaching is of vital importance.

Mannheim, Germany — Bernd-Joachim Ertelt
Winnipeg, Canada — William E. Schulz
Mannheim, Germany — Andreas Frey

Contents

About the Authors

Bernd-Joachim Ertelt, Ph. D. is a Professor of Vocational and Business Education at the University of Applied Labour Studies of the Federal Employment Agency, Mannheim/Germany, at the University of Czestochowa/Poland (UJD), and (until 2020) at the Catholic University of Lublin/Poland (KUL). He works also as a lecturer at the University of Mannheim. Since 2018, he is visiting Professor at the National University of Mongolia (NUM). Furthermore Prof. Ertelt has since 1972 been involved in the development and implementation of academic qualifications programmes for professional counsellors at home and abroad. He has published numerous articles on counselling and education and has participated in many international and European projects related to counselling and educational guidance.

William E. Schulz, Ph. D. is Professor Emeritus at the University of Manitoba/Canada. Since 1971, he has conducted many research projects on counselling and created a series of training programmes for counsellors at Human Resources Development, Canada. Professor Schulz has contributed significantly to the development of counselling ethics in Canada and other countries. He has been a co-editor of professional journals and is the author of numerous publications on counselling methodology and ethics at national and international levels. He has been an expert in training programmes for educational and vocational guidance in various countries. He recently received the Manitoba Career Development Award of Excellence for Lifetime Achievement in Career Development, renamed in his honour.

Andreas Frey is **a** Professor of Vocational and Business Education at the University of Applied Labour Studies of the Federal Employment Agency at Mannheim/Germany, Visiting Professor at the University of Czestochowa/Poland, and at the Swiss Federal University of Vocational Education at Zollikofen/Swiss. He is a co-editor of professional journals and is the author of numerous publications on diagnostic, education, and competence development at national and international levels. He has received various national awards for his research achievements.

Chapter 1
Main Trends in Counselling

We have been teaching courses on counselling theories for nearly five decades and we are still amazed at how new theories keep emerging and are the focus of interest for a while and then sink back into insignificance. One reason for this may be the glaring lack of systematic European studies on the effectiveness of guidance approaches, especially in the field of educational and career guidance (cf. Hofer, 1997, 2015, cf. also Grawe et al., 2001).

At the 1999 conference of the American Counselling Association, new theories were again added to the more than 250 (cf. Ivey et al., 2002, p. 97), including "impact therapy", "filial therapy" and "floral therapy", which are now available to practitioners in the therapeutic and non-therapeutic fields.

Those approaches that continue to exert the greatest influence and have spawned a number of offshoots are what Allen E. Ivey calls the "three forces of guidance":

1. The psychodynamic theory
2. The cognitive-behavioural theory
3. The existential-humanist theory

1.1 The First Force: Psychodynamic Theory

This approach has influenced many theorists. For example, not only was the work of Alfred Adler, Erik Erikson and Carl G. Jung influenced by Freud's theory of psychoanalysis but to some extent also that of Fritz Perls (Gestalt Therapy), Eric Berne (Transactional Analysis) and Bandler and Grinder (Neurolinguistic Programming).

Updated translation of chapter 1 from: Handbuch Beratungskompetenz, 4th ed. by Bernd-Joachim Ertelt & William E. Schulz, 2019, Springer Verlag.

B.-J. Ertelt et al., *Counsellor Competencies*,
https://doi.org/10.1007/978-3-030-87413-1_1

Psychodynamic counselling focuses on the unconscious processes that influence clients' behaviour. It is an "uncovering" therapy insofar as the past is analysed to find out how it affects the clients' present behaviour.

Ivey et al. (1997, p. 210) have defined the main aspects of psychodynamic therapy as follows:

1. Childhood experiences are important, and to fully understand a client you need their full developmental history.
2. An important part of the developmental history is the people with whom the clients have mainly dealt.
3. Clients know nothing about the influence of the unconscious on their needs, nor about the determination of present behaviour by their past.
4. Accordingly, clients are strongly influenced in their lives by forces outside of awareness.
5. Psychodynamic counselling is designed to help clients find out how their past affects the present.

Some of the main techniques and strategies of psychodynamic counselling have enriched counselling enormously. Free association encourages clients to say whatever comes to mind, in an attempt to help clients, find underlying factors below their level of consciousness. In psychodynamic counselling, counsellor and client rely heavily on interpretation. This requires a great deal of counsellors skills if they are to help clients attach greater meaning to their needs, desires, aspirations, and patterns of behaviour that stem from unconscious motivations. Another main strategy of psychodynamic counselling is dream interpretation, often paired with free association.

Psychoanalytic theories have been repeatedly shown to have scientific credibility. Fisher and Greenberg (1977) compiled and contrasted over 2000 research papers on psychoanalysis; they concluded that much of it supported Freud's general theory of subconscious motivation. Freud was instrumental in helping therapists and counsellors to better understand the meaning of ego defence reactions, resistance to counselling, transference, and past events. The psychoanalytic approach contributed immeasurably to a better understanding of the role of early childhood experience in clients' later problems and possible resulting stress. "Speech" therapy, introduced by Freud, is now found in every major counselling model.

But one of the main disadvantages of psychoanalytic counselling and therapy is that analysing takes a lot of time. Similarly, many psychoanalytic ideas (penis envy, Oedipus complex, castration anxiety, to name but a few) can be problematic for counsellor and client alike. However, the psychoanalytic model is still useful for understanding early childhood experiences as well as human behaviour as a whole. Freud and his students developed concepts that look at the human being from a social, biological and psychological perspective.

1.2 The Second Force: Cognitive-Behavioural Theory

While in the 1960s and 1970s the Person-Centred counselling approach of Carl Rogers was the preferred counselling theory, in the 1990's Cognitive-Behavioural counselling became the preferred counselling approach. In the 1960s and 1970s, Behavioural counselling and Cognitive counselling were still clearly separated from each other in terms of approach, but in the last two decades, the two approaches have moved towards each other in a significant way. The widely used approaches of Albert Ellis (Rational-Emotive Behavioural Counselling), Aaron Beck (Cognitive Therapy), William Glasser (Reality Therapy) and Arnold Lazarus (Multidimensional Counselling) are more cognitively oriented, but the more behaviourally oriented approaches of Joseph Wolpe, Albert Bandura, John Krumboltz and others continue to influence the work of many counsellors.

Behavioural counselling first developed in the USA, where an optimistic, fast-paced, forward-looking scientific and "what works" approach to counselling was readily accepted.

Ellis (1973, 1980, 1987, 1992, 2004), Meichenbaum (1985, 1991, 1994) and Beck (1987, 1991, 1993) were prominent theorists who helped to ensure that behavioural counselling gradually shifted its focus in the cognitive-behaviourist direction. Although William Glasser downplayed the importance of this theory for years (when control theory did not yet exist), he should be included among the names mentioned above as one who advanced cognitive behavioural counselling. All these authors emphasised that people should be helped to change their thinking or cognitions and that this changed thinking should be followed by changed behaviour.

According to Rational-Emotive Behaviour Therapy, everyone has an innate potential to think rationally and irrationally, with these ways of thinking affecting emotion and behaviour (Fig. 1.1).

The counsellor's task is to examine critically the client's irrational beliefs (dispute, D). Ellis (1980) described the main mechanisms of rational-emotive behaviour therapy (REBT) by showing how three main irrational beliefs stir up emotions:

1. I must perform well and gain recognition for it; otherwise, I am considered a failed person.
2. Others must treat me just as considerately and kindly as I expect them to; if they do not, the social environment should blame them, condemn them, and punish them for their inconsideration.

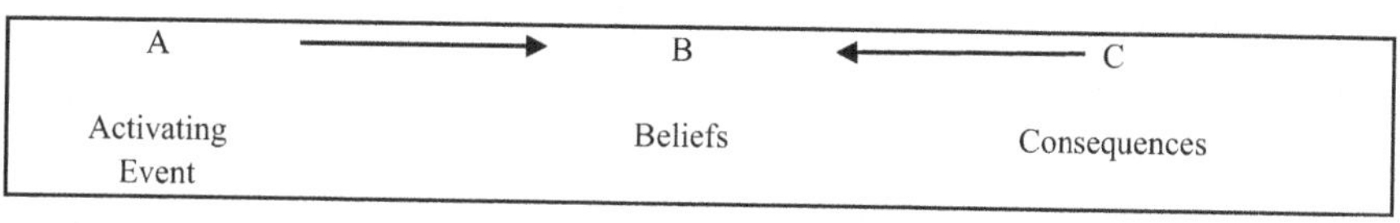

Fig. 1.1 ABC model according to Ellis

3. The conditions under which I live must be designed in such a way that I can get practically everything I want conveniently, quickly, and easily and do not actually have to accept anything I do not want.

These irrational beliefs lead to very unproductive feelings and attitudes:

1. Worthlessness ("I am worthless if I don't perform as well and gain as much recognition for it as I need to").
2. Dramatising ("It's terrible, awful or horrible that I don't perform as required").
3. "I-can't-stop-it" behaviour ("I can't stand what is happening to me and shouldn't be happening").

The following example will illustrate this approach.

Example
Julia is constantly in turmoil because of her relationships with her circle of friends.

One day she came to class complaining that her "best friend" had not sat next to her at lunch (A—triggering event) and expressed her anger and annoyance about it (C—emotional consequence). Julia assumed that if her friend did not sit with her, it must mean that her friend did not like her anymore, that she (Julia) wouldn't know anyone and would never get friends again (B—irrational beliefs). In addition, Julia demanded that her friend behaves in a very specific way, saying that otherwise it would be terrible. To help Julia deal with this problem, Ellis would encourage her to fight these irrational beliefs through disputation (D). He could ask her questions such as the following to help her frame the problem and be less upset and angry:

1. Just because your girlfriend sat with someone else, does that necessarily mean she does not like you anymore or that she will never be your best friend again?
2. Is there a law that says she cannot sit with others just because you are friends?
3. Why does the fact that it sat with someone else mean you are no good?
4. Suppose she is sitting with someone else again tomorrow. What will you choose? Will you walk around feeling miserable, or will you find someone else to sit with?
5. If you cannot determine what your girlfriend does, what can you determine?

Like Ellis, Meichenbaum added a cognitive component to counselling. Meichenbaum's model, often described as a *cognitive behavioural modification*, aims primarily to help clients modify their verbal self-descriptions through cognitive restructuring.

Self-instructional training has been used successfully by Meichenbaum and others for decades. This technique encourages clients to keep track of their self-expressions and replace them with more appropriate expressions. Clients are encouraged to practice these expressions as homework in stress-free situations.

In *stress immunisation*, Meichenbaum (1985) tries to combine Socratic questioning, instruction, restructuring, problem-solving, relaxation training, presentation of one's imagination, reinforcement, environmental change, and self-monitoring. This stress immunisation consists of three phases:

- Acquisition of skills
- Testing
- Application and permanent use

Like Beck, Meichenbaum sees counselling sessions with clients as cooperative and warm; acceptance and understanding are important dimensions. After an analysis of the problem situations under consideration, the skill acquisition and testing phases are designed to help clients learn and implement specific coping techniques. The main objective of the application and implementation phase is to ensure that clients practice the skills learned in the interview, making extensive use of role-plays and simulations to practise coping techniques.

Aaron Beck's Cognitive model of therapy (very similar to Albert Ellis' model) emphasises the importance of belief systems in determining what people feel and do. Beck (1987) focuses on understanding maladaptive beliefs and uses a wide range of techniques to correct maladaptive thinking. Beck also addresses thoughts of which his clients may not be aware and important belief systems of clients, which he calls cognitive schemas. He distinguishes two basic types of cognitive schemas: positive (adaptive) and negative (poorly adaptive). These schemas give space to distortions. Common biases include:

- *Dichotomous thinking* (all or nothing)
  "If I don't get an A, I've failed."
- *Selective abstraction*
  Selective focus on one-off failures instead of the many successes
- *Arbitrary inference* (impulsive conclusions)
- Know what someone else is thinking or that something bad is about to happen.
- *Building up to a catastrophe*
- Such exaggeration of an event until fear arises.
- *Enlargement or reduction*
  when small imperfections appear enlarged, and pluses appear diminished.
- *Over-generalisations*
  Establish a rule based on one or two negative events.
- *Labelling*
  develop an inappropriate sense of self (extreme generalisation) ("I have no friends, I'm a total failure!").
- *Personalisation*
  Personalise an unrelated event and give it too much importance ("Whenever I'm on my way to a job interview, there's so much traffic jam!").

If cognitive distortions are frequent, anxiety, depression or other disorders may occur.

Beck (1987) places greater emphasis on the client-counsellor relationship than counsellors using the rational-emotive method. He sees this relationship as a collaboration: in the first session, time is taken not only to assess the problem but also to build a collaborative partnership. This is done through guided analysis (Socratic dialogue), which is designed to help clients examine their cognitive distortions. In addition to guided analysis, the counsellor uses three key questions in cognitive counselling to help clients examine their negative thinking:

1. Where is the proof of your conviction?
2. How can you interpret this event differently?
3. If this is true, what is the impact?

Homework is an important part of cognitive counselling. After each session, there is specific homework that is reviewed in the next session.

The last of the four cognitive-behavioural models mentioned is Glasser's Reality Therapy. Like Ellis, Meichenbaum and Beck, Glasser has done a great deal for the further development of Cognitive-Behavioural counselling. Glasser emphasises that people are responsible for their own behaviour. To explain individual motivation, he expanded Powers' (1973) control system theory and developed a system of five needs. These needs are: Possession, Recognition, Fun, Freedom and Survival. According to Glasser (1984, 1998), these needs serve as motivators for all behaviour.

The contributions of Cognitive-Behavioural approaches to counselling were considerable. *Action* was placed at the centre. Homework assignments were designed to get clients to practise new behaviours. Many new and different techniques were formulated and tested with clients, successfully practised. Moreover, the representatives of this Cognitive-Behavioural direction have done much to demythologise the whole counselling process. They use an educational model that promotes not only the working atmosphere between counsellor and client but also the client's self-help.

1.3 The Third Force: Existential-Humanistic Approach

Ivey et al. (1997) refer to the existential-humanistic theories as the third force in counselling. These theories usually include life counselling, logotherapy, formative therapy and especially person-centred counselling. The person-centred approach of Carl Rogers had the greatest influence on a changed view of counselling, as this theory was not only a system of counselling but a "state of mind on the *human condition*" (Ivey et al., 1997, p. 350). In this view, a relationship between two equal partners prevails in counselling. The equivalence of both is a necessary and sufficient condition for the client's change and positive development. Rogers (1977) believed that the goal of counselling was not simply to solve problems. The goal, he said, was to enable clients to develop in such a way that they could cope with present and future problems.

According to Person-Centred counselling, it is important to create a trusting, warm, empathic counselling atmosphere. Rogers (1987, p. 39) considers the following six conditions necessary to achieve such a personality change:

1. Two people are in psychological contact.
2. The client feels incongruence.
3. The counsellor is congruent or integrated in the relationship.
4. The counsellor feels unconditional positive regard, respect or empathetic acceptance towards the client.
5. The counsellor feels empathic understanding of the client's inner frame of reference and strives to communicate this perception to the client.
6. The mediation of unconditional positive attention is achieved by the counsellor.

Since Ivey's refined skills of attentive listening, paraphrasing and reflection of feelings are based on the counselling variables of respect, empathy, and sincerity that counsellors express, further exploration of these concepts is warranted.

1.4 Respect for the Other

Respect or unconditional positive regard and compassionate acceptance refer to behaviour where the counsellor does not judge or otherwise evaluate clients but accepts them as they are. The following example shows the difference between high and low respect.

Example
One employee says to another, "If I had done what I thought was best instead of listening to the plant manager, my foreman wouldn't be so furious with me now".

Non-respectful reactions:

"What did you do?"
"Who is your foreman?"
"If you think you're in trouble, let me tell you what my supervisor got me into the other day."

Respectful reactions:

"This is very unpleasant. Would you like to talk to me about it?"
"By not following your own good judgement, you got into trouble. But what else could you have done?"

1.5 Empathy

In Person-Centred counselling, the counsellor tries to "slip into the client's skin", but without ever forgetting that it is just as if "I were in his skin". In this way, an objective relationship is maintained. If counsellors can grasp the private inner world of clients, then change and growth are quite possible. The following example tries to explain the difference between real empathy and little or no empathy:

Example
"Since I started high school, I've been looking forward to graduating and getting a job, and now it looks like I won't be able to find a job when I graduate. There is very high unemployment, I'll never get a job!"

Low empathic reactions:

"Sure, it's not easy to get work."
"I know how you feel."
"Part-time work would perhaps bring in enough money to meet your needs."

Highly empathic reactions:

"You're really disappointed that you can't find a job right after you finish high school."
"You think you will never find a job because of high unemployment, and that is very annoying."

Research has repeatedly shown the importance of the relational level in counselling. Lambert and Bergin (1994) examined several dimensions of counselling and summarised their findings as follows:

> Interpersonal, social, and affective factors common to all therapies still appear as the great stimulators of patient improvement. Not surprisingly, helping people deal with depression, inadequacies, anxiety, and inner conflict, as well as helping them build sustainable relationships and make sense of life, is much easier to accomplish in a therapeutic relationship characterised by trust, warmth, acceptance, and human wisdom (p. 181).

1.6 Authenticity (Congruence)

Authenticity in the counsellor's behaviour is of crucial importance for every counselling activity and plays an important role in multicultural counselling. Authenticity means, above all, that the counsellor does not play a role, but remains himself in the relationship with the client. The counsellor's behaviour has a clear effect on the client. The following example illustrates levels of authenticity:

Example
A teacher is nervous because a group of parents wants to visit her class, which is often restless. A pupil says to the teacher: "Mrs Heinrich, aren't you a bit nervous about our parents inspecting our class this morning?"

Non-genuine reactions:

"If you embarrass me in front of the parents, you'll be sorry."
"Teachers are used to this kind of thing."

Sincere reactions:

"Yeah, I have a few jitters."
"Yes, I am excited. I know I need your cooperation to make a good impression on your parents."

Ivey adopted these counselling attitudes from Rogers in his inclusive, multicultural approach. Attentive listening and understanding how clients perceive events are an important part of Multicultural counselling. The humanistic relational aspects of Person-centred counselling shed light on human relationships and the importance of listening more than any other model.

Corey (2001, p. 187 f.) listed the contributions of Humanistic psychology and especially of Carl Rogers' Person-centred approach: his work was used in over 30 countries, his writings were translated into 12 languages. His influence was indeed cross-cultural and his impact global:

1. In many European countries his approach influenced communication, education, and counselling.
2. Japan, Australia, South America, and Mexico have adopted Person-Centred approaches in their counselling.
3. Large workshops were held to try to improve intercultural communication in South Africa, Ireland, Poland, Italy, Japan, Mexico, and many other countries.

References

Beck, A. (1987). Cognitive therapy. In J. Zeig (Ed.), *The evolution of psychotherapy* (pp. 149–178). Brunner/Mazel.

Beck, A. (1991). Cognitive therapy: A 30-year retrospective. *American Psychologist, 46*(4), 368–376.

Beck, A. (1993). Cognitive therapy: Past, present, and future. *Journal of Consulting and Clinical Psychology, 61*(2), 194–198.

Corey, G. (2001). *Theory and practice of counseling and psychotherapy* (6th ed.). Wadsworth & Thomson Learning.

Ellis, A. (1973). *Humanistic psychotherapy: The rational-emotive approach.* Julian Press.

Ellis, A. (1980). Overview of the clinical theory of rational-emotive therapy. In R. Grieger & J. Boyd (Eds.), *Rational-emotive therapy: A skill-based approach* (pp. 1–31). Van Nostrand Reinhold.

Ellis, A. (1987). The evolution of rational-emotive therapy (RET) and cognitive behavior therapy (CBT). In J. Zeig (Ed.), *The evolution of psychotherapy* (pp. 107–132). Brunner/Mazel.

Ellis, A. (1992). Brief therapy: The rational-emotive method. In S. H. Budman, M. F. Hoyt, & S. Friedman (Eds.), *The first session in brief therapy*. Guilford Press.

Ellis, A. (2004). *The road to tolerance: The philosophy of rational emotive behavior therapy.* Prometheus Books.

Fisher, S., & Greenberg, R. (1977). *The scientific credibility of Freud's theories and therapy.* Basic Books.

Glasser, W. (1984). *Control theory.* Harper & Row.

Glasser, W. (1998). *Choice theory.* Harper & Collins.

Grawe, K., Donati, R., & Bernauer, F. (2001). *Psychotherapie im Wandel – Von der Konfession zur Profession* [Psychotherapy in transition – From confession to profession] (5th ed.). Göttingen: Hogrefe.

Hofer, M. (1997). Geleitwort. In B. J. Ertelt und W. E. Schulz (Hrsg.), *Beratung in Bildung und Beruf* [Foreword. In B. J. Ertelt & W. E. Schulz (Eds.), *Guidance in education and work*]. Rosenberger: Leonberg.

Hofer, M. (2015). Theoriebildung im Bereich der Beratung. [Theory building in the field of guidance]. In B. J. Ertelt, A. Frey, & M. Scharpf (Hrsg.), *Berufsberatung als Wissenschaft – Vier Jahrzehnte akademische Ausbildung für Berufsberaterinnen und Berufsberater in Mannheim* (S. 135–144) [Career guidance as a science – Four decades of academic training for career guidance counsellors in Mannheim (pp. 135–144). Hamburg: Kovač.

Ivey, A., Bradford-Ivey, M., & Simek-Morgan, L. (1997). *Counseling and psychotherapy* (4th ed.). Allyn & Bacon.

Ivey, A., D'Andrea, M., Ivey, M., & Simek-Morgan, L. (2002). *Theories of counseling and psychotherapy* (5th ed.). Allyn & Bacon.

Lambert, M., & Bergin, A. (1994). The effectiveness of psychotherapy. In A. Bergin & S. Garfield (Eds.), *Handbook of psychotherapy and behavior change* (4th ed.). Wiley.

Meichenbaum, D. (1985). *Stress inoculation training*. Pergamon Press.

Meichenbaum, D. (1991). Evolution of cognitive-behavior therapy. In J. Zeig (Ed.), *The evolution of psychology II*. Brunner/Mazel.

Meichenbaum, D. (1994). *A clinical handbook/practical therapy manual for assessing and treating adults with Post-Traumatic Disorder (PTSD)*. Institute Press.

Powers, N. (1973). *Behavior; the control of perception*. Aldine.

Rogers, C. (1977). *Carl Rogers on personal power: Inner strength and its revolutionary impact*. Delacorte Press.

Rogers, C. (1987). The underlying theory: Drawn from experiences with individuals and groups. *Counseling and Values, 32*(1), 38–45.

Chapter 2
The Microcounselling Model by Ivey

2.1 Development and Status of the Model

2.1.1 Integration of Theories and Multicultural Counselling

It would go far too far in this chapter to list all of Ivey's contributions to the field of theory integration and multicultural counselling. We have chosen to look at only the five editions of "Counselling and Psychotherapy" (Ivey et al., 1987, 1993, 1997a, 2002; Ivey & Simek-Downing, 1980) in more detail.

But we would also like to refer to the highly recommended ninth edition of Intentional Interviewing—Facilitating Client Development in a Multicultural Society (Ivey et al., 2018).

In their first edition of "Counselling and Psychotherapy", the authors not only emphasise the importance of the counselling interview as a decision-making process, but also touch on the many skills involved in microcounselling. The important question in this book is:

> Which therapeutic procedures should be used for which individual, when and under which conditions?

The idea of a general counselling theory was not new. But because of the wide acceptance of Ivey's microcounselling, his main assumptions about an integrated approach had an immense impact on the way counsellors were trained and educated. The importance of multicultural counselling was also quite evident in Ivey's first edition (Ivey & Simek-Downing, 1980):

> All helping approaches and techniques are ultimately concerned with freeing people to generate the greatest possible number of verbal and non-verbal statements and constructs, thus freeing them for further purposeful action (p. 171).

Updated translation of chapter 2 from: Handbuch Beratungskompetenz, 4th ed. by Bernd-Joachim Ertelt & William E. Schulz, 2019, Springer Verlag.

B.-J. Ertelt et al., *Counsellor Competencies*,
https://doi.org/10.1007/978-3-030-87413-1_2

> In different cultural groups, skills will have different patterns of application. A pattern of use that is appropriate in one culture may be less effective in another (p. 174).

In their second edition in 1987, the authors continued their attempts to unify theories. They examined 13 of the most important counselling theories and defined their general theory or meta-theory as a

> Theory for the purpose of understanding various theories' underlying constructs—especially the search for harmony and connections between and among alternative theories and methods. Applied to counselling and psychotherapy, general theory serves to develop a unified and systematic formulation of skills, theory and practice in the helping process (p. XI).

In this edition, Ivey et al. (1987) emphasised the importance of culture even more: the first chapter is entirely devoted to cultural intentionality. Cultural intentionality means that counsellors must have three main skills:

1. The ability to generate a maximum of thoughts, words, and behaviours to communicate with oneself and others within a given culture.
2. The ability to generate the maximum number of thoughts, words, and behaviours to communicate with a variety of different groups and individuals within and outside that culture.
3. The ability to formulate plans, respond to many opportunities available in a culture and reflect on these responses (p. 10).

In the second edition, the authors also paid more attention to Feminist Therapy, recognising that women in general are more "relational" and men more "linear" thinking.

In the third edition (Ivey et al., 1993), even greater emphasis is placed on multicultural counselling. With multicultural counselling, counsellors appreciate the importance of the impact of family and culture on clients' realities. In short, cultural awareness becomes the foreground rather than the background. Fukuyuama (1990) makes a convincing case that multicultural counselling must do the following:

1. Do not define culture too narrowly and include such aspects as gender, age, race, and ethnicity.
2. Draw attention to the dangers of template thinking.
3. Emphasise the importance of language in counselling.
4. Call for loyalty and pride in all cultures and family ties.
5. Provide information on the processes of socialisation and oppression.
6. Show the importance of gender roles.
7. Help individuals develop their identity within a culture and a sense of self-worth.
8. Facilitate understanding of the individuals' own world view and show how this view is related to family and culture.

Ivey et al. (1993) summarise the main characteristics of Multicultural Counselling as follows:

- Multicultural counselling is both a theory in itself and a general theoretical orientation for all other counselling theories.
- Since most counselling theories have a "male" European-North American basis, there is a need to add a multicultural dimension to counselling theory.
- Feminist counselling and Afrocentric theory have shown that it is possible to develop new counselling theories from a cultural frame of reference.
- Multicultural counselling emphasises that family, group, and cultural interventions are the first step to make sure that counselling is a necessary part of the counselling process.

The fourth edition of Counselling and Psychotherapy (Ivey et al., 1997a) has been supplemented with additional chapters on multicultural counselling that place even greater emphasis on the "culturally intentional" counsellor. A larger section of the book (pp. 131–203) is devoted to integrating multicultural counselling theory (MCT) and practice into a universal approach to counselling. The goal of Ivey et al. (1997a) is,

> ... to free individuals, families, groups, and organizations so that they can generate new ways of thinking, feeling, and acting and thereby live intentionally [...] MCT is not opposition to cognitive-behavioral, psychodynamic, or existential-humanistic approaches but rather seeks to add culture as a centre while respecting older traditions (p. 138).

In this edition there have been a number of further additions; additions which again show that Ivey is ahead of the game when it comes to counselling. Topics, strategies, and techniques from solution-focused brief counselling, family counselling and spirituality have been added and integrated into multicultural counselling.

Since we have included a chapter on solution-focused brief counselling in this book, Ivey's multicultural counselling combined with solution-focused brief counselling seems particularly interesting to us. The focus on finding solutions in solution-focused counselling is enhanced by the greater attention multicultural counselling pays to social and family influences, to establishing an empathic, caring relationship, and to the inclusion of family and multicultural issues.

In the fifth edition of "Theories of Counseling and Psychotherapy" (Ivey et al., 2004), the authors have revised many chapters and especially given more emphasis to multicultural counselling. A new section on family counselling and psychotherapy has also been added. In it, the authors deal with the origins of perspectivity on the family and offer a systemic perspective on this.

In short, Ivey et al. (2004, p. 394) emphasise that every family is strongly influenced by a web of relationships, rules and role expectations from the neighbourhood, the media, work and school.

The systemic guidance models can be classified according to the following orientations:

(a) Historical (authors: Bowen; Ackermann; Sharff)
(b) Interactional/behavioural (authors: Minuchin; Harley; Liberman)
(c) Existential (authors: Whitaker; Napier; Satir)
(d) Ecological/postmodern (authors: Watzlawick; Anderson; Neimeyer)
(e) Integrative (Authors: Brenzlin; Pinsof; Ivey)

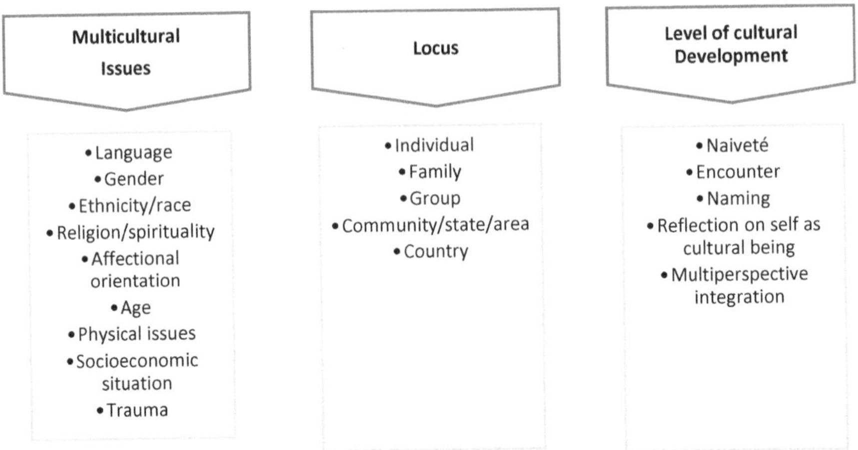

Fig. 2.1 Multicultural dimensions (according to Ivey et al., 2002)

The new edition also contains a range of useful information on using the portfolio method to further develop competences in guidance training. Of particular interest is the model described by Ivey et al. with the acronym RESPECTFUL, which is intended to help guide practitioners further develop their multicultural competences.

R—*religious/spiritual identity*
E—*economic background*
S—*sexual identity*
P—*psychological maturity*
E—*ethnical/racial identity*
C—*chronological/developmental challenges*
T—*various forms of traumata and threats to* well-being
F—*family background and history*
U—*unique physical characteristics*
L—*location of residence and language differences*

Ivey assumes that these ten factors are decisive in many ways for the development and personal well-being of the client (see also the Multicultural Cube according to Ivey et al. (2002), Fig. 2.1).

Finally, the fifth edition also offers a common website (www.ablongman.com/ivey5e) with many links to other subject-related resources, professional organisations, and ethics guidelines.

2.1.2 *Microcounselling and Intentional Counselling*

While Ivey places great emphasis on theory integration and multicultural counselling as a fourth force in the five editions of "Counselling and Psychotherapy", in the six editions of his book "Intentional Interviewing and Counselling" he focuses more on teaching counsellors skills and strategies to facilitate client development.

Even before the first edition in 1983, Ivey had worked extensively on basic techniques of attentive listening and other communication skills, but with this book, he puts together an excellent guidebook. Each chapter of the book deals with a specific skill or set of skills for a counselling interview and is structured as follows:

- Introduction to the skill and an exercise to facilitate understanding of the skill.
- A role-played conversation to demonstrate the skill, followed by more details about the skill.
- A summary of the chapter, practical exercises and self-assessment scales to help the user identify, apply and teach the skill.

In the second edition in 1988, Ivey makes a number of significant changes. For example, the skills are grouped into clearer units.

In the second edition, Ivey devotes a great deal of attention to confrontation skills, including a "Confrontation Effectiveness Scale". The necessity and ability to point out discrepancies, contradictions and mixed expressions of the client is, according to Ivey, a very important aspect of counselling skills.

A second important addition in this edition was the assessment of the client's developmental stage. According to Ivey, it is essential that counsellors adapt their conversational style to the client's developmental stage. Ivey (1988, p. 177) outlines these developmental stages as follows:

Stage 1: Pre-operational

The client is stuck because he has no alternatives or at best a limited range of options.

Stage 2: Concrete operations

The client knows some of the problem points, has certain skills but does not know how to use them. For example, an employee who has been promoted to a new position of which he only partially understands.

Stage 3: Formal operations directed towards the self

The client needs little help from others. For example, an employee who is generally used to working independently works satisfactorily but has difficulty with a particular problem.

Stage 4: Reciprocal or dialectical

The counsellor who lets clients develop their own goals and works with them as equal partners. Feminist counselling, for example, is an approach that aligns with this stage 4.

In the third edition of "Intentional Interviewing and Counselling" (Ivey, 1994), Ivey emphasised the need for multicultural awareness on the part of the counsellor. He went into detail about influencing skills such as logical consequences, directives, giving information and feedback. A section on focusing skills was also added.

In the fourth and fifth editions of Intentional Interviewing and Counselling (Ivey & Bradford-Ivey, 1999, 2002), Ivey described in more detail the six skills of

The Indivisible Self: An Evidenced-Based Model of Wellness (Myers & Sweeney, 2005)	
Creative Self	Thinking, Emotions, Control, Work, Positive Humor
Coping Self	Leisure, Stress Management, Self-Worth, Realistic, Beliefs
Social Self	Friendship, Love
Essential Self	Spirituality, Gender Identity, Cultural Identity, Self-Care
Physical Self	Exercise, Nutrition

Contexts			
Local (safety)	Institutional (policies & laws)	Global (world events)	Chronometrical (lifespan)
Family Neighborhood Community	Education Religion Government Business/Industry	Politics Culture Global Events Environment Media	Perpetual Positive Purposeful

Fig. 2.2 The indivisible self: an empirical model of well-being

counselling influence; namely, reframing, logical consequences, self-revelation, feedback, information and statements, and giving directives. These extensions seem to be particularly valuable for career counsellors, case managers and school counsellors, as they can help the counselee to design new scenarios, in the sense of solution-oriented counselling.

In the sixth edition of their book, Ivey and Ivey (2007) have again added a number of new aspects. Chapter 2 deals with questions of ethics, multicultural competence, and "wellness". By "wellness" Ivey and Ivey (2007, p. 488) understand the orientation towards optimal health and well-being. Body, mind, and soul should be connected in such a way that people can live fulfilled lives. The underlying "wellness" model comes from Sweeney and Myers (2005) and can be characterised as follows (Fig. 2.2).

Other additions in this edition include:

- A guide for the reader to become aware of the meaning and direction of life.
- Recent research in neuropsychology provides evidence that effective counselling not only advances thinking but also contributes to brain development.
- Each chapter begins with a case study and detailed comments on it from national and international experts.
- In Chap. 14 on integrating individual skills, the reader will find a number of suggestions and strategies for conducting initial consultations.

A CD-ROM with video units on reflection of feelings, ethical and multicultural issues complete the new publication by Ivey and Ivey. In another study, Daniels (2007) analysed 450 empirical studies on "micro-skills" (the data is available on the CD-ROM of the sixth edition of Ivey & Ivey, 2007 available). The main conclusions are:

- The counselling skills can be classified extremely reliably. Microcounselling appears to be more effective for training the skills than other forms of mediation.
- In order for the skills to be transferred to the current counselling situation permanent application is required.
- Scientific studies of counsellors, social workers, nurses and similar professionals in Japan, the Netherlands, Sweden, Canada and Africa show the intercultural validity of microcounselling skills.
- The conscious use of these skills in counselling evidently leads to commitment and satisfaction on the part of the client.
- Teaching communication skills to clients can be effective (Ivey & Ivey, 2007, p. 219).

In 2001, John Littrell asked Allen Ivey in an interview what he considered to be his greatest contribution. The answer was (in excerpts): "I think that the 'microskills' are probably remembered. One of the nicest things about it is that terms like 'attentive behaviour' etc., which are used by the counsellor educators to teach 'microskills' have now found their way into the literature and are no longer associated with my name . . ." (p. 118).

2.1.3 Research on Microcounselling

In the 1970s, in the wake of the first edition of "Microcounseling: Innovations in Interviewing Training" by Ivey and Authier (1978), hundreds of papers on microtraining appeared on the book market. Parker (1972) used the method to teach affective understanding and responding to 20 Master's students. Immediately after placement, those who had undergone microcounselling performed significantly better than the comparison group. Shea (1975) used microcounselling to teach future counsellors counselling confronting and growth-oriented behaviours. Data analysis revealed that those who had undergone microcounselling showed improved counselling behaviour in practice by emphasising strengths and by 'encouraging action'. Belle (1976) compared microcounselling with "traditional" attentive listening training. In terms of attention and verbal behaviour, the microcounselling group was significantly better than the comparison group.

Kasford and Gustafson (1978) reviewed the large body of literature on microcounselling. Kerrebrock (1971) trained school counsellors in attentive listening, emotion reflection and emotion expression, and he found that the group trained in microcounselling used the latter two skills much more frequently. Scroggins and Ivey (1976), using the approach with dormitory counsellors, found that they performed significantly better than the comparison group in minimal encouragement, paraphrasing, emotion reflection and summarising.

A number of studies also argued for retention and generalisation of microcounselling skills. Gluckstern (1973) found that trainees trained in microskills retained their skills during a six-month refresher course. Guttmann and Haase (1972) found that counsellors were able to use the skills after microtraining and held on to the emotion reflection and summary skills in actual counselling sessions.

In the first half of the 1980s, Ertelt and Schulz implemented the training program "Microcounseling for counselling support of vocational decision making" into the first academic program for career guidance counsellors in Germany at the University of Applied Labour Studies of the Federal Labour Administration in Mannheim. The students were trained in combining MC-skills with descriptive decision-making models with particular attention to the heuristic behaviour of their clients (Ertelt & Schulz, 1985, p. 169). This was an important step in the development of the "Information-Structural Methodology of Counselling" (see Chap. 5).

In the 1990s, Daniels (1998) and Daniels et al. (1997) provided an additional and comprehensive endorsement of Ivey's approach to counselling training. In addition, Baker and Daniels (1989), Baker et al. (1990) provided reviews of all the literature in the field of microcounselling. Baker and Daniels (1989) meta-analytically reviewed the microcounselling approach. The average effects of 81 accessible studies were calculated and the results showed that the overall positive effects of microcounselling fell into the category of "pronounced effect".

The research findings suggest that the microcounselling approach is very effective in teaching basic communication skills. It is also well established through research that microcounselling is an appropriate way to teach more advanced counselling skills such as self-disclosure, confrontation and reflection on feelings and meanings. Microcounselling training has also led to a stronger integration of skills training into actual counselling practice.

In an extensive interview in the Journal of Counselling and Development (Littrell, 2001), Ivey talked about the influences on his counselling and the many changes in his personal approach to counselling before he developed his microcounselling skills approach. In this interview, Ivey readily admitted that he was initially a very Rogers-oriented Client-Centred or Person-Centred counsellor. But he soon realised that he needed to be much more directive in his approach to vocational and career counselling. Consequently, he adopted the more directional counselling used by Trait-Factor counsellors. In the 1960s and 1970s, the only choice seemed to be between the non-directive (somewhat like Carl Rogers) and the more directive approaches to counselling, or becoming Freudian was an additional choice. Later, Ivey became a convinced behaviourist and abandoned all other approaches. He began to question why he kept switching from one theory to another and realised that all counselling approaches had their value. Thus, he began to develop skills strategies for the cognitive-behavioural models, the relational approaches, and other theoretical directions because he believed that using microskills would help counsellors not only learn counselling skills but also integrate them into specific counselling strategies.

Allen Ivey was a leader in promoting multicultural awareness, knowledge, and skills in the training of counsellors. He recognised the need to explore cultural environments and that microskills differed from culture to culture. This led to the definition of culture-centred skills and their inclusion in the qualification process, as well as to the sensitisation towards communication patterns of ethnic groups, which may be different from those of the counsellors. The latter must be able to help counselees with comprehensive culturally specific concepts, taking into account gender, religion, nationality, economic status, and sexual orientation. Subsequently, Ivey's later writings (Ivey et al., 2009) encouraged counsellors to see counselees in their own cultural context. Ivey notes that professional, multiculturally oriented counsellors are aware of the differences between themselves and their counselees, without trying to make them conform to their own perceptions.

Hansen et al. (2000) drew up a list of minimum multicultural competences for counsellors:

1. Awareness of own cultural heritage (see Exercise 4, Sect. 2.3).
2. Knowing how theories, practices and societal values change over time.
3. Knowledge of prejudice and discrimination in own counselling practice (see Exercise 3, Sect. 2.3).
4. Know how social and political influences (e.g. poverty and stereotyping) affect people's lives.
5. Knowledge of culture-specific diagnostic categories.
6. Knowledge of views regarding illness and counselling needs.
7. Knowledge of culture-specific assessment procedures.
8. Knowledge about family structures, gender roles, values and beliefs of different ethnic groups.
9. Knowing when theoretical orientations need to be adapted.
10. Knowing how to assess one's own multicultural competence.
11. Ability to modify assessment tools.
12. Ability to plan and implement effective treatment plans and interventions without bias (see Exercises 6 and 7, Sect. 2.3).

2.2 Counselling and Intentional Conversation from a Multicultural Perspective

2.2.1 Tenets of Multicultural Counselling

In Chap. 1, we summarised the three counselling forces, namely psychodynamic, cognitive and existential-humanistic. Ivey et al. (1997a) refer to multicultural counselling as the fourth counselling force.

The six key tenets detailed by Ivey et al. (2002, pp. 291–360) are based on the multicultural work of Donald Wing Sue (1995).

1. Multicultural guidance is an integrative metatheory of guidance.
2. Counsellor and client identities are formed within several levels of experience and context. The totality of these experiences and contexts is the focus of counselling.
3. The development of a client's cultural identity is a major determinant of both counsellor and client attitudes towards themselves, others of the same group, members of another group and the dominant group.

4. The effectiveness of counselling increases when the counsellor uses techniques, strategies and goals that are compatible with the client's life experiences and cultural values.
5. Traditional individual counselling is only one of many theoretical techniques and strategies; others involve larger social units, system interventions and prevention.
6. Multicultural counselling emphasises the importance of expanding personal awareness, also regarding family, group, and other structures. It draws on many methods of help from many cultures.

1. *Multicultural guidance as a meta-theory*

   Multicultural guidance is a meta-theoretical approach. It takes into account that all guidance takes place within a cultural context and serves as an integrative framework for all guidance. All counselling theories are developed in a specific cultural context and are shaped by that culture. Multicultural counselling seeks to help clients see their problems from a cultural perspective and find culturally appropriate solutions. Ivey et al. (2002, p. 297) point out that multicultural counselling theory is concerned with cultural intentionality and that the aim of multicultural counselling is to free clients to generate new ways of thinking, feeling, and acting and thereby live purposefully. Multicultural counselling is thus not at all opposed to the first three (psychodynamic, cognitive, and existential-humanistic) counselling forces, but rather seeks to add culture as a central element for all counselling.

   Nwachuku and Ivey (1991) have developed steps that can be helpful in adding cultural references to counselling theory. This three-step process consists of examining a specific culture and identifying important personal and interpersonal characteristics of that culture. Secondly, concrete skills and strategies are extracted from this culture that one might use in the counselling situation. Finally, the new approach or theory and its associated skills and strategies are tested in practice. Exercise 1 in the following section may help to understand culturally relevant theories of helping.
2. *Multi-layered contexts and experiences*

   All experiences and contexts need to be taken into account in multicultural counselling. For example, in many Western counselling theories, counsellors focus almost exclusively on what each individual client can do to help themselves. In other cultures, more balance is needed; for example, the family, the individual and the community need to be considered. The traditional focus on independence and self-reliance may need to be complemented by relationships with others, interdependence, and connectedness.

   Ivey et al. (2002) have given several examples of how to add a multicultural dimension to techniques and strategies of existing theories. The existential-humanistic strategy—active listening and reflection of feelings—can be multiculturally grounded by an additional focus on cultural and relational issues. Comparably, the irrational client beliefs tackled in cognitive-behavioural theory may not be irrational at all when examined from a different cultural perspective.

Multicultural counselling involves paying attention to the different stages of human development. The strategy of life review is very important. Giving meaning to the past in order to help in the present and future is an important part of multicultural counselling. Exercise 2 in the next section will help counsellors to think about clients multiculturally.

3. *Cultural identity*

Multicultural counsellors seek to expand their awareness of cultural issues in themselves and their clients. Perhaps counsellors go through the following four stages cognitively, emotionally, and behaviourally as outlined by Ponterotto (1988):

Stage 1: Before perception

The counsellor has not yet thought about the multicultural implications of counselling and treats all clients the same.

Stage 2: Perception

The counsellor finds himself at the mercy of multicultural problems and is confused by the many implications.

Stage 3: Overeagerness/Defensiveness

Faced with the challenge of multicultural issues, some counsellors become overactive advocates of multiculturalism, while others "creep into a silent defensive posture".

Stage 4: Integration

Counsellors respect cultural differences and can appreciate how personal family and cultural background might affect their counselling.

4. *Culturally appropriate strategies*

This fourth tenet of multicultural counselling is perhaps the most important when related to the intended effects of this unit on Ivey's work; that is, to present his work in such a way that counsellors can begin to use strategies and techniques helpful in multiculturally embedded situations through reading and practical exercises.

Like feminist therapy, multicultural counselling sees both social context and mechanisms of oppression as important. This similarity would suggest complementary counselling strategies, such as storytelling, gender and/or culture-specific analysis, analysis of minority oppression, and informing others about oppression and contextual issues.

For multicultural counselling, the well-known "golden rule" can be rephrased as follows: "Do *not* do to others what you would have them do to you, because they may want something else". An important component of multicultural counselling is therefore the alert awareness of the counsellor; an awareness of the importance of the family and community with many groups and also an awareness of the so-called "multicultural cube" (Ivey et al., 2002, p. 39).

Exercise 5 in the next section is designed to help counsellors assess themselves as multicultural persons for the first time.

5. *Multicultural counselling alternatives*

   In addition to traditional individual counselling, there is a whole range of counselling alternatives. These involve the resources of an extended family, people in the community, spiritual counsellors, authorities, and many(s) others.

   Systems therapy (Attneave, 1969, 1982) is a method of involving not only the individual and family but also society and the social environment. This approach to therapy is in line with the idea of collaboration and the use of different approaches with different clients.

   Another multicultural alternative is *informal counselling*. One form of informal counselling is traditional healing, which is practised in many parts of the world. Achebe (1986) describes the main elements of traditional healing as follows:

   1. The healer invokes the "spirit of the gods" through practices that vary from burning incense to prayer.
   2. The healer proves his powers and explains the healing process.
   3. The client communicates his concern.
   4. The healer diagnoses the problem.
   5. Specific interventions, usually involving the family and/or society, are proposed.

As can be seen from this brief outline of traditional healing, it is certainly not in conflict with the traditional methods of "Western" counselling theories, be they cognitive, psychoanalytical, or existential-humanistic. In more recent times, these western approaches, just like traditional healing, have increasingly included culture, family, and society.

6. *Expansion of consciousness*

   Multicultural counselling emphasises the importance of broadening personal awareness, including of family, groups, and other structures. This means that multicultural counselling is often highly educational as counsellors educate clients about the cultural and social context of their concerns and needs. Sharing stories, either as an individual to a counsellor or in a group setting, is one method of expanding reflective awareness. In a group setting, for example, familiar ideas are shared by group members and gave new meanings to these ideas.

2.2.2 Overview of Counselling Skills

Before multicultural counselling developed, little attention was paid to ethnic and cultural aspects of counselling. While multicultural counselling supports mainstream counselling approaches, it also requires increased attention to cultural aspects.

Before studying Ivey's intentional model of conversation, the counsellor to be trained is asked to assess himself culturally again. The first five exercises in the next section (p. 60) were created for this purpose:

Exercise 1	Counselling Model "RESPECTFUL"
Exercise 2	Generating Culturally Relevant Theory
Exercise 3	Life Stage Review
Exercise 4	Your Personal Cultural Identity
Exercise 5	Developing Multiculturalism

The books by Ivey (1983, 1988, 1994) and those by Ivey et al. (1997b, 1997c), Ivey and Bradford-Ivey (1999), and Ivey et al. (2018) on listening and influencing skills, interviewing and counselling are practical guides to help counsellors learn and practise the skills needed for counselling and apply these skills in multicultural situations.

Ivey and Ivey (2007, p. 439) have summarised the steps of intentional conversation in a diagram (see Fig. 2.3). The base of Ivey's pyramid is the "culturally and individually appropriate" listening behaviour. This behaviour will be the first of the skills examined below. The "basic sequence of listening" will then examine and practise a number of skills: open and closed questions, paraphrasing, encouraging, reflecting on feelings, and summarising.

Next, Ivey and Ivey describe the five stages of a conversation. These five stages are compatible with a number of theoretical approaches, particularly the cognitive approaches. Similar to the problem-solving process of behavioural counselling and

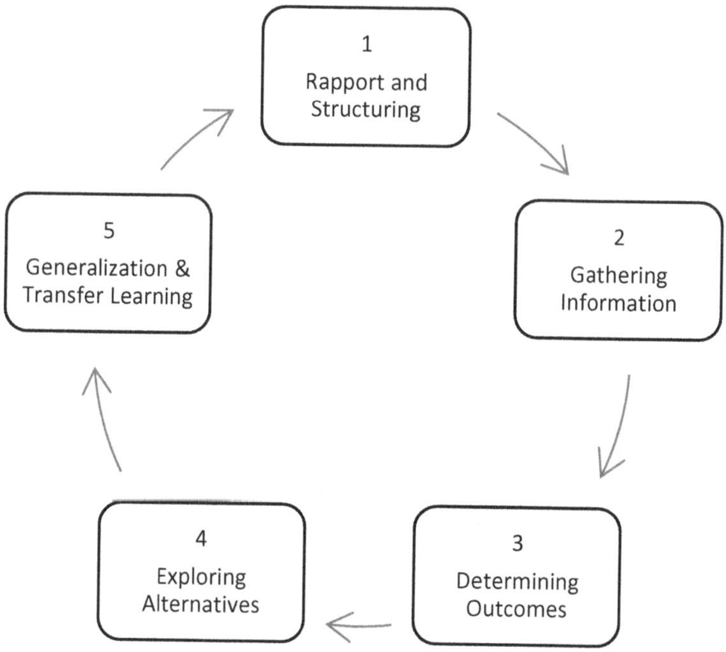

Fig. 2.3 Structured counselling interview according to Ivey

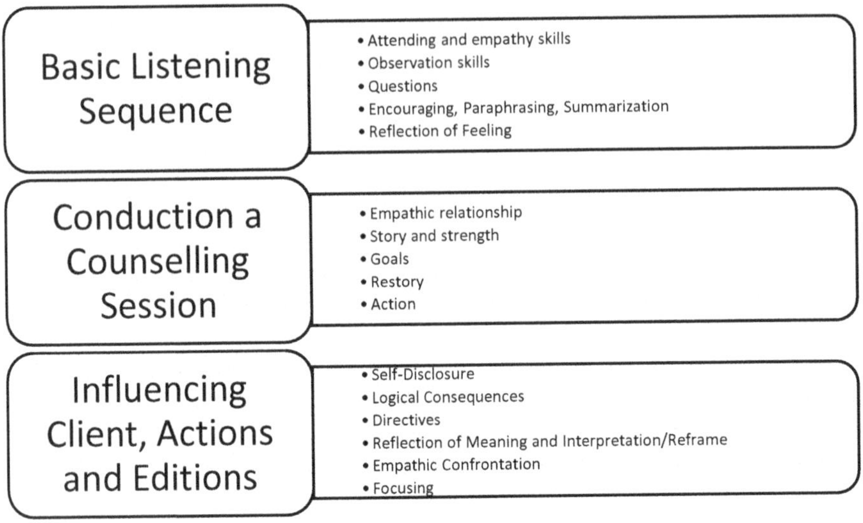

Fig. 2.4 Counselling interview skills (according to Ivey et al., 2018)

the cognitive approaches of Ellis, Meichenbaum, Beck and Glasser, Ivey and Ivey (1999, 2007) elaborate on the following five steps:

1. Build a relationship and structure the conversation.
2. Clearly define the problem.
3. Set a goal.
4. Look for alternatives and address disagreements.
5. Generalise counselling to daily life.

With Fig. 2.4 counsellors can start to assign numerous skills to the different stages. Based on Ivey et al. (2018, p. 12) triangle, the sections of Ivey's schema that are most relevant for career counselling are the following:

At the initial stage of relationship building, open-ended questions, paraphrasing and reflection of feelings are often used to help clients talk about themselves. At the second stage—gathering information and clarifying the problem—counsellors continue to use open-ended questions and paraphrases but make heavy use of encouragement and possibly self-disclosure and end this stage with a summary.

In recording results, many skills from the first two steps are used. The tool of focusing is used as well as additional summarising and encouraging.

At the fourth stage, client and counsellor begin to explore alternatives and confront the client with discrepancies in their statements. The skills often used at this stage are meaning reflection, feedback, information, confrontation and influencing skills and strategies, such as change of perspective, logical consequences, and directives.

At the final stage, the action plan is transferred to everyday life, and counsellors often provide summaries, feedback, and additional information.

Helping change often requires counsellors to have "higher" skills, such as confrontation, focusing and meaning reflection. The next section of the pyramid introduces the skills of influencing, including directives (specific instructions for action) to clients, interpretation and reframing of clients' feelings and behaviours, logical consequences of clients' actions, feedback, informing and giving advice, and self-disclosure by the counsellor.

At the top of the counselling pyramid, counsellors learn to integrate different skills into different theories, and they gradually understand that different theories require different skills, different situations require different types of skills, and different cultures require different patterns of skill use. All this will hopefully lead to counsellors developing their own personal counselling style.

2.2.3 Attentive Behaviour

Counsellors devote themselves to clients in order to encourage them to talk. By addressing them in a culturally appropriate way, counsellors communicate to their clients that they are interested in what the clients are saying. With some attention, counsellors also learn how clients respond and adjust their own attentional behaviour to reflect cultural differences. Ivey and Ivey (1999, 2007) describe the four qualities of attention as follows:

1. *Visual (eye contact).* When you want to talk to people, you should look at them.
2. *Vocal.* The tone of voice and rate of speech of the counsellor should consistently indicate: "I am interested in what you are saying".
3. *Pay attention to what is said.* Follow the client's words and stay on their topic.
4. *Body language.* Counsellors must show expressive facial expressions, lean forward slightly, and look directly at clients.

These are the four expressions of attention that are valued by European-North American clients. However, counsellors need to improve their cultural awareness. Counsellors need to adapt their attention behaviour accordingly with members of other cultures. For example, with careful observation of clients, the counsellor will be more likely to notice that:

(a) Physical touching is more common among the French than in the English.
(b) Europeans and Americans communicate at arm's length, while Arabs prefer a distance of barely 1/2 m when conversing.
(c) A smile indicates discomfort in some situations in Japan.
(d) Eye contact is inappropriate for some indigenous cultures.

One part of the attention behaviour that is sometimes forgotten by counsellors, especially beginners, is *silence.* Sometimes the best help is to say nothing and just be there for the client. Silence pauses should not be too long so as not to unsettle the client, but clients need time to reflect in silence.

Attentive behaviour can also be taught to clients. When clients are taught to be more attentive to others, they focus their attention more on others than on themselves. So, when they are depressed or sad, this focus on being attentive to others can help alleviate their own feelings of dejection and sadness.

Exercise 6 in the next section is designed to help you learn more about yourself and your attention behaviour.

2.2.4 The Basic Sequence of Listening

The basic listening sequence consists of the skills of asking questions, encouraging, paraphrasing, reflecting on feelings and summarising. The skills in this section are designed to give clients an opportunity to share their concerns.

Questions
Open questions are meant to "open up" a conversation and get clients to talk freely and openly. Closed questions lead to shorter answers and are mostly meant to get specific information. Ivey and Ivey (1999) provide a set of key characteristics of open and closed questions:

1. *Questions help to start a conversation.*

   "What would you like to talk about today?"
   "How did your job search go last week?"

2. *Open questions help clients to provide more detailed explanations.*

   "Could you tell me more about what your colleague said?"
   "What else did your boss say?"

3. *Questions help to find out more about the clients' concerns and experiences.*

   "What exactly does your boss do to make you so angry?"
   "Could you give me a specific example?"

4. *Questions are needed for accurate assessment.* The questions of who, what, when, where how and why provide the counsellor with a procedure to make a more accurate assessment.

   "When did your problems with colleagues start?"
   "How did they behave towards you?"

5. *In open questions, the first word sometimes determines the direction of the answer.*

   What-questions lead to facts:

   "What are you going to do?"

   How-questions can lead to the discussion of processes and feelings:

"What do you think about it?"

Why questions are used to discuss reasons:

"Why do you think this happened?" What-questions are the most open:

"Could you give me a specific example?"

6. *Questions can be used excessively and incorrectly.* Too many questions or too many closed questions are asked.

   Why questions that put clients on the defensive.
   Steering the conversation through questions. Some cultures do not respond positively to someone who asks a lot of questions.

7. *Questions to help clients find plus points.*
   Remarkably similar to solution-focused brief counselling, Ivey also recommends questions to help clients see their strengths. Clients are given feedback on the challenge of strengths and asked about exceptions to the rule so that clients can more easily see exceptions to their problems and needs.
8. *Questions to evaluate the ongoing conversation.* You can use questions to set the pace of a conversation, open questions to get clients to say more, and closed questions to narrow the focus of the conversation.

Practical exercises on the questioning technique are provided by Exercise 7 in the next section.

Encourage

It is important that clients feel the empathy of the counsellor to be understood from their own point of view. The skills of encouraging, paraphrasing, reflecting feelings and summarising can be helpful in this regard.

Open gestures, head nods and positive facial expressions encourage clients to keep talking. Comments like "hmm" or "ah-ah" and repetition of keywords also serve as encouragement. For example, a client says: "I am so angry about what my foreman did". To which the counsellor simply says, "Angry?" This repetition of the keyword helps steer the conversation or get to the point. Similar to the repetition of keywords is the rephrased rendition of what the client said: "You got angry with your foreman". Rephrased renditions also serve to encourage the client.

Paraphrase

Ivey and Ivey (2007, p. 161) describe the goal of paraphrasing as the "facilitated client exploration and clarification of problem issues". Simple paraphrases are almost like rephrased renditions or repetition of keywords. However, when clients have complex problems, it is much more difficult to accurately relate the ideas and perceptions they have expressed to the client.

Ivey and Ivey (2007, p. 161) comment on some essential dimensions of good paraphrases:

1. If a sensory hook is necessary, use as much as possible the way the client takes in information.

   Visual—"It looks like you are saying …".
   Kinesthetic—"So the situation touches you like …" Auditory—"It sounds like …"

2. The client's keywords and ideas are expressed in a condensed form.
   Client: "I was offered a job in another city. I like the city and I would earn quite a bit more money. But my wife and children have no interest at all in moving away. I have this great job offer, but no one is really happy about it." Counsellor: "You're really excited about the new job offer you got, but there are a few other points you need to consider".
3. The paraphrase is checked for accuracy. Usually, this check is done by a short question at the end of the paraphrase.

   "Did I understand you correctly there?"
   "Is that about it?"

   Usually, the reaction tells the counsellor whether he or she has paraphrased accurately or not (see Exercise 8 in the next section).

Reflection of the Feelings
While paraphrases are mainly concerned with the content of the client's statements, emotional reflections are concerned with the client's emotions. All the elementary skills of listening, questioning, encouraging, paraphrasing, reflecting on feelings and summarising are used to make the client understand that they are being listened to and understood (empathy). Feeling reflections come very close to the essence of empathy, as good reflections of feeling make (sometimes hidden) emotions clear to the client.

Not all emotions need to be addressed, and not all emotions are explored in detail. Through attentive listening, counsellors will notice when to explore the emotions a client expresses in a little more detail, when simply taking note of the emotions is appropriate, and when to keep emotions in mind for possible discussion later.

Exercise 9 in the next section is designed to teach counsellors the techniques of reflecting on feelings. Ivey and Ivey (2007, p. 194) provide the following overview of the emotion reflection technique:

1. Similar to paraphrase, a (visual, auditory, kinaesthetic) sentence stem is used.
2. The stem is followed by a short paraphrase with an emotional word.
   "Jonathan, you seem upset about your appointment with the boss last week."
3. Try to reflect in the present tense. "You are still angry about what happened when …"
4. Perhaps you still need to clarify whether the reflection of feelings is appropriate.

Summary

Summaries are long paraphrases. Summaries can recapitulate an entire conversation or even key elements from several conversations. Here are some examples of summaries:

At the beginning of the conversation

The last time we met, we talked about all the problems you had with the foreman of your construction crew. Today you say things are going much better. We talked about one thing you could try, which is to ignore what the boss says negatively. How did that go?

At the end of a conversation

Today we started by talking about how your plan to ignore the negative comments from your foreman didn't work as well as you had hoped. After that we discussed some other strategies and after going through each one you decided that you ....

(see Exercises 9 and 10 in the next section)

2.2.5 The Five-Step Conversation Structure

The skills in the basic listening sequence should help counsellors to encourage clients to describe their situation—the main problems, the essential facts and how they are affected by them. As a next step, Ivey and Ivey (1999) suggest using a problem-solving approach that includes the following five stages:

1. Relationship and structuring.
2. Gather information, define the problem, and identify strengths.
3. Set goals.
4. Identify alternatives and point out possible contradictions to the client.
5. Generalisation and transfer of what has been learned to everyday life.

1. *Relationship and structuring*

   Like most counselling theories, Ivey's model starts with establishing a relationship with the client. The relationship-building skills of paying attention to the client, calling the client by name from time to time, and carefully observing the client's behaviour are among the most important skills. Then the counsellor asks:

   "Could you tell me how I can help you?" Structuring is the second stage of this first phase, and it involves informing clients of the intended effects and general procedures of a conversation and letting them know what they can hope to gain from it.

   Since the first part of the conversation sets the tone for all the subsequent work between counsellor and client, it is very important that the counsellor is attentive to multicultural sensitivities. Some cultural groups expect a long period of relationship building, others require a very formal approach, while still others expect a lot of structuring from the counsellor.

2. *Collect information*

   The second phase of Ivey's approach is also similar to many other counselling models, as in this phase clients are encouraged to tell their story and explain why they have come for counselling and what their problem is.

   All the skills of the basic listening sequence—open and closed questions, paraphrasing, encouragement, and summarising—are used by the counsellor to encourage clients to tell their story in detail.

   Ivey and Ivey (2007, p. 231) point out two multicultural considerations here. First, some clients may prefer the counsellor to use words such as "challenge", "story" or "question" rather than "problem". Secondly, some clients might prefer to establish clear goals (level three) before they are willing to "tell their story".
3. *Set goals*

   What does the client want? What are the client's goals? This question is especially important in career counselling, where many clients come to the counsellor with vague, fuzzy concerns. In solution-focused brief counselling (Chap. 4), the focus is almost exclusively on steps to achieve the goal, and little or no attention is paid to phase two, where the client is supposed to tell his story or provide information to the counsellor.

   Once the goal and desired outcome are clearly stated, it is easier for the counsellor to address the specific issues. For example, in the case of upcoming professional decisions, a counsellor might say:

   > You are just telling me that you would love to be a teacher, but you don't know if you can handle the scientific work, nor if you can afford a four-year teacher training course . . . But you also mention that you really like working with children and that your family is willing to support you financially in some way . . .

4. Identify alternatives and point out contradictions

   This next phase is known in many counselling approaches as the handling phase. The purpose of this phase is to help clients find solutions or help for their problems or needs. This is typically done by way of problem-solving, i.e. the concern and the goal are defined, alternative solutions are generated and specific action is decided. Useful questions in this phase could be:

   > "What alternatives are open to you?"
   > "What has worked well for you in the past?"
   > "Which of these alternatives would you like to try first?"
   > "What are the strengths and disadvantages of this action plan?"

5. Generalisation and transfer of learning to everyday life

   Sometimes the most difficult part of counselling is to motivate clients to find new ways of dealing with their problems or concerns. Clients will not automatically transfer what they have learned to their real situation once they have left counselling. To facilitate this transfer of learning, one or more of the following techniques can be used to advantage:

   (a) Roleplays
   (b) Specific homework assignments

(c) Keeping a record of behaviour
(d) Aftercare

(See Exercise 14 in the next section).

2.2.6 *Three Skills that Guide Action*

The skills of confrontation, focusing and meaning reflection are good for helping clients to move into the action phase.

Confrontation (see Exercise 15)
The word "confrontation" often has a negative connotation, many prefer the word "challenge". Confrontation can be made less harsh if counsellors consciously ask clients to challenge inconsistencies, discrepancies or "mixed messages" in their behaviour, feelings, and thoughts. It must be made clear that the confrontation is not directed against the client.

The aim of confrontation is to make clients change as desired and realise their full potential. However, caution is advised. Some cultures do not tolerate even a mild form of confrontation. On the other hand, other clients respond very well to direct confrontation with energetic, positive, and helpful responses. The first part of confrontation involves identifying mixed messages, inconsistencies and discrepancies, e.g. the job seeker who claims to be a very hard worker but puts little or no "work" into finding a job. Or the employee who says that everything is going great at work but obviously has no friends at work.

What is the best way to address contradictory behaviour in a gentle and helpful way?

- Perhaps a simple question will make clients aware of their problems: "How do you reconcile both?"
- Summarising the discrepancies or mixed messages can provide clients with useful specific, non-judgmental facts:
  "On the one hand, I see that you are a very hard worker, on the other hand, now that you are dismissed, I realise that . . ."
- Positive feedback is another gentle way to resolve discrepancies.
  or discrepancies: "I can see that they tried very hard to stand up to their foreman. Your efforts went in the right direction. Maybe you can do more. Do you want to try this?"

The final part of the confrontation or challenge in a positive sense includes evaluating the changes the clients intend to make and giving them the necessary feedback to spur them on to greater activity. When clients recognise and admit that there are discrepancies or contradictory behaviour, they are usually willing to make adjustments and work towards better solutions.

Focus (see Exercise 16)

Ivey and Ivey (2007, p. 294) state that "focusing makes client observations more accurate by selectively attending to certain aspects of client statements". Focusing is intended to help clients see their problems and concerns in a different light. There are a number of different types of focusing:

1. *Client focus*
   "What are you thinking right now?"
   To help the client explore feelings.
2. *Advisor focus*
   "I sense that you are still angry. I know I would have felt the same way."
   Self-disclosure can lead to further discussion.
3. *Focus on others*
   "Could you say a little more about how Horst (a colleague) might describe this incident." Should let the client know the other point of view.
4. *Thematic focus*
   "I would be interested to hear what actually happened exactly when ..." Encourages discussion of the topic.
5. *Family focus*
   "How does your family fit into all this?" The influence of the family is very important in many situations.
6. *Cultural/environmental/contextual focus*
   "We know that your supervisor had to work his way up from the bottom. How does that affect your relationship?"

   Focusing can be helpful with all clients, although some may want the focus to be mainly on themselves, while for others the focus should be more on the family and community.

Reflection on Meaning (see Exercise 17)

The person-centred theory of Carl Rogers (1987) and the further development of reflection of feelings according to Gazda et al. (1999) refer to stages of reflection, from the reflection of feelings on the surface to advancing to subliminal feelings. Ivey uses the term meaning reflection to refer to high levels of empathy or, to use Gazda et al.'s (1999) terminology: level four, advanced accurate empathy.

Meaning reflection is concerned with detecting hidden feelings and helping clients explore core values and goals in their lives. Counsellors need to help clients find the true meanings hidden behind their feelings, thoughts and behaviours.Ivey and Ivey (1999) identify a number of ways in which counsellors can reflect on meaning. To help clients trace meaning, questions can be asked:

"What significance did that have for you?"
"What did you intend when you did that?"

Meanings are often explored through reflection on feelings:

"It sounds like you still have anger in your stomach about ..."
"Your concern, indeed, fear, of losing your job is ..."

2.2.7 *Influencing Skills for Change*

Ivey and Ivey (2007, p. 351) explain six other skills that can lead clients to change. These skills are:

1. *Recasting*—enabling the client to look at situations differently.
2. *Logical consequences*—helping clients to explore possible outcomes and alternative courses of action.
3. *Self-disclosure*—briefly telling clients about the counsellor's experience to encourage trust and openness.
4. *Feedback*—telling clients how they are seen by others and the counsellor.
5. *Giving information*—providing clients with new information and ideas; very useful in career counselling.
6. *Directives*—giving clients specific strategies and courses of action.

Change of Perspective (see Exercise 18)
With a reframing, counsellors enable the client to look at their situation or problem differently. In a career counselling interview, the recast might look something like this:

Client: I am miserable. I've been unemployed for three months and it looks like there are no jobs out there for me. I'm sure my whole family considers me a real failure.
Counsellor: Being miserable because you don't have a job is very real for someone like you who has always had a good job. One thing that we might lose sight of is your professional achievements and skills and how these skills could be used differently from your last job. Let's look at these specific skills from a transferability perspective.

Logical Consequences (see Exercise 19)
Logical consequences are those results that follow naturally from a particular action. For example, the unemployed person who rarely looks for work is likely to remain unemployed for some time. Or a teacher who needs a certain amount of quiet in the classroom when lecturing the material will tell the students that students who disrupt the lesson will be sent out of the classroom after a single warning.

Logical consequences can also be very positive. Rewards offered by teachers and employers are examples of positive logical consequences. Ivey and Ivey (2007, p. 367) suggest the following steps for counsellors who want to make logical consequences clear to clients:

1. Counsellors should make sure that they understand the situation from the client's perspective.
2. They should encourage clients to explore the positive and negative consequences of alternatives.
3. They should provide clients with information on the positive and negative consequences of alternatives.

4. They should summarise all positive and negative consequences.
5. You should let the clients decide what they want to do.

Logical consequences should be presented gently and factually to help clients consider their alternatives more fully.

Self-revelation (see Exercise 20)
Self-revelation begets self-revelation. So, if counsellors are willing to engage in meaningful self-disclosure, clients will also get the courage to talk more about their situation. Self-disclosure should always be brief, relevant, and closely related to what has happened to the client. Immediately after the self-disclosure, the focus should be back on the client. Self-disclosure often begins with an "I" statement and empathetic words:

> I am really pleased that you managed to stand up to your boss last week. My own experience of dealing with a boss were similar. At that time, I felt used and underestimated. But let's get back to your positive experience last week.

Feedback (see Exercise 21)
Clients need to understand themselves, but they also need to know how others see them. Feedback is the process of providing clients with information not only about how others see them but also about their behaviours or performance. The following are some guidelines on how to give feedback:

1. Feedback is best received when the client asks for it.
2. Give encouraging feedback on things where the client can make a difference.
3. When giving feedback, be specific, precise, concrete and do not judge.
4. Carefully go over with the client how the feedback was received.

Feedback is always given with the intention of helping clients to change their behaviour. Clients need to recognise what they are already doing well and then expand on it.

Giving Information (see Exercise 22)
Information, advice and instruction play an important role in career guidance. As with feedback, counsellors must be precise, concrete and focused when providing information or advice.

Clients who come to the counsellor with career concerns often need direct instruction on how to look for work, how to make a CV, how to have a good interview and how to advance professionally. When informing, counsellors need to make sure that clients are open to this information, that the informing is done accurately, and that the information is fully understood by the clients.

Giving Directives (see Exercise 23)
Giving directives is an elementary building block of solution-oriented brief counselling presented in Chap. 4. Solution-focused counsellors listen carefully to clients and give them directives on how to apply what has already worked well in the past. Clients benefit from directives to specific actions that they can also implement.

The following is a short list of different directive strategies that can be helpful in counselling situations:

1. *Instructions for action*

   "When you applied for jobs in the past, it worked out well for you. For next week, I would like ..."

2. *Figurative ideas*

   "Close your eyes and imagine that a human resources manager asks you a tricky question. What does he say? What do you answer?"

3. *Hotseat ("Hot Chair")*

   "Talk to your colleague Mr. Frank as if he were sitting in this empty chair. Now go to the empty chair and answer as you think Mr Frank would."

4. *Paradoxical instructions*

   "Mrs Peters, I notice that you mostly give in to others and are not forceful enough. I want you to deliberately give in at least once a day next week when someone asks you to do something. Pay attention to how you behave and how others react."

5. *Roleplay*

   "We now want to hear your answers to these questions in a role play. I'll start with ..."

6. *Change of perspective*

   "We've been talking for quite a while now about what went wrong in the conversation. Could we also talk about a few things that went okay and follow up on that?"

7. *Teaching/Homework*

   "During the next week, I want you to practically apply the skills we have just demonstrated in the role play. Especially ..."

8. *Meditation*

   "Concentrate on this one point. Relax. Breathe deeply and relax some more. Try to let go of all other thoughts."

9. *Group work*

   "I want each of you in this practice group to play the interview leader, the candidate and the observer."

10. *Language change*

    "Try replacing the one word I have often heard you use with others ... Say 'I will...' instead of 'I should ...', and say 'I won't' instead of 'I can't'."

11. *Systematic desensitisation*

    "We will list in order the many things that cause you anxiety. Pick out what causes the least anxiety and do relaxation exercises at the same time."

12. *Relaxation*

> "Let's start the relaxation exercises by first tensing muscles and then relaxing them. Let's start with the arms ...".

These selected directive strategies have been shown to be successful in terms of a number of counselling theories. Directives help clients to become active.

In conclusion, it should be noted: Of course, all the counselling procedures presented here are presented as suggestions. Counsellors should know that every client and every situation is different and even the best plans sometimes need to be modified. As counsellors, we also have our preferences for a certain style and skills. It is difficult to ensure balance in the many skills Ivey presents. Finally, and most importantly, clients are culturally different and therefore some counselling skills and strategies are appropriate for them and others less so. All clients are unique and need to be treated as individuals.

2.3 Competence Development Exercises

Preface to the Exercises

"Microcounselling" was developed to break down the skills commonly used in effective counselling and guidance. The breakdown of skills makes it easier for counsellors in training to understand the whole counselling process. Microcounselling as training consists of reading about the different skills, modelling the skills, exercises and applying the skills in practice. The 23 exercises in this chapter are meant to provide visual material for the previous chapter.

Exercise 1

The "RESPECTFUL" advisory model

(*See* D'Andrea & Daniels, 1997; Ivey et al., 2004)

Step 1	
Religious/spiritual identity	can play an important role in shaping the client's views on different life experiences.
Economic background, social class	there is a strong link to the client's attitudes, values and behaviours. Counsellors need to critically examine their assumptions and preconceptions when meeting clients of different social levels.
Gender identity	refers to gender-typical roles and sexual orientation. The latter includes bisexuality, heterosexuality and homosexuality.
Psychological maturity	refers to the way people mature from childhood to adulthood. Children for example are able to think about themselves and their experiences in a complex way.
Ethnic identity	refers to the differences between people of different ethnic groups. In a pluralistic society, counsellors need to be open to human diversity and group identity.

(continued)

Time and developmental challenges	draw attention to the tasks people face as they move from infancy through childhood and adolescence to adulthood. Counsellors encounter many such developmental challenges with their clients.
Trauma and other threats to well-being	for successful counselling, knowledge of the different ways to assess the challenges that are placed on the stress factors acting on the client are indispensable.
Family background and family history	different family constellations (e.g. complete, single parent, divorced) require the counsellor to constantly review his/her family picture.
Special physical characteristics	counsellors need to be sensitive and knowledgeable about issues of physical characteristics, especially for clients with physical limitations.
Region of residence and language differences	it is important for counsellors to reflect on their own stereotypes and prejudices towards people from other regions.

Step 2

RESPECTFUL—Application to the Self

You can use the RESPECTFUL components to assess yourself. To do this, you should enter your position on the respective descriptions in keywords in the following scheme:

R	
E	
S	
P	
E	
C	
T	
F	
U	
L	

Exercise 2

Develop a culturally relevant theory

(*See* Nwachuku & Ivey, 1991; Ivey et al., 1997a)

Choose a specific group (e.g. Turkish immigrants) to start building a culturally relevant theory.	
Step 1	***Examine the culture***
1.	What are the important personal and interpersonal characteristics of this culture?
2.	What is the cultural attitude towards individual and relational problem points?
3.	Who are the natural helpers?
4.	How are decisions made?
5.	How are children brought up and what do the subsequent developmental steps look like
6.	How is change viewed?
7.	How is language used? For example, are metaphors or storytelling an important part of a conversation?
8.	What are the main problems this cultural group has to deal with, among others? Are they overpowering?

Step 2	***Determine skills and strategies***	
1.	What is the natural way of helping in this culture?	
2.	Develop a family or community genogram.	
3.	Which specific skills, techniques and strategies from the following theories can be helpful	
	a	Psychodynamic theory
	b	Cognitive theory
	c	Existential-humanistic theory

Step 3	*Test the new theory*
1.	What contributions have the clients made to your jointly developed theory?
2.	What needs to be changed in your theory?

Exercise 3

Life stage review

[*According to* Ivey et al. (1997a, p. 156)]

Each stage of life (e.g. early childhood, puberty and adolescence, early phase of adulthood) is examined retrospectively by asking yourself the following questions:	
Environment	
1	What was your family situation like during this phase?
2	What important events happened in your family during this period of your life?
3	Where did you get support from during this phase?
4	How is your family or extended family today?
5	How do these environmental factors affect your worries today (e.g. dissatisfaction at work or unsuccessful search for a satisfying job)?

Life stage stories	
1	Tell a story from this phase of your life that is of outstanding importance to you.
2	Tell other stories from this phase of life.

Multicultural problem issues	
1	How did religion, ethnic status, gender-typical behaviour or other multicultural areas affect your development during this phase?
2	Who were your heroes?
3	Who did you admire and respect?
4	How are these multicultural imprints related to your current concerns (e.g. job, failure at school, no friends)?

Exercise 4

Your personal cultural identity
[*According to* Ivey et al. (1997a, p. 166)]

Keeping in mind Ponterotto's (1988) four-stage model of cultural identity (pre-awareness stage, awareness stage, overzealousness or defensiveness, integration) intended for white European-North American counsellors, consider the following questions:	
1	At what stage are you in your personal journey as a Turkish-German, German American or other ethnic/racial identity
2	Think back to an earlier part of your life and think about how your ethnic identity was different then. How did you think and feel then? What made you change?
3	In your work with clients, can you identify dimensions of the above phases (pre-awareness, awareness, overzealousness or defensiveness, integration)?

Exercise 5

Multicultural development

So that you can more easily perceive how your cultural background gives you strength, but also sets limits:	
Step 1	*Examine multicultural problem areas*
Investigate the following points by exploring your level of cultural identity (naivety, encounter, naming, reflection on oneself as a cultural being and integration):	
a	Language
b	Gender
c	Ethnicity/race
d	Religion/Spirituality
e	Affective orientation
f	Age
g	Physical problems
h	Socio-economic situation
i	Trauma (e.g. rape, AIDS)

Step 2	*Family of origin*
Look back at the family you come from. How did your family as a whole deal with issues of cultural identity?	

Step 3	*Examine the biases*
How well can you work with people who are different?	
a.	Different gender
b.	Another language
c.	Poverty
d.	Other religion
e.	Old people
f.	Disabled people

Exercise 6

Counselling a client from a minority group

In a small group (4–6 participants) a minority in their own or another country is selected and typical characteristics of a jobseeker from this minority are defined. A

15-min counselling session is then conducted in a role play, with one person taking the role of the job seeker. Afterwards, the group members give feedback to the counsellor on his/her cultural adaptability to the job seeker.

Exercise 7
Identifying multicultural competences

A client, Gregor M., lives in an extremely poor neighbourhood of the city. He comes to the employment agency because his mother has told him that if he does not try to find a job, they will not let him live with her and his five siblings. How would you advise this advice seeker? Write a short summary of the counselling for this case and identify the multicultural competences that would be particularly helpful for Gregor M.

Exercise 8
Practise attention behaviour

Remember: high attention includes at least these four dimensions:	
1.	Appropriate eye contact
2.	Alert body language
3.	Voice sound
4.	Verbal following

Group exercise for three persons	
Counsellor	practices attention behaviour in this role play.
Client	discusses real situations or situations presented in the role play.
Observer	gives feedback on the counsellor's verbal and non-verbal behaviour.

1.	Clients talks for about 4 min about their past or present professional interests.
2.	The counsellor practices attention behaviour, with only a few verbal comments or questions.
3.	After these 4 min, the observer gives strength-building feedback based on the checklist at the end of this exercise. Example of feedback: • Not so helpful: "You did a great job with the attentive listening". • Strength challenging: "When you looked the client straight in the face and kept good eye contact, I noticed that he relaxed and talked more. I would like to challenge you to maintain this kind of attention. It seems to work well for you".
4.	The roles are exchanged so that everyone plays each role.

Checklist for attentive behaviour	
A.	Examples of when appropriate eye contact was used.
B.	Examples of less appropriate eye contact
C.	Comment on the rate of speech, volume, and tone of the counsellor
D.	An example of when the counsellor was right on the money
E.	An example of when the consultant could have done a better job.
F.	Comment on the balance between the counsellor's and client's parts of speech.

Exercise 9

Use open questions	
Closed question:	Do you have a job? Do you enjoy it?
Open question:	Tell me about your job? Describe a few things you like about the job.

Group exercise for three persons	
Counsellor	Practises open questions in this role play.
Client	Talks about a real or role-played situation.
Observer	Gives feedback to the counsellor.

1.	Clients are asked to talk for about 5–10 min about an important event in their life (job loss, career planning, school problems, other)?
2.	The counsellor mainly uses open questions to bring out not only facts and reasons but also feelings. A variety of what, how, why and could(s) questions should be used. (Note: A few closed questions should be interspersed in the open questions).
3.	The observer gives feedback to the counsellor using the checklist at the end of this exercise.
4.	The three roles are swapped so that everyone plays each role.

Checklist for open questions	
A.	Examples of each of the four basic open questions:
	What:
	How:
	Why:
	Could(s)
B.	Examples of one or two appropriate closed questions:
C.	Suggestions on how to make one or two closed questions better:
D.	Comment on the counsellor's attention behaviour (eye contact, body language, manner of speaking and following the client's statements):

Exercise 10

Minimal encouragement to speak and paraphrase

While open-ended questions are often used to get the client talking, minimal "encouragers" facilitate the continuation of the conversation

Minimum encouragers	
1. *Non-verbal minimal encouragers*	Attentive behaviour, leaning forward, head nodding
2. *Verbal minimal encouragers*	"So?" "Oh?" "Well?" "Then?" "Tell me more." Repetition of one or two keywords Hm-hm" "Ah-ha" Exact reproduction of the client's last statement
3. *Silence*	Simply waiting in silence is an encouragement for clients to talk that cannot be underestimated.

Working in pairs	
1.	List and discuss the minimal encouragements you prefer to use. Use all three types (non-verbal, verbal, silence).
2.	Add to the list of frequently used verbal minimal encouragements.
3.	What minimal encouragement was used when you both discussed this exercise?
4.	Since Ivey advocates learning skills using the "do - apply - teach" method, you are now to make a plan for how you might use minimal encouragement more often and more effectively. And how would you teach this skill to others?

Paraphrases

Paraphrasing means repeating the essential. Effective paraphrasing promotes discussion, shows understanding and seeks clarity.

Group exercise (3–5 participants)	
1.	Choose a topic for discussion (e.g. ethnic relations in your community, counselling for minorities or problems in the workplace). Allow 15–20 min for this discussion.
2.	After a group member has said something, the person who wishes to respond must first paraphrase what has been said and only then give his or her comment.
3.	This goes on and on after every discussion contribution by a group member.
4.	After 20 min, assess the impact of the paraphrases on all group members using the following checklist as a guide.

Checklist for paraphrases	
A.	Give examples of paraphrases that showed that someone clearly understood what someone else said.
B.	How were paraphrases used to gain clarity?
C.	Were some paraphrases too long? Too short?
D.	Comment on the other skills used during the discussion in your group: a. Open questions -
	b. Closed questions
	c. Attentive behaviour –
	d. Minimum encouragers

Exercise 11

Reflect feelings

Naming feelings	
1	The counsellors need to be able to recognise and name feelings. Work in pairs and list other words that express a feeling in addition to the four basic words below:

sour	glad	sad	frightened
Anger	Joy	miserable	shy
Hate	happy	violated	concerned
angry	Exited	Dept	Fear

2.	Take turns trying to demonstrate a couple of the feelings listed above and identify the feeling or feelings that the other person is demonstrating

Reflect feeling	
As a reminder, effective reflection on feelings consists of the following steps (Ivey et al., 1997b, p. 73):	
a.	Name the feeling
b.	Use a sentence structure such as "Apparently you feel that . . ."

(continued)

	"I sense with you that . . ." "It sounds like you feel that . . ."
c.	For further clarification, you may want to paraphrase the context. "Apparently you feel disappointment every time you meet with others after work."
d.	If you are not sure of the feeling, you can clarify this with the client. "Is that about it?" "Is that right?"

1.	Distribute the roles of counsellor, client and two observers.
2.	The client has to play a role in which he can express his emotions well.
3.	The observers give feedback using the following checklist as a guide.
4.	Change roles after 5–7 min.

Checklist for reflecting on feelings	
A.	List emotions that the client expresses.
B.	Were these emotions accurately reflected by the counsellor? Give examples.
C.	What other skills did the counsellor use in this mock conversation?

Exercise 12

The skill of summarising

The purpose of the summary is to help the client reconcile their behaviours, thoughts, and feelings. An accurate summary can help the client move from exploration to active problem-solving.

Exercise for two

Role play the following scenes to highlight points in the conversation where the skill of summarising can be very helpful:

a.	Start a second conversation by summarising the first conversation. "In our last session we talked about . . ."
b.	Clarification of a complex situation. "Could we stop here for a moment and see how far we have come in terms of your professional goals . . ."
c.	Going from one topic to the next. "To that point, you said . . . Where do you want to go next now?"
d.	Summary of the entire conversation. "Today we started with a discussion . . . then we talked about . . . finally and at last we both agreed . . ."
e.	Compile common themes or ideas from several conversations. "In the last conversation you said . . .; today you say . . ."

Exercise 13

Review basic listening skills

This exercise is designed to practise the skills from Exercises 5–9 as a whole, namely:

a. Attentive behaviour
b. Open and closed questions
c. Encouragement and paraphrases
d. Emotional reflection
e. Summary

1.	Form a working group and take turns playing the role of counsellor, client, observer 1 and observer 2 (observer 1 can give written feedback and observer 2 oral feedback).
2.	Determine a topic and make sure that the client provides the counsellor with both content and feelings.
3.	Use the following form [according to Ivey et al. (1997a, p. 59)] to provide feedback.

Basic listening skills										
		Attentive behaviour	**Closed questions**	**Open questions**	**Min. encouragement**	**Paraphrases**	**Emotional reflection**	**Summary**	**Other**	

Statement of the Client	Important words on the part of the Counsellor

Exercise 14

Conversation structure

Conduct a counselling interview in groups of three (counsellor, client, observer) using as many attentive listening skills as possible. The observer later gives feedback on the structure of the conversation and on each of the five stages.

Stage 1: Relationship and structure	1.	Give examples of how the relationship was built.
	2.	How was the conversation structured?
Stage 2: Gather information	3.	What skills were used to get the client to tell his story?
	4.	Give a few examples of encouragement from the counsellor.
Stage 3: Determine results	5.	What goals have been set?
	6.	Has the client expressed the goal? How?
Stage 4: Explore alternatives	7.	Make a list of the alternatives you are considering.
	8.	How were the strengths and weaknesses of each alternative assessed?
Stage 5: Generalisation	9.	What specific action plans have been drawn up?
	10.	What follow-up care was planned?

Exercise 15

Challenge clients

Challenging or confronting consists of supportively pointing out discrepancies and contradictions that clients express in their thoughts, behaviours, or attitudes.

Group exercise	
1.	In groups of three (observer, counsellor, client), the counsellor uses attentive listening skills to get to the client's "story".
2.	The client picks out a "story" where they have mixed feelings or disagreements with someone.
3.	The counsellor tries to make challenging comments to encourage the client to look at discrepancies, distortions or inconsistencies.
4.	The observer uses the following checklist to give feedback to the client and counsellor.

Checklist for challenges	
A.	Comment briefly on how the counsellor's challenging remarks pointed to a discrepancy in attitudes, thoughts, or behaviours.
B.	Was the challenge a statement based on observable facts? Was the challenge non-judgemental and non-judgmental?
C.	What came out of the counsellor making challenging or confronting remarks (denial, partial examination, full examination)?

Exercise 16

Focus the conversation

Focusing on the client's story is a good way to assess the client's situation. One could focus on one or all of the following dimensions:

a.	Client focus: "You are feeling rejected and very discouraged right now".
b.	Counsellor focus: "Something similar happened to me at work".
c.	Other focus: "Tell me more about your work colleagues".
d.	Thematic focus: "I see you have a number of worries. Among them, not getting ahead at work, not earning enough money, the urge to move away, and maybe other worries".
e.	Family focus: "Tell me more about how your family influences your decision".
f.	Cultural focus/environmental focus: "They said that all the people they work with have more money because they don't have financial commitments like you".

1.	Form a working group with 3–5 participants and play the counsellor and client roles alternately.
2.	Take the scenes depicted in the roleplays and have each counsellor illuminate different dimensions (client, counsellor, family, etc.).
3.	The observers should comment on the results of the illumination of different dimensions

Exercise 17

Reflection on meaning

1.	Practise the skill of meaning reflection in groups of three (client, counsellor, one or two observers).
2.	Now practise with reversed roles for 5 min, using one or more of the following sentence stems as a stimulus to use the meaning reflection: • "The most important event in my life . . ." • "My family is . . ." • "What I would really like from a profession is . . ." • "My thoughts on what is really important are . . ."
3.	Give specific feedback to the counsellor by focusing your attention on how the counsellor reflects on the meaning of the key words used by the client.

a.	What points in particular were of concern in the conversation?
b.	List the meaning questions and meaning reflections used in the conversation.
c.	Comment on the effectiveness of the meaning reflection skill used by the counsellor.

Exercise 18

The skill of recasting

In so-called narrative counselling, counsellors make it easy for clients to tell or reframe their life stories in new, more positive ways. As Ivey et al. (1997c, p. 87) **put it: "To recast a problem or concern is to change the nature of that problem. To rename or recast a life story may be enough to change a life". In short, reframing a client's story is an attempt to see the story from a different, more positive perspective.**

Small group exercise

1.	The counsellor, using as many listening and influencing skills as possible, should put forward the idea that the client may want to look at the situation from a new perspective. "I have heard about your trouble in the workplace. Now let's talk for a while about how you might see it in a new light".
2.	Several role plays with different approaches to recasting should be tried: (a) Naming. By naming something specifically, the client can sometimes look at their problem differently. "How would you name or talk about your problem differently?" (b) Positive recasting. By focusing on the client's strengths, he sees some of the things he does well. "For example, when does it ever happen that you and your boss get along, and then what do you do?" (c) Focusing recasting. Directly asking the client to look at the situation from a different perspective. "Tell me what your best friend would say about this very situation".
3.	Evaluate the skills of the recast using the following checklist as a guide:

Checklist for recasts	
A.	Has the counsellor managed to sufficiently draw the client out before using a recasting technique? Take a stand.
B.	How effective was the recast? Naming: Positive recast: Focusing recast:
C.	Has the counsellor managed to sufficiently draw the client out before using a recasting technique? Take a stand.

Exercise 19

Logical consequences **Practise using the five steps of logical sequences in pairs:** **1. Understanding the situation** **2. Examination of the consequences** **3. Data on the consequences** **4. Summary of the consequences** **5. Decision of the client**	
Take your own situation or the following short case: Mr. Jung, an assembly line worker, often has to do many of the unpleasant tasks because other workers ask him to. He never resists and reluctantly does what he is told to do.	
1)	Summarise Mr. Jung's problem using "If ... then ..." sentences in their own words.
2)	Ask Mr Jung specific questions about the positive and negative consequences of his behaviour.
3)	Give him feedback on the possible consequences if he continues to behave in this non-forceful way. Use "If...then..." sentences.
4)	Summarise the differences between the feedback just given and Mr Jung's view of things.
5)	Encourage him to make his own decision.

Exercise 20

Relevant self-revelation **Self-disclosure means that the counsellor shares personal experiences with the client in order to help him/her to explore his/her own problems more deeply. The benefit only becomes apparent with the client's reaction.**	
Exercise for two	
1)	As in the previous exercise, a client and a counsellor do a five-minute role play, followed by self-disclosure feedback and discussion.
2)	Use the same predicament as in the previous exercise but include a relevant self-revelation from the counsellor. Afterwards, the counsellor should go through with the client how the client reacted to it. Use the following checklist to guide the discussion after the five-minute role play.
Checklist for self-disclosure	
A.	*Comment on the following characteristics of the counsellor's self-disclosure:* *Honest:* *Situationally relevant:* *Short and to the point:* *Present or past:* *The client's problem remained the "pivot":*
B.	Did the counsellor check the client's reaction to the self-disclosure? Take a stand.

Exercise 21

Giving feedback to clients **Feedback for clients means telling them how others see them and their actions. Feedback is done in the following way:** **1. Careful observation of the client** **2. Concise, accurate, specific feedback in a non-judgmental way** **3. Checking the effect of the feedback on the client.**	
Exercise for two	
1.	A client and a counsellor do a five-minute role play followed byfeedback and discussion.
2.	The counsellor presents a problem situation (e.g. family constraints, pressure at work, working too hard, little time for family, few friends at work) and then provides the client with feedback on how the client 'comes across' to them in that situation. Use the feedback checklist to assess the feedback.
Feedback checklist	
A.	Was the feedback concrete and specific? Give an example.
B.	Was the feedback non-judgmental and non-evaluative? Give an example.
C.	Did the counsellor focus on the client's strengths when giving feedback? Give an example.
D.	Was the focus on facts and data rather than impressions? Give an example.
E.	Has the counsellor checked the impact of his/her feedback on the client? Give an example.

Exercise 22

Give information. **The following stimulus questions are designed to get you to explore issues around information, teaching and counselling activities.**	
1)	If a counsellor is practising a counselling session and it is not going well, what do you say to the client?
2)	How do you react to someone who gives you advice?
3)	Comment on useful advice you have been given and how you have been given that advice.
4)	What kind of instruction or teaching do you like? Why?
5)	How could you best use each of the following in your counselling work: a) Provide information: b) express an opinion or give advice: c) Make proposals: d) Teach:

Exercise 23

Give directives

Directives play an important role in many guidance models. If you give the right directives, it often leads to the clients' following instructions from the counsellors. Among the directives often used are: imagery, role play, group work, recasting, relaxation and paradoxical instructions.

Exercise in threes

1.	The counsellor draws the client out on a particular problem or concern and gives a total of three directives. After each directive, check how the client has received it and then move on to the next directive. The directives can be taken from the "list of directives".
2.	The observer gives feedback.
3.	Practise with alternating roles so that in the end everyone has played all the roles.

Directive list [Ivey: *Intentional Interviewing and Counseling* (1994)]	
1.	Instructions for action "I want you to try next week to . . ."
2.	Figurative ideas "Close your eyes and describe your ideal working day".
3.	Hotseat ("Empty Chair") "Talk to your boss as if he were sitting in this chair. Now go to the chair and answer as your boss would".
4.	Paradoxical instructions "Keep doing what you're doing . . ."
5.	Role plays "We will now try to role play your repartee with your superior, but this time try . . ."
6.	New version "Identify a negative experience or thought and identify something positive about it. Focus only on the positive about it and place it in the overall problem".
7.	Conselee Homework "Practice this vigorous expression with your supervisor for a week".
8.	Meditation "Concentrate on this one point. Relax yourself. Concentrate on your breathing. Let go of all other thoughts".
9.	Group work "I want you to do the following in your small group: . . ."
10.	Language change "I want you to change 'should' to 'would like'. Change 'can't' to 'won't'".
11.	Systematic desensitisation "View fear triggers in a relaxed way in a systematic hierarchy".
12.	Relaxation "Tighten and relax muscles".

References

Achebe, C. (1986). *The world of the ogbanje*. Fourth Dimension Publishers.

Attneave, C. (1969). Therapy in tribal settings and urban network intervention. *Family Process, 8*(2), 192–210.

Attneave, C. (1982). American Indian and Alaskan native families: Emigrants in their own homeland. In J. P. McGoldrick & J. Giordano (Eds.), *Ethnicity and family therapy* (pp. 55–83). Guilford.

Baker, S., & Daniels, T. (1989). Integrating research on the microcounseling program: A meta-analysis. *Journal of Counseling Psychology, 36*(2), 213.

Baker, S., Daniels, T., & Greeley, A. (1990). Systematic training of graduate-level counselors: Narrative and meta-analysis reviews of three major programs. *The Counseling Psychologist, 18*(3), 355–421.

Belle, R. (1976). *The effects of microcounseling on attending behavior of counselor trainees*. Dissertation Abstracts International, 37, 2626A, University Microfilms, No. 76–21, 802.

D'Andrea, M., & Daniels, J. (1997). RESPECTFUL counseling: A new way of thinking about diversity counseling. *Counseling Today, 40*(6), 30, 31, 34.

Daniels, T. (1998). *Microcounseling: A summary of literature*. Sir Wilfred Grenfell College (Unpublished manuscript).

Daniels, T. (2007). A review of research on microcounseling: 1967-present. In A. Ivey & M. Ivey (Eds.), *Intentional interviewing and counseling: Your interactive resource (CD-ROM)* (3rd ed.). Brooks/Cole.

Daniels, T., Rigogio-DiGilio, S., & Ivey, A. (1997). Microcounseling: A training and supervision paradigm. In E. Watkins (Ed.), *Handbook of psychotherapy supervision*. Wiley.

Ertelt, B. J., & Schulz, W. E. (1985). Microcounseling für beraterische Hilfen bei beruflichen Entscheidungsproblemen [Microcounseling for support in vocational decision making]. In A. E. Ivey & J. Authier (Eds.), *Microcounseling – Neue Wege im Kommunikationstraining* (pp. 169–197). BRATT.

Fukuyuama, M. (1990). Taking a universal approach to multicultural counseling. *Counselor Education and Supervision, 30*, 6–17.

Gazda, G., Asbury, F., Balzer, F., Childers, W., Phelps, R., & Walters, S. (1999). *Human relations development* (6th ed.). Allyn & Bacon.

Gluckstern, N. (1973). Training parents as drug counselors in the community. *Personnel and Guidance Journal, 51*, 676–680.

Guttmann, M., & Haase, R. (1972). The generalization of microcounseling skills from training periods to actual counseling setting. *Counselor Education and Supervision, 12*, 98–107.

Hansen, N., Pepitone-Arreola-Rockwell, F., & Greene, A. (2000). *Professional Psychology: Research and Practice, 3*(6), 652–660.

Ivey, A. (1983). *Intentional interviewing and counseling*. Brooks/Cole.

Ivey, A. (1988). *Intentional interviewing and counseling* (2nd ed.). Brooks/Cole.

Ivey, A. (1994). *Intentional interviewing and counseling* (3rd ed.). Brooks/Cole.

Ivey, A., & Authier, J. (1978). *Microcounseling* (2nd ed.). Thomas.

Ivey, A., & Bradford-Ivey, M. (1999). *Intentional interviewing & counseling* (4th ed.). Brooks/Cole.

Ivey, A., & Bradford-Ivey, M. (2002). *Intentional interviewing & counseling* (5th ed.). Brooks/Cole.

Ivey, A., & Ivey, M. (2007). *Intentional interviewing and counseling* (6 Aufl.). Brooks/Cole.

Ivey, A., & Simek-Downing, L. (1980). *Counseling and psychotherapy*. Prentice-Hall.

Ivey, A., Bradford-Ivey, M., & Simek-Dowining, L. (1987). *Counseling and psychotherapy* (2nd ed.). Prentice-Hall.

Ivey, A., Bradford-Ivey, M., & Simek-Morgan, L. (1993). *Counseling and psychotherapy* (3rd ed.). Allyn & Bacon.

Ivey, A., Bradford-Ivey, M., & Simek-Morgan, L. (1997a). *Counseling and psychotherapy* (4th ed.). Allyn & Bacon.

Ivey, A., Gluckstern, N., & Bradford-Ivey, M. (1997b). *Basic influencing skills*. Microtraining Associates.

Ivey, A., Gluckstern, N., & Bradford-Ivey, M. (1997c). *Basic attending skills* (3rd ed.). Microtraining Associates.

Ivey, A., D'Andrea, M., Ivey, M., & Simek-Morgan, L. (2002). *Theories of counseling and psychotherapy* (5. Aufl.). Allyn & Bacon.

Ivey, A., D'Andrea, M., Bradford-Ivey, M., & Simek-Morgan, L. (2004). *Theories of counseling and psychotherapy: A multicultural perspective* (5th ed.). Allyn & Bacon.

Ivey, A., Bradford Ivey, M., & Zalaquett, C. (2009). *Intentional interviewing and counseling: Facilitating client development in a multicultural society*. Cengage Learning Brooks/Cole.

Ivey, A., Bradford Ivey, M., & Zalaquett, C. (2018). *Intentional interviewing and counseling: Facilitating client development in a multicultural society* (9th ed.). Cengage Learning Brooks/Cole.

Kasford, J., & Gustafson, K. (1978). Research related to microtraining. In A. Ivey & J. Authier (Eds.), *Microcounseling: Innovations in interviewing, counseling, psychotherapy and psychoeducation*. Springfield.

Kerrebrock, R. (1971). *Application of the microcounseling method using videotape recordings to the training of teachers in basic counseling techniques*. Unpublished dissertation, Los Angeles,

University of Southern California. Dissertation Abstracts International, 32:740A, University Microfilms, No. 71-21, 470.
Littrell, J. (2001). Allen E. Ivey: Transforming counselling theory and practice. *Journal of Counselling & Development, 79*(2), 105–118.
Nwachuku, U., & Ivey, A. (1991). Culture specific counseling: An alternative approach. *Journal of Counseling and Development, 70*, 106–151.
Parker, R. (1972). *The effects of microcounseling with counseling practicum students*. Dissertation Abstracts International, 33, 4096A, University Microfilms, No. 72-32, 726.
Ponterotto, J. (1988). Racial consciousness development among white counselor trainees. *Journal of Multicultural Counseling and Development, 16*, 146–156.
Rogers, C. (1987). The underlying theory: Drawn from experiences with individuals and groups. *Counseling and Values, 32*(1), 38–45.
Scroggins, W., & Ivey, A. (1976). *An evaluation of microcounseling as a model to train resident staff.* University of Alabama. Unpublished manuscript.
Shea, J. (1975). *An evaluation of the effectiveness of microcounseling in training counselors to use selected behaviors in an urban field practice*. Dissertation Abstracts International, 36, 3419A, University Microfilms, No. 75-27, 072.
Sue, D. (1995). Toward a theory of multicultural counseling and therapy. In J. Banks & C. Banks (Eds.), *Handbook of research on multicultural education*. Macmillan.
Sweeney, T., & Myers, J. (2005). Optimizing human development for helping. In A. Ivey, M. Ivey, J. Meyers, & Sweeney (Eds.), *Developmental strategies for helpers* ((2nd ed., pp. 39–68). Microtraining.

Chapter 3
Egan's Model of Problem-Management

3.1 Development and Status of the Model

3.1.1 Introduction

Gerard Egan is professor emeritus of organisational development and psychology at the Centre for Organisational Development at Loyola University in Chicago. "The skilled helper" is probably the most widely used specialist text for counselling professions worldwide and has been translated into both European and Asian languages and was also given central consideration in the counselling concept of the Federal Employment Agency Germany (cf. Rübner & Sprengard, 2010). The practical approach to problem-solving and the opening up of possibilities is, among a number of other reasons, responsible for the unbroken popularity of the book (Egan, 1998, 2018):

1. Problem-solving is one of the most researched paradigms in psychology.
2. Problem-solving and exploring possibilities for action are part of almost every kind of help. The reason for this is probably that the approach focuses on the needs of the person seeking advice and is not dominated by a theory.
3. The problem-solving process or model is universal at its core; therefore, it can be easily adapted to cultural differences.
4. It is a very practical model. Each case is a study in itself; goals are set and progress towards those goals is monitored.
5. Counsellors quickly understand the problem-solving process and this understanding allows them to become partners in counselling.
6. The counselling sessions become laboratories for better-designed problem-solving.

Updated translation of chapter 3 from: Handbuch Beratungskompetenz, 4th ed. by Bernd-Joachim Ertelt & William E. Schulz, 2019, Springer Verlag.

B.-J. Ertelt et al., *Counsellor Competencies*,
https://doi.org/10.1007/978-3-030-87413-1_3

7. Helpers can use the problem-solving framework to organise a wide range of help methods. It becomes a tool for them to perceive the best of research and new methods and to integrate them into practice.

Egan recognised from the outset that there was a tension between behavioural science psychology on the one hand and humanistic psychology on the other. When "The Skilled Helper" was first introduced and extensively reviewed, Egan received positive comments from both camps, with behaviourists viewing the model as a humanistic way to introduce behaviourist, action-oriented concepts, and representatives of humanistic psychology viewing it as a behaviourist way to spread humanistic ideas. In all editions, Egan tried to combine the two psychological directions, recognising that the behaviourist counselling technique always needed humanising.

3.1.2 The Development of Egan's Model

All editions of Egan's book "The Skilled Helper" emphasize two principles:

1. The aim is to help those seeking counselling to cope better with the problems in their lives and to better activate unused or underused resources. Clients are successful to the extent that they are involved in the help or counselling process and implement what they have learned in the counselling to deal effectively with problematic situations.
2. The clients should be encouraged to help themselves with the challenges of daily life. Counsellors are only professional to the extent that they can support clients in developing their own skills. Counselling skills should enable clients to act independently. In this sense, Egan (2007) sees counselling as an attempt to help clients become more socially and emotionally mature. He defined maturity in terms of self-management, which includes self-awareness, self-control and action orientation. Mature personalities are also capable of good interpersonal relationships and they have empathy and communicative competence. They constantly strive to understand the world in which they live.

When Egan (1975) first presented his approach, he called it a model for systematic helping and interpersonal relationship building. His work was strongly influenced by three interrelated sources:

1. The work of Robert Carkhuff and other counselling skills training systems,
2. The theory of social imprinting, and
3. Learning theory and the basic assumptions about maintenance and change of behaviour.

Although Carkhuff (1971, 1973) was strongly influenced by Carl Rogers (1965), especially with regard to the use of communicative skills and attentive listening, he extended Rogers' relational theory and added a handling phase. Carkhuff's well-thought-out, scientific model appealed to Egan. He was impressed by the way Carkhuff detailed the requirements and characteristics of each of the three stages of his model. Egan also used Carkhuff's approach to identify the skills the counsellor needs to be effective. Many of the skills (and gradations of skills) described also appear in Egan's model: empathic understanding, various degrees of respect and genuineness, correctness or attention to detail, confrontation, and others.

Brammer (1973) also developed a systematic skills training programme that influenced Egan's work. Brammer's model, like Egan's, could be called eclectic. Brammer expanded Carkhuff's list of counselling skills and added 20 specific skills that he felt would be beneficial to counselling.

Egan was also influenced by Ivey and his colleagues (Hackney et al., 1970; Ivey, 1971, 1972) in developing his systematic, skills-based model of counselling assistance (see Chap. 2).

Egan included two other models of help, Hackney and Nye's (1973) model of discrimination and Kagan's micro-manufacturing approach to counsellor training. Hackney and Nye found it especially important to set goals and plan behavioural interventions to help the client in achieving their goals, Kagan (1973, p. 44) put the essence of his training approach in the following words:

The general teaching strategy [...] has evolved as a step-by-step sequence of lessons starting with a didactic notion of concepts, then moving on to simulation exercises, interpersonal affective stress, video and psychological feedback, studying one's own inaction, feedback from clients, and finally understanding and dealing with complex bilateral differences of opinion that occur when two people enter into relationship.

Egan sees helping as a socially influenced process. He emphasises the importance of the helper's first step being to respond positively to the client. This creates a basis for being able to influence the person seeking advice by means of proven professionalism, trustworthiness, and attractiveness. Egan also uses this influence on question and challenge the client's attitudes. Skills such as active listening, attention, empathy, and summary are used by Egan to make social influence possible.

Of greater influence on the Egan model were, thirdly, learning, and behavioural theory and its principles. These insights were important because Egan (1975, p. 6 f.) saw counselling as helping people to change their behaviour. Individuals should make significant changes in themselves and in their environment, improve their destructive behaviour towards themselves and others, and acquire skills that will enable them to live more effectively. Egan encouraged all his students to acquire a wide range of skills—based on learning principles—in problem-solving and behaviour change.

Thus, Egan's model represents the integration of three influences in a three-stage development model. Egan saw himself as a mediator who is in touch with the best in research and theory and adapts this to the needs of the practitioner.

Gerard Egan has written more than 15 works on counselling and communication. He has continually made changes in his approach to reflect the many changes in counselling over the last decade. For example, support for counselling from most American government agencies is limited to just a few sessions, as longer-term models are seen as too expensive. Also, the emphasis is no longer only on an empathic relationship, but increasingly on client activation and problem-solving.

In recent years, EGAN has emphasised cognitive and affective behaviours (Egan, 2010; Egan et al., 2013).

However, listening and understanding remain at the core of his model, but he also sees that people often need to be asked to make multiple efforts. This is why problem management is more prominent in the new editions of "The Skilled Helper".

In our first three exercises on EGAN's counselling model, we take into account the fact that he continues to emphasise the importance of emotions; but this does not contradict the increasing focus on goal setting, procedures and the decision-making process. EGAN does not ignore the importance of the past, but instead of focusing on the causes of problems, possibilities for a better future are explored. Therefore, from the beginning of counselling, Egan's model of helping encourages step-by-step actions in terms of problem-solving (Egan, 2010).

Exercises 13 and 14 help to illustrate this approach and to better understand what EGAN calls "The Way Forward".

In 2018, EGAN released a new version of "The Skilled Helper" specifically for Europe, the Middle East and Africa. It is intended for counsellors who have not been under the strong influence of counselling models that emphasise relational counselling. Therefore, EGAN focuses much more on relationship building skills and specifically on empathic responding. A number of suggestions are made for this (Egan, 2018, p. 98):

- Consider empathy as a value in its own right, a way of being.
- Pay conscious attention to the client's point of view.
- Look out for culture-specific cues and key messages.
- Pay attention to non-verbal cues.
- Be restrained in your answers.
- Practice empathy in all phases of your counselling,
- Remembering that empathy is only one tool among many.

As Egan's approach for counsellors in Europe, the Middle East and Africa is more relational, it suggests some approaches for dealing with clients' personal problems:

- Help to overcome and identify possible obstacles and blockages (see Exercise 22).
- Help in the development of action-related self-commitments.
- Helping people to help themselves.

3.1.3 *Model of Assistance and Interpersonal Relationship Building*

In his book "The Skilled Helper" (1975, p. 30), Egan gave an "overview of an organic or developmental model of helping and interpersonal relationship building". The model includes a pre-help phase and three stages.

Pre-help or pre-communication phase:

Pay attention

Goal of the helper: To pay attention to the other person, both physically and psychologically, to devote oneself completely to the other person, to work with the other person.

Stage I: Reacting/Self-Exploration

Goal of the helper: Respond. Respond to clients and their expressions with care and empathy; establish a relationship of effective community work with clients; facilitate clients' self-exploration.

Client's goal: Self-exploration. To explore experiences, behaviours and feelings relevant to the client's life problems; to explore the ways in which the client is living ineffectively.

Stage II: Integrative understanding/dynamic self-understanding

Goal of the helper: Integrative understanding. The helper starts by assembling the data provided by the client in the self-exploration phase. He sees guiding behavioural motives or patterns and helps the other to identify them. He helps the other to see the "bigger picture". He teaches the client to go about this integration process himself.

Client's goal: dynamic self-understanding. Develop self-understanding that recognises the need for a turnaround and the need for action; learn from the helper the ability to put the bigger picture together for him- or herself; identify resources, especially unused ones.

Stage III: Facilitate/act

Goal of the facilitator: Facilitate action. To work with the client to develop specific programmes of action; to help the client to act on a new understanding of him/herself; to identify with the client a wide range of different ways and means of seeking to change behaviour in a constructive way; to provide guidance and instructions for programmes of action.

Goal of the client: Taking action, living more effectively. To learn the skills needed to live more effectively and to deal with the social-emotional dimensions of life; to discard self-destructive and other destructive behaviour patterns; and, to develop new resources.

In Stage I, the counsellor lays a foundation for social influence in the client's life. A good relationship is established, and the counsellor becomes a counsellor who works with clients in their attempts to cope with their problem.

In Stage II, the counsellor assists clients in their efforts to understand guiding principles in their life. This stage can also be understood as an influencing process, as the counsellor uses the basis established in Stage I (through expertise, trust, contact) to influence the clients' perceptions, i.e. to help them to a more realistic perception of themselves, their environment and the interaction between both. In the course of Stage II, clients become increasingly clear about the need for action, and in Stage III, helper and client work out action programmes together. These usually include problem-solving techniques, decision-making methods, behaviour change programmes, homework and training in interpersonal and other skills (Egan, 1975, p. 49).

In the second edition (1982), Egan clearly describes his three-stage solution approach as a *problem management model.* Counsellors are advisors who help to manage problems. Greater emphasis is placed on goal setting in stage II of the helping process. This stage is described by Egan (1982, p. 51) is characterised as follows:

Stage II: Setting goals based on dynamic understanding

The counsellor helps the counselee to synthesise the data obtained in the self-exploration phase; helps the client to develop those new perspectives that are necessary for goal setting and facilitates the goal-setting process.

This shift towards greater emphasis on goal setting continues in the third edition of "The Skilled Helper"(1986). In fact, Stage II is now called "goal setting" instead of "integrative understanding". What is new is the idea of helping clients construct a new scenario. Egan thus bridges the ideas of self-understanding to goal setting. Since people come to counsellors because their current situation is problematic, the counsellor's goal must be to help the client envision a better scenario. This includes more constructive behaviour patterns and the goals of the corresponding help process.

In his fourth edition (1990), Egan makes a number of additional changes to his model. The second and third steps of Stage I are reversed: questioning (third step) is thus included earlier in the counselling interview. Those seeking counselling are more likely to be able to deal with their problems if they first critically examine blind spots such as problem distortions, misinterpretations, motivational deficits, and lack of problem awareness.

The client's actions become increasingly important, as do client knowledge, goal setting and strategy planning. But it seems even more important to get the person seeking advice to act. And that means not only helping them to build a better future and committing them to a programme of action, but also helping them to choose the best strategies to implement.

Egan (1990) also emphasises the importance of practical experience. The best counsellors are mediators, i.e. professionals who base their practice on both action research with clients and current scientific knowledge. The recognition of the importance of counselling practice led Egan to describe his model less as a sequence of developmental stages and steps, but rather as a *series of ground rules* that could serve as guidelines for practitioners. Since the early 1990s at the latest, Egan no longer wanted to offer a how-to book with standard recipes.

The fifth edition (1994) of "The Skilled Helper" is almost 100 pages shorter than the fourth edition of 1990, but no changes in content have been made. Egan continues to strongly advocate the approach of problem-solving and opportunity development. The final chapter of the fourth edition, in which Egan discusses the counselling period and the conclusion of counselling, has been greatly shortened.

In the sixth edition (1998), the increasing influence of brief therapy and the more strictly regulated health care in the USA (where health insurance only pays for a limited number of sessions with a counsellor or therapist) is evident. Egan places an even stronger emphasis on clients taking advantage of untapped opportunities. As with some forms of brief therapy, Egan (1998) looks for the strengths that clients bring to the conversation. He notes that by focusing on possible solutions, clients can often manage their own problems (p. XVI). However, all this should be done quickly and efficiently.

In the sixth edition of 1998, Egan places particular emphasis on the *preventive use of communication and problem-solving skills*.

The learning of these skills is often left to chance, but ideally, they are taught and shaped in many areas, including at home, at school and in the community.

In updating our book on counselling competence, we were made aware—in a similar way to Egan—of the growing importance of multiculturalism in counselling. Already in his booklet "Skilled Helping Around the World" (2002a), Egan states that we should "appreciate and learn from diversity rather than looking down on it or just 'tolerating' it. People thereby develop empathy for the living environment and a place in it. Without giving up one's own views and values, one realises that there are many ways of life and that one is not necessarily 'better' than the other" (p. 1).

Multiculturalism in counselling contributes to equality and justice in all countries. It is essential for counsellors to recognise the relationship between characteristics (ethnicity, sexual orientation, socio-economic status, national origin, physical characteristics, gender, etc.) and the issues and problems that affect clients.

There are currently many contributions on the need for multicultural competence of counsellors. According to our observations, two frequently repeated views stand side by side:

- "Remember that not everyone is exactly like you. And, if you are uncomfortable with the differences, look first to yourself and your prejudices".
- "Multiculturally oriented counsellors often make two mistakes: they focus on the specific and unique of their clients rather than the universal; or they see the general rather than the specific and unique".

Obviously, there is a need for mediation between the two views. Egan (2002a, p. 11) offers a number of good suggestions in this regard:

- Counsellors should be aware of their own cultural background, how they present themselves and how they are perceived by clients.
- Counsellors should be aware of their cultural biases towards certain groups and people.
- Counsellors should positively perceive the ways in which diversity contributes to the dynamic appearance of each client.
- Counsellors should always be aware of the ways in which poverty, stereotyping, discrimination, oppression and prejudice affect particular groups and individuals.
- Counsellors have to take into account that Western-oriented theories may not always be appropriate for other cultures. Counsellors should essentially know the family structures and gender roles of their clients.
- Counsellors should consider differences in interaction styles, language differences and non-verbal communication.
- Counsellors should master different procedures in which the cultural variable plays a role.

- Counsellors must be able to assess their multicultural competence and be motivated to further develop their knowledge and skills.

3.1.4 Theory Influences

Egan's model of problem management is primarily a practical approach, but it is not therefore untheoretical. Rather, it is an *integrative approach* that borrows from many counselling theories. The model is primarily based on learning theory and the principles underlying behaviour change. However, because it is a problem-solving approach, the model draws heavily on research on problem-solving and decision-making. It has also been influenced by Rogers' (1965) relationship theory and communication skills.

The work of numerous behaviourists influenced Egan and his model; they include Bandura (1969), Eysenck (1965), Goldstein (1966), Krumboltz (1966), Maier (1960) and B. F. Skinner (1953). Most behaviourist-oriented counsellors work with the client. These counsellors are expected to have training and experience in behaviour therapy. For the behaviourists, the counselling focus is on helping the counselee analyse behaviour, pinpoint problems and select goals. The behaviour counsellor should be skilled in using techniques to help clients determine and solve a wide range of problems. Egan incorporated many of these ideas into the second and third stages of his counselling model. Counsellors help counselees determine a preferred scenario so that goals can be accurately stated. In the third stage, Egan helps clients in the same way that behaviourists do, develop action plans and put them into action. Egan also uses the behaviourists' concepts of self-contracts, self-monitoring, and self-reinforcement.

Carl Rogers' work is well known in its main features; however, in order to make the direct influence on Egan's model clear, the main aspects of Rogers' work are summarised below:

Rogers' theory focuses on the human being. At its core, it is an amalgamation of views about people and their relationships rather than a treatise on counselling techniques. Rogers emphasises understanding the world of the counselee from his or her perspective (phenomenological point of view). Therefore, it becomes important to make the relationship level with the client as close as possible so that genuine trust and understanding emerge.

Roger (1961) has a very positive view of humanity. He sees people as essentially rational, accepting, forward-looking and full of potential. People have an inherent tendency to develop and grow positively. These positive realisation tendencies can be promoted by counsellors who are sincere or congruent; i.e. the counsellors are not the doer, rather they bring their experience fully to bear. Egan (1975) accepts this notion of Roger's authenticity and notes that the communication of this authenticity in behaviour involves the following:

- Being free from playing a role
- Spontaneity
- Unopposing
- Consistency, and
- Participation in the self (p. 91).

Empathy and respect (unconditional positive regard) for clients play an important role in Rogers' theory. Empathic understanding means that the counsellor knows, on both a cognitive and a deeper affective level, what it is like to be someone else while maintaining his or her own autonomy. Unconditional positive awareness is characterised more by a total than a conditional acceptance of a client.

Egan (1975) states that deference is an asset for successful counsellors and is demonstrated to clients as follows (p. 97 f.):

- Be there for the client.
- Support the clients as a unique individual and help them develop their uniqueness.
- Believe in the client's potential for self-direction.
- Commit to working with the client.
- Assume that the client feels committed to change.

Listening, warmth, understanding, sincerity, empathy, and attention are part of most counselling efforts and training today. Egan and many others have Rogers to thank for his influence in terms of theory.

Despite the theoretical influences on his model, however, it should not be forgotten that Egan relied more and more on his practical instincts in each new edition of his model. In the preface to the fourth edition (1990) of "The Skilled Helper", Egan notes that "research findings are often so inconsistent and contradictory that it is difficult to formulate a coherent approach to practice" (p. VI). Egan is in full agreement with Morrow-Bradley and Elliott (1986) statement:

Psychotherapy researchers have almost unanimously pointed out that (a) psychotherapy research should yield useful information for practising therapists, (b) such research has not yet taken place, and (c) this problem needs to be remedied (p. 188).

Egan does not think that practitioners should break with research, but they should put more emphasis on their own insights. There are many excellent practitioners "on the front line" who update their practice through action research and who are also willing to share their knowledge with others. Egan always paid attention to the voices from the field; the result has been an effective model for problem-solving. Egan realized that people seeking advice are not interested in theories, but in results (1994, p. 14). To this end, he presented a comprehensive, curricular plan (2002b, p. 17) (see Fig. 3.1).

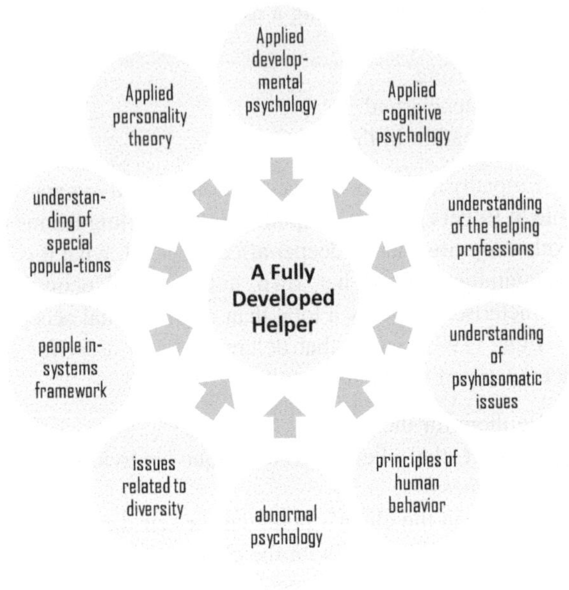

Fig. 3.1 Sample plan for counsellors according to Egan (2002b)

3.1.5 *Strengths and Weaknesses of the Model*

Egan (1994) points out that there has always been a certain tension between practitioners and theorists/researchers. Counsellors and other helping professions need to help clients immediately and would readily use any strategy that not only works but works quickly. Researchers often take the longer, more cautious route, claiming that their meagre results are not yet ripe for implementation into practice. Researchers often take the longer, more caution route, claiming that their meagre results are not yet ripe for implementation into practice. Often these researchers criticise practitioners for using methods that have not been fully researched.

With his model of problem management, Egan succeeded in showing the importance of another role: the role of the mediator. *Mediators* are closely related to validated theory and research and, most importantly, to the needs of practitioners in their work with clients. In short, Egan has tried (successfully) to translate the best of theory and research (Rogers, 1980; Carkhuff, 1969; Bandura, 1969; Krumboltz, 1966, to name but a few) into his very application-oriented model. The worldwide acceptance of his approach supports Egan's conviction that learning and problem-solving are the cornerstones of any counselling approach. He has provided (1996) a clear logical basis for the use of his approach for counsellors/helpers:

1. Problem-solving has been intensively researched and is therefore not based on unproven theory.
2. Opening up new possibilities for those seeking advice is an important part of the help.

3. The problem-solving process is universal and easy to adapt to cultural differences.
4. The process is clear and practical when goals are set and progress towards the goal is planned.
5. The process can be made easy to understand for those seeking advice, and they become partners in the process.
6. Once the process is learned, clients can apply it to other problem areas in their lives.
7. The simple, three-stage basic framework can easily adapt new methods and research findings.
8. Problem management can be used preventively.

Egan's approach did much to demystify the whole counselling process. The three stages of his guidance model are clear and understandable. The method can be applied to many different target groups within a very short time. The present and the future come into focus, the clients work with quickly realisable goals.

Egan's model is timely as billing arrangements (limited funds for counselling sessions) increasingly influence what counsellors do. The model focuses directly on what clients bring to the conversation and how to use these strengths to reduce problems by focusing on opportunities for action.

But the model also has weaknesses. Like most learning theory approaches to counselling, Egan's model tends to shift the solution onto the client. The weakness is that if clients come from a repressive environment, be it family, cultural background or circle of acquaintances, they have to return to this environment after counselling and may believe that the causes of the problem lie with them rather than in the social environment.

Little attention is paid in Egan's help model to factors such as insight, ego strength, self-actualisation, or subconscious factors. Another weakness is that the emphasis (cognitive-behavioural influence) is on goal setting and action planning, possibly at the expense of affective factors. Extensive use of confrontation, questioning, enquiry and brainstorming can become detrimental to a therapeutic relationship and may undermine long-term progress with the client.

Egan's model largely ignores the genesis of problems and thus fails to provide the counsellee with insights and a deeper understanding of the problem.

For effective practice, the counsellor must not only be able to understand Egan's model but must also be able to apply techniques and plan actions. Thus, counsellors should be well trained in behavioural techniques and learning theories. Egan, on the other hand, does not clearly explain how the insights of learning theory should actually be put into practice. Not every counsellor has the attitude or aptitude to apply behavioural techniques appropriately. This requires a lot of practice, skill, hard work and practice.

In Egan's model, the helper works as a cooperative counsellor. But often too little time is spent understanding the psychological or social factors that contribute to the solution of the concern. Similarly, the assumption that every counsellor has the ability to implement a solution to a problem is often made, which is not always the case. Finally, in a counselling approach, the objectivity of the helper is indispensable. But will the counsellor's perceptions always correspond sufficiently with objective indicators regarding the client's problem?

To some extent, Egan's approach does not look at the whole person, but only explains certain behaviours. Coupled with this criticism is that inexperienced counsellors start applying techniques too quickly. Gilliland et al. (1989, p. 47) criticise approaches such as Egan's for programming the client towards minimal or just tolerable levels of behaviour, reinforcing conformity, stifling creativity and ignoring the client's needs for self-fulfilment, self-actualisation and feelings of self-worth. To be fair to Egan: He himself partially addressed this criticism, modified his second stage, as explained in the following chapter, and had the clients think more deeply about their preferred scenario.

3.2 The Problem-Management

3.2.1 The Three-Stage Advisory Model

To explain the process of his model, Egan (2002b, p. 25, 2018, p. 173) states that at some point clients with difficulties have to answer four basic questions:

1. *Current scenario*: What problems should I work on? The answers to this question reflect the current state of affairs or the current scenario of the client.
2. *Preferred scenario*: What do I need or want instead of what I have? Answers to this question represent the preferred state of affairs or the preferred scenario.
3. *Strategies*: What do I have to do to get what I need or want? Answers to this question generate action strategies to achieve the goal.
4. *Act*: How do I bring all this about? Answers to this question help clients move from a planning mode to action or "arranging".

These questions can be broken down schematically to show Egan's three-stage guidance model (see Fig. 3.2).

Egan (1998, p. 25) provides a simplified case to demonstrate how his model works. It is clear that this is not a detailed account of how the conversation unfolds from session to session, but rather a condensed overview of the process in the three stages of this problem-solving model.

> **Example** *Current scenario*: What problems is Maria facing? Maria, a 37-year-old single mother, has two children of primary school age. Since her husband disappeared, she has been working two jobs to earn enough money to support herself and her children. She observes how she becomes more tired and angry every day. At times, she takes out her anger and frustration at work,

(continued)

and because of her frequent outbursts of anger, she is at risk of losing the job. She has also started taking out her anger on the children. Although she does not mistreat her children, she never really has time to devote to them fully.

In desperation, Maria seeks out a counsellor who listens carefully to her story and helps her to elaborate on some important aspects. By digging a little deeper, the counsellor learns that Maria has done nothing to find her missing husband so that he could be ordered to pay alimony. The counsellor also finds out that Maria has a drafting diploma from a technical college. She has skills and talents that are lying idle, which increases her anger because she feels severely under-utilised. In addition, Maria has no social life worth mentioning because of the two jobs and the educational and domestic demands.

After a few counselling sessions, Maria begins to really understand her own situation for the first time. Although there are no dramatic changes in her life, she feels less stressed and angry because of her greater self-understanding. Although she had previously seen herself as a "doer" (after all, she had two jobs and raised two children), she now realises that she had done little to overcome her real problems. Instead, she had developed a *victim mentality*.

This is a brief sketch of Maria's current scenario. The counsellor mainly followed Egan's model in his approach so that Maria could actively participate in the help process.

The three steps of Stage I

- *Step A—The story.*

  The counsellor helps Maria to tell her story with enough detail to help her get to the goal-setting stage ("What do I really want?") of the help process. By

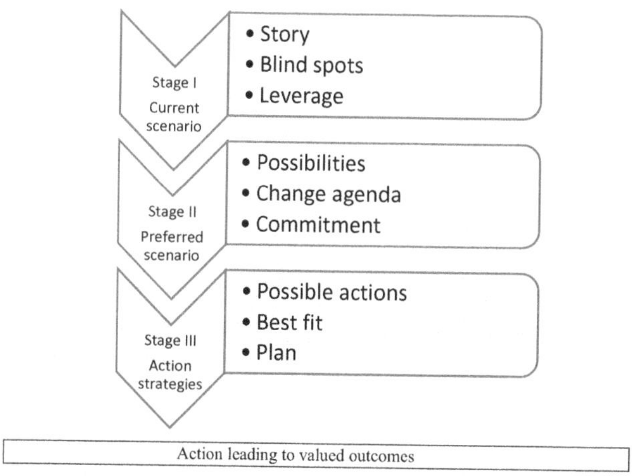

Fig. 3.2 The three-stage counselling model according to Egan

helping the counsellor to understand her problem and what is going on with her life, she has a better chance of doing something about it.

- *Step B—Blind spots.*
  In the course of this step, a counsellor helps the client to identify the blind spots that prevent her from seeing her problem situation and unused opportunities realistically and from successfully shaping the helping process. Maria's counsellor has to help her identify such blind spots and to develop new perspectives.
- *Step C—The right choice of problems to work on.*
  Maria has to work on something that brings about change.
  It is important that the counsellor and Maria focus on her problems and untapped opportunities that can lead to significant change.

"Focusing" means tackling the problem that is currently most pressing for the client. Through a strictly purpose- and result-oriented approach, counsellors want to set immediate stimuli for the client's action. In the last part of Step 1, clients are encouraged to ask themselves questions like the following (Egan, 2002b, p. 239, 2018, p. 175):

- Which problem should I really tackle?
- Which central aspect would bring about a fundamental change in my life?
- How would solving one problem affect the others?
- Where should I best start?
- What problem do I need to address if I am aiming for quick success?

Focusing aims to ensure that clients leave counselling with the best possible outcome.

The three steps of Level II

At this stage, counsellors help the person seeking counselling to recognise what they need and want, i.e. to develop a preferred scenario. For example, what would Maria's life be like if it were more bearable or even fulfilling? Many counsellors start from the

"What's wrong?" of Stage I directly to "What can I do about it?" of Stage III. But Stage II helps clients discover what they really want. It has a profound impact on the whole helping process.

Example *Preferred scenario*:

Within this stage, the counsellor encourages looking into the future. In discussions with the counsellor, Maria discovers many things she would like: a better-paid job, a job that requires her to think and make decisions, better relationships with her children, time for herself, a nicer flat, a few luxuries, a meal in a restaurant now and then, a trip to the cinema and maybe even a car. She also expresses the desire to have less guilt and aggression. She also wants financial help from her husband to support their children.

Maria is encouraged to structure and prioritise her needs and wants. She realises that in order to get out of the impasse, she first needs a better-paid job that allows her more time at home, resulting in a better relationship with her children and also some kind of social life. Just setting priorities makes her think of ways to realise them. The counsellor helps Maria to filter her wishes even more, for example, by asking her to describe in more detail what a better relationship with her children would look like. The counsellor also talks about specific occupations that would fit her needs and desires.

- *Step A—Possibilities for a better future.*
  By using techniques such as divergent thinking and brainstorming, counsellor and client use their imagination to design a better future. Once clients have a more accurate sense of what they really want, they are more able to identify the most important problem points in their lives.
- *Step B—The change catalogue.*
  The counsellor helps the person seeking advice to formulate realistic and appealing goals in order to address the problems and untapped opportunities identified in Step A. Maria's initial list of changes included getting a better job, improving her relationship with her children, and having a better social life.
- *Step C—Self-realisation.*
  Counselling enables clients to find incentives that help them to pursue new goals with perseverance. To achieve this, Maria will need courage and will have to do a lot of work.

The three steps of Level III

Level III defines what needs to be done ("action strategies") to help the client move from priority setting to problem-solving. Here Maria has to ask herself: "What do I have to do to get what I need or want?"

Example *Action strategies:*

During individual counselling, the counsellor encourages Maria to join a "Job Finding Club". Here Maria learns a lot about job search while working with other group members. She talks about the job she wants and she explores what she has to do to get them. Being with other people in a similar situation also allows Maria to restart her own social life. All this helps to relieve her stress about the fact that she feels she has no time for herself. At the same time, she can continue to focus on getting a better-paid job and rebuilding her relationship with the children.

- *Step A—Possible actions.*
  Let the client realise that there are many different ways to achieve goals. Hasty and disorganised action often leads to a partially filled goal. Thinking calmly about many different ways to reach the goal is usually time well spent.
- *Step B—Select best-fit strategies.*

Both—counsellor and Maria—work on finding strategies.

They focus on the ones that best suit Maria's talents, style, resources, temperament, and schedule.

- *Step C—Design a plan.*

  Finally, client and counsellor work on actions that help to achieve the goals set.

3.2.2 Level I Process and Skills

The micro-skills of attentive listening can be summarised in the acronym SOLER (see Exercise 1)

S (squarely)—Openly face the person seeking advice, i.e. adopt a posture that indicates involvement. "I am here with you, I am here for you." Posture should express involvement. It should be noted, however, that communication skills are a delicate matter when there are cultural differences. If it seems too threatening for certain cultures or anyone else to look the other person full in the face, then the counsellor must change his or her posture accordingly.

O (open)—Adopt an open posture. Crossed arms or crossed legs are often interpreted as diminished interest in others. Counsellors should always be aware of the following during the conversation:

"To what extent does my current attitude proclaim openness and willingness to be there for the client?"

L (leaning)—Leaning slightly forward towards the client indicates attention. "I am with you, I am interested in you and what you have to say." In a broader sense, the word "leaning" can refer to a kind of physical flexibility or responsiveness that is conducive to communication with the client.

E (eye contact)—It is important that counsellors maintain good eye contact with the client. However, this does not mean staring. Eye contact also has multicultural and gender implications. Counsellors should always be aware of this.

R (relaxed)—Counsellors must appear relaxed or natural in their relationship with clients. This means avoiding disruptive body language or nervous facial expressions.

The point is that a respectful, sincere, helping attitude easily loses its influence if the client does not find this attitude reflected in external, non-verbal behaviour.

Egan (2002b, p. 71) summarises the main aspects of attention in the following ten questions:

1. What is my attitude towards the client?
2. How would I rate the quality of my presence to the client?

3. To what extent does my non-verbal behaviour indicate willingness to work with the client?
4. What attitudes am I expressing with my non-verbal behaviour?
5. What attitudes am I expressing with my verbal behaviour?
6. To what extent does the client experience me as effectively present in working with them?
7. To what extent does my non-verbal behaviour reinforce my attitudes?
8. What keeps me from giving the client my full attention?
9. What do I do to stop this?
10. How could I become even more effective for this person?

Active listening

Like other authors, including Ivey et al. (1997, 2002), Rogers (1965), Carkhuff (1969), Eisenberg and Strayer (1987), Egan has shown counsellors the importance of understanding clients' verbal messages, experiences, behaviours and associated affects or emotions. Problem situations become much clearer when they are expressed as specific experiences, behaviours and feelings related to specific situations.

Conversations about experiences often focus on what people do or do not do. Sometimes it is implicitly made clear that others are to be blamed for the problems. "At home she does nothing but watch TV. At work I often think about it and then I can't concentrate". Constantly talking about their *experiences* also gives clients the opportunity to avoid their own responsibility.

Clients usually want to talk less about their own *behaviour*, because all people have behaviours that are not always helpful. "I haven't even started looking for a job because I know there are no vacancies here"; "When things do not go well at home, instead of looking for a job, I phone some friends and we go out and have a drink". Affects refer to feelings and emotions that accompany or underlie clients' experiences and behaviours. When clients tell their story, it is a mixture of experiences, behaviours and affects. It is the counsellor's job to help clients 'embellish' their accounts with other essential experiences, behaviours and feelings.

Actively listening to clients is not as easy as it may seem. Many obstacles can get in the way. Counsellors do not listen adequately if they are distracted by their own thoughts or problems. In listening, counsellors may judge what the other person is saying as right/wrong, good/bad, or acceptable/unacceptable. Too often this judgmental listening leads to giving advice, perhaps advice that puts clients before themselves.

Bias, prejudice, and cultural filters prevent active listening, so counsellors need to know themselves to counteract such influences. Many counsellors also focus too much on the information to be gained from the clients instead of taking in the totality of the clients' experiences, behaviours, and feelings.

Besides focusing on data, some counsellors are quick to pigeonhole clients into a particular diagnostic category. It is precisely this pigeonholing that can lead to observational typing (neurotic, paranoid, borderline, etc.) and can get in the way of good active listening.

Exercise 2 aims to help the reader better understand active listening.

Empathy

Empathy is the communication of understanding the other person. That is, the other person must realise that he or she is fully understood by the helper. Empathy seems to mean something different to various authors and counsellors. Schulz (1996), for example, describes empathy as one of the three crucial counselling attitudes (sincerity, respect, and empathy) in building cooperative relationships between helper and client. For Schulz, empathy is more than the ability to reflect a feeling, which is often used to show a certain aspect of empathy. He understands empathy in a comprehensive sense as accepting, affirming, and understanding another person.

Egan, on the other hand, defines empathy more narrowly, as a skill rather than an attitude and/or philosophy. The exercises he offers (see Sect. 3.2) are not dissimilar to the skill of reflecting a feeling according to Gaza et al. (1995) and Ivey et al. (2002). However, to be fair to Egan, he does point out that empathy should ideally be considered "a way of being", even though he usually describes empathy as a skill in his writings.

Elementary empathy is expressed by Egan in the following formula: "You feel . . . (correctly label the emotion shown by the client) . . . *because* . . .". (correctly name the experiences or behaviours that evoke the emotion).

Example *Client* (enthusiastic): I threw all caution to the wind and confronted him with his sarcasm (action) and it actually worked. Not only did he apologise, but he behaved for the rest of the trip . . . (description of the rest of the trip).

Helper: You feel wonderful because you took a chance and it paid off.

Understanding feelings can be expressed in different ways:

Through short statements: e.g. "You feel down"; "You are delighted"; "You are angry".

Through idioms: e.g. "You are devastated"; "You are floating on clouds"; "You have your back against the wall".

By what is implied in statements about the behaviour: e.g. "You would like to give up" (feeling of despair is implied); "You would like to hug him" (feeling of joy is implied).

By what is implied in disclosed experiences: e.g. "You feel that you are being trampled on" (implicit feeling: being victimised); "You think they will be caught soon" (implicit feeling: concern about being arrested).

It is important that counsellors listen for key messages and the context of the messages. It is important for counsellors to pay attention to what is most important to the client. This can also mean focusing either more on experiences, more on actions or more on feelings and not on all three aspects at the same time. If empathy is practised with restraint and flexibility, it can be used to keep clients focused on important issues. Counsellors must never forget that empathy helps clients to see themselves and their problem situations more clearly and to deal with them more effectively.

Enquiry

Not all clients will respond to attentive listening and empathy with openness. And while it is very important for counsellors to respond with empathy when clients do not describe their current situation in enough detail, it may also sometimes be necessary to encourage and prod clients to explore their concerns in more detail if they do not do so on their own. The *skill of skilful questioning* is another important communication skill to move the counselling process forward. As the purpose of enquiry is to help clients explore their problems more fully, enquiry can be useful at every stage and step of the helping process, as it promotes focus and direction.

Enquiry can take many forms:

1. Statements: “It is not clear to me which of these two options you would choose”.
2. Ask: “Why don’t you tell me what you mean when you say ‘the boss never gets it’”.
3. Questions: “What exactly could get in the way of you realising your plan?”
4. Minimal encouragement: “Yes”, “Continue”, nodding head, “I understand”, “hm” or “aha”.
5. Silence: The helper says nothing but leans forward slightly and waits tensely for the client to continue talking.

Exploratory questions can be used in many counselling situations, for example, to help clients formulate vague and abstract things more concretely.

Client: “The boss treats me badly”.
Counsellor: “What does he actually do?”
Client: “He talks about me behind my back and he always gives me the hardest assignments”.

Enquiry can be used to help clients move forward within each step of the process and from one stage to the next balanced view of their problem situations. Sometimes clients only want to present the negative aspects and fail to look at the positive sides as well.

Client: “Sometimes at the end of a hard day’s work I’m just not at my best. I rant and rave to myself”.
Counsellor: “You work hard and you are tired at the end of the day. What about the rest of the day?”

Enquiry can be used to help clients move forward within each step of the process and from one stage to the next. In the first example, the counsellor helps a client brainstorm ways to meet people and make friends.

Counsellor: “Which of the leisure activities or hobbies that you enjoy could help you meet other people?”

Client: "Well, I like playing tennis and going to the cinema. I also like book clubs and discussing books".

In another example, the counsellor uses follow-up questions to help the client move to another stage of the counselling process.

Client: "I don't want to retire and then just be a bagger in the supermarket".
Counsellor: "You have explained in detail what you are doing, now I wonder if you can also set out what you really need and want?"

Exercise 4 gives the reader an opportunity to combine empathy and probing/inquiry.

Process
When people seek counselling, they must be made to feel welcome. They should be encouraged to tell how things are going for them at the moment. Clients need to feel that they are being paid attention to and listened to, that the counsellor is really trying to understand them from their perspective. In short, a cooperative relationship is established. To fully engage in this process, counsellors use basic communication skills.

When Egan practices communication skills with future counsellors, he emphasises the need to master these skills professionally. Doing exercises (see Sect. 3.3) and applying the skills practically in the group is only helpful if they become an everyday communication style. Students are asked to constantly develop these skills in dealing with others through empathy, attentive listening, questioning, and summarising.

Stage I of the help process is indeed the *assessment stage*, where the helper tries to find out what is wrong, what resources are not being used and what opportunities are being missed. In order to do this, it is necessary to explore what is currently motivating the client. It is not about putting the client in a particular diagnostic box, but rather about being open to any form of information or understanding. At this stage, key questions need to be clarified, the seriousness of the problems needs to be assessed and the past should be talked about constructively. As clients tell their stories, counsellors look for potential in it and help clients explore untapped possibilities.

Like Ivey, mentioned in the previous chapter, Egan's model puts a lot of emphasis on learning the key skills of communication, which are used at every stage and step of his model. Unlike Rogers (1965, 1980) and his Person-Centred approach, the communication or relationship between counsellor and client is not the main helping process, but rather the tool for better interaction with clients. The teaching of these skills is not dissimilar to the microcounselling skills of Ivey's model presented earlier. Egan (1998, p. 60) emphasises that the teaching of micro-skills must be constantly related to the needs of the clients and integrated into the whole three-step helping process.

Basic communication skills
Pay attention

Effective attention lets clients know that the counsellor is standing with them and enables the counsellor to listen carefully to their concerns. Attentive presence of the counsellor can encourage clients to open up, feel trust and explore their concerns and problems.

Summary

Like probing questions, summaries can be used to give focus and direction to a conversation. Summaries can be used to great advantage as an introduction at the beginning of a new session, because they prove to the client that the counsellor has listened attentively in the earlier conversation. After the summary, the client should be encouraged to take the initiative to move forward.

A summary can also be used to give focus to a session that seems to be going nowhere. Similarly, a session in which the client seems to have said everything on a particular topic and now seems stuck.

Of course, at the end of each stage of the counselling session, there should be a summary as a conversation-saving activity.

Advanced communication

The advanced communication skills: Questioning, Advanced Empathy, Information Sharing, Self-Revelation, Authenticity and Focusing are used throughout the stages in Egan's model, but can be particularly helpful during Step 1 in order to:

- Clarify key issues/problems
- Talk productively about the past
- Search for resources
- Tap into untapped opportunities
- Deal with blind spots
- Identify themes in the clients' representations
- To establish relationships that may be useful to them

Egan does not believe that Carl Roger's Person-Centred approach—with its emphasis on sincerity, respect, and empathy—is sufficient, but that clients sometimes simply need to be *challenged.* Egan's (1998) principle for this is simple:

> Ask clients to question themselves, to change ways of thinking and acting that keep them stuck in the quagmire of problem situations and prevent them from identifying and opening up possibilities. If they do not comply with the request, they are asked directly to change (p. 147).

Asking clients to change is ultimately what the following skills are about (see also Exercise 6).

Advanced empathy

Advanced empathy involves moving on to meanings of which the client is as yet hardly aware. Often the counsellor senses the story behind the story: What is the client only half saying? What is he hinting at? What is he saying in a confused way? What hidden message is behind the explicit communication? (Egan, 2002b, p. 200; 2018, p. 80 ff.).

The most basic form of advanced empathy is to help clients express more strongly what they really mean.

Client: (hesitantly): "I think I could wait until the personnel office answers. But I don't think it would be wrong to call and ask about the decision on the job".

Counsellor: "You're thinking of calling, but if I'm not mistaken, you're not too keen on it".

Advanced empathy can be used to help clients make connections among their experiences, behaviours, and feelings.

A part-time working student, who is preparing for his final exams and wants to get married after the exam, talks about his fears of not living up to the expectations of others and about his constant exhaustion.

Counsellor: "There might be a simpler explanation for your anxiety and fatigue. First, you work really hard at your job. Secondly, striving for top marks in your exams can cause stress. And thirdly, marriage preparations bring additional emotional stress. Even 'Superman' would have problems with all this".

Client: "I realise now that I may want to do too many things at once. But all my life I have been taught by my parents to tackle everything that comes my way straight away".

By asking the client to examine all the factors, the counsellor helps the client to make connections between different circumstances. The client gradually realises that family expectations play a role in his anxiety and stress.

Advanced empathy has been described as elementary empathy plus a hunch or assumption. Allowing clients to share in the counsellor's educated guesses can help them to see their concerns more clearly and to set goals and act on them. Assumptions can help clients identify guiding principles, take more responsibility for only partially conscious experiences and feelings, and draw logical conclusions from what they say.

Designing information processes

Egan's model is very useful in educational and vocational counselling, where those seeking advice often fail to make satisfactory progress because of a lack of information. Information can help clients at any of the three levels of the model. The skill of designing information processes is classified under the skills of questioning because they help clients to develop new perspectives on their problems and shows them how others have acted. Clients should not be overwhelmed with information but stimulated by it. Counsellors must take special care to ensure that the information given is both clear and relevant. Of course, the information given should be neutral and not misused to impose the counsellor's values. Exercise 7 provides the reader with several examples where the method of designing information processes could be helpful.

Self-disclosure

All the skills described in Step I are designed to help clients tell their stories. Sometimes when counsellors share their experiences, behaviours and feelings, clients are more willing to say more about their own experiences. In this respect, the counsellor's self-disclosure proves to be a form of model learning. Egan (2002b, p. 207 ff., 2018, p. 144 ff.) suggests that counsellor's self-disclosure is challenging because it is a form of intimacy; and secondly, counsellor disclosures commonly want to say to the client, "You can do this too".

For self-disclosure to be most helpful, statements must be selective, focused, and appropriate. The client's concerns must always remain the pivotal point.

Immediacy

In Egan's goal-oriented, action-focused model, direct talk or immediacy becomes an important prompting skill. Directness can help in a number of situations:

1. When there is friction or tension between counsellor and client, it is important to address this tension immediately.
2. If it appears that the client does not fully trust the counselling process and/or the counsellor, the counsellor must investigate this lack of trust.
3. When conversations seem to become aimless, the counsellor must investigate the lack of progress.
4. If cultural diversity results in too much social distance, it is imperative for the counsellor to address this issue.

It is often easier for a helper not to explore tensions, lack of trust, goal-less conversations or social distance. However, counsellors should keep in mind that immediacy is a tool to activate the client and thus to move the whole conversation forward.

Focusing

Stage I of Egan's helping process also involves helping clients to see through their problems and opportunities, to work on the right things and to keep the goal in mind during the assistance process. Focusing means helping the client to achieve positive results quickly. The counsellor should therefore focus on those problems that cause the client the most distress. If at all possible, the counsellor should start with a solvable sub-problem of a larger problem situation.

Egan often uses the focusing technique introduced by Arnold Lazarus (1981). This involves asking a client to describe their problems in one word. Next, the client is asked to put the word into a one-sentence that would describe the problem. The counsellor then moves from this sentence to a more detailed description of the problem. The procedure is a simple way of giving a conversation a clear goal and can be used at any stage of Egan's helping process.

3.2.3 Level II Process and Skills

Process

Within Level II, counsellors help clients answer two crucial questions:

- What do you want? (Preferred scenario)
- What do you have to do to get what you want?

More precisely, this stage contains three steps:

Step 1: Help the client to identify the possibilities for a better future, i.e. determine some of the ways the client can do this.
Step 2: Assuming there are a few options for the client, which one would s/he choose?
Step 3: Help clients commit to change.

As described earlier, Egan's model has evolved over the years. In his revised model of 1998, Egan shifts the emphasis even more to strategies for action. In contrast, fully understanding the origin of problems and changing them through insight takes a back seat. An important aspect of Stage II is goal setting. Goals are needed for the client to act and to show the client the way. Locke and Latham (1984) outline the power of goals this way:

- Goals focus the attention and action of clients.
- Goals mobilise the energy and power of the clients.
- Goals motivate clients to look for strategies to achieve them.
- Goals, if formulated correctly, strengthen the motivation and perseverance of the clients.

Developing a feeling for the right route and exploring the possibilities for a better future are the contents of level II. To let results come before the mind's eye can achieve a lot. But it is equally dangerous to formulate strategies for action before the client has a clear idea of the desired results.

So what are useful techniques or skills that Egan uses to identify possibilities for a better future (preferred scenario)?

Level II Skills

Divergent thinking

As shown in Exercise 10, divergent thinking is used to help clients answer the question: "What do I want? Divergent or lateral thinking implies that there is more than one way to solve a problem or explore a possibility. De Bono (1987, 1992) has described thoughtful techniques for helping clients to think laterally. You can even ask clients to put on hats of different colours to encourage this. Only the creative, coloured hats are worn, as there is little value in being neutral (white hat) or pessimistic (black hat) at this level of counselling. If one wears the red hat, facts are played down and emotions, hunches, feelings and impressions are emphasised. The judgement is made "from the gut". The yellow hat is the very positive one. Clients are encouraged to look for good news, benefits and suggestions for improvement. De Bono's green hat symbolises creative thinking. Clients are asked to be inventive, to look at things differently, to explore alternatives, to go beyond the obvious and to look for interesting solutions.

In short, counsellors need to get clients to overcome fears, fixed habits and dependence on others. In positive terms, this means making clients flexible, persistent and optimistic and preparing them to take appropriate risks.

Brainstorming

Brainstorming is a common strategy used to encourage non-value-added divergent thinking. The rules for this simple, idea-generating stimulating technique are: to refrain from any evaluation, to produce as many ideas as possible, to use a certain idea as a starting point for further ideas, to discard the usual boundaries of thinking and to produce even more ideas by using special item lists. Exercise 11 shows what can be done to develop non-judgemental suggestions.

Formulation of goals

Helping clients formulate goals is an important skill that counsellors need to learn. Useful goals usually have the following characteristics:

- They are formulated as outcomes rather than activities.
- They are specific, realistic and challenging.
- They are flexible.
- They are within a reasonable time frame.

Counsellors can achieve much greater cooperation in goal setting if they continue to use the collaborative strategy of brainstorming as well as the communication skills presented in Stage I of Egan's helping process. Egan (1998) asked counsellors who set goals together with clients the following questions:

1. Is your goal linguistically oriented towards results?
2. Is the goal specific? How do you know you have achieved the goal?
3. Can the goal be realised?
4. Is it possible to hold on to the realisation of the goal over a long period of time?
5. Is the goal compatible with your values?
6. Have you set a realistic timeframe for achieving the goal?

Obtain a voluntary commitment

Although engaging the client's commitment is not such a specific skill as paraphrasing, asking open-ended questions or reflecting feelings, it is an important part of the last step in Step II of Egan's model of helping. There is already a big difference between a client who is supposed to agree to a goal and a client who does not slacken in achieving his goal through action. What can the counsellor do to achieve an ongoing commitment from clients? Counsellors can help clients by:

1. Presenting goals in a more attractive way
2. Helping clients to become more involved in their problems
3. Helping clients to deal with competing programmes of action

Counsellors can help clients make goals more appealing by pointing out the benefits of individual goals and the consequences of not acting on a goal. For example, if a client continues as before, she will continue to have a job that only pays minimum wage, but if she works on her goal of furthering her education, her prospects for a higher salary and job satisfaction will increase enormously.

Clients need to take full ownership of a goal in order to make a longer-term self-commitment. If it is more the counsellor's goal than the client's, the client will blame the counsellor in case of failure. Self-contracts are therefore a good way and also serve to bring the goals more into focus.

Clients will often see other important tasks in their lives that run counter to goal realisation, such as responsibilities for the family, current work or even leisure interests and social life. Counsellors can help by making clients aware of competing tasks and emphasising the need to find a work/life balance without losing sight of the appealing side of goal realisation.

3.2.4 Level III Process and Skills

Process

Level III is about the activities needed to achieve the outcomes planned in the previous level. At Level III, counsellors try to bridge the gap between the resources and the needs or wants of the clients. Clients have to brainstorm many strategies that might help them to achieve their goals. If clients have difficulties in doing this, counsellors can initiate the process by making their own suggestions. However, the main responsibility of assessing the value of approaches and ultimately selecting them lies with the client.

Client: "I could try one more thing, but that's it".
Counsellor: "I'll give you a few examples of what others have done who have had a similar problem. Would that be OK".

An important part of Level III is the identification of resources for the client, such as resources from others, role models, the community, career organisations or oneself.

Other people, such as neighbours, friends and relatives, can be very helpful to someone who is having difficulty finding work. They may have job tips and they can also provide a lot of encouragement and motivation during the job search period. The same goes for identification figures. Having someone as a role model, who does what the client wants to do or who has the attitudes that might be helpful to the client, is an important resource. Some organisations may be willing to help clients; organisations such as Alcoholics Anonymous or Unemployment Initiatives. There may also be programmes, courses or workshops that are of considerable help to the client. In most cities, there are programmes for people who want to become more self-confident or to cope with frustration, depression or grief.

It is important to remember that all clients are ultimately on their own. Thus, counsellors need to help clients establish relationships with appropriate agencies as soon as possible. The counsellor must provide knowledge of community and regional networks.

After this initial step in Stage III, clients need to decide what the best strategies are for their situation and resources and then create a step-by-step change plan.

The approach chosen should be specific and realistic enough to allow the client to arrive at a solution to the problem. Most clients find it easier to choose a strategy if they first try out a few possibilities. For example, a high school graduate who has to decide between several fields of study can seek counselling at a career centre or ask successful people in the field about their interests. Another way to determine the best strategy is the balance matrix method. A sample can be found in Exercise 18.

Finally, clients are asked to make specific plans. A good plan identifies the activities or actions required to achieve the goal or sub-goal, arranges the activities in a logical order and sets a time frame for the successful completion of each major action step.

A good counsellor will also prepare his clients for the time when they are on their own. This includes alternative plans of action for phases in which things do not go so well for the client. This preparation helps clients to develop more responsibility in situations where their plans do not work but they have to make a decision. Alternative plans do not need to be complicated and can be prepared with a counsellor's question: "If this doesn't work, what will you do?"

In summary, the three steps at Level III are to:

1. Help clients develop possible strategies for achieving their goals (what do clients need to do to get what they want)
2. Help clients choose strategies that are related to their preferences and resources
3. Help clients develop a step-by-step action plan

Level III Skills

Assessing personal skills

Many clients do not have the life experience or the ability to cope with their problem situation. This being the case, practising skills according to Egan's counselling model becomes very important. Other clients are not aware of their potentials and need help to assess their personal skills. Exercise 16 provides a helpful checklist for this lack of awareness.

As indicated in the description of this stage, the counsellor also helps the client to access role models, community, and relevant organisations, as well as meetings with people who have similar problems.

Determination of the procedure

Egan asks clients a series of questions to help them choose strategies. Typical questions to check a particular course of action include:

1. Do you understand what you need to do with this strategy?
2. Will you make it in the planned timeframe?
3. Does this strategy suit you personally?
4. Will it take you where you want to go?

Balance sheet matrix method

When clients have to make decisions, a kind of balance matrix can be helpful. This involves weighing whether both benefits and costs are acceptable. A less structured approach is to evaluate strategies with questions such as the following:

1. How does this strategy benefit me and others?
2. What are the costs of this strategy for me and others?

Use supporting forces

Before clients leave counselling with the intention of following a plan of action, counsellors can reinforce clients' motivations and make it easier for them by making them think of possible help they may get from themselves and others; help such as the following:

- Pride
- A promise to oneself
- Trying something new
- Encouragement from the family
- Encouragement from friends
- Good feeling you get from acting on goals
- Financial resources
- Deferring current pleasures

Exercises 20 and 21 have been included so that counselling students can examine themselves in relation to multiculturalism in their own lives, families, and world-views. Egan (2002b, p. 52, 2018, p. 42) lists some principles for integrating these views into her counselling methodology:

- Put the client's needs first in all considerations.
- Identify the client's perceptions and focus on them.
- Base the counselling methods on the client's ideas and not on social or political guidelines.
- Make sure that your own value system does not negatively influence the client's interests.
- Avoid cultural stereotypes, because groups often have greater differences within them than between them.
- Do not meet cultural diversity with definitions that are too narrow.
- Create an atmosphere of professional tolerance.

3.3 Competence Development Exercises

It was important to Egan not only to present a model of helping but also to provide counsellors with a set of techniques and skills to make his approach actually work. These techniques and skills include:

1. Basic and advanced communication skills
2. Building sustainable relationships with clients
3. Helping clients to question themselves
4. Problem clarification

5. Setting goals
6. Developing action plans
7. Implementing plans
8. On-going evaluation

Egan (1975, 1982, 1986, 1990, 1994, 1998, 2002a, 2002b, 2007, 2010, 2018) and Egan et al. (2013) use a standard approach to teaching and practising skills. The first step is *cognitive understanding.* Counsellors in training are encouraged to develop a cognitive understanding of a particular skill. This is usually achieved through reading and lectures. *Clarification is* done through guided discussions about what the students have read or heard. The third step in this process is *model learning.* Experienced instructors provide a model for the use of a particular skill. This can be done live or via films and video sequences. Next, *written exercises* (such as those in this section) are provided on the skill. The purpose of the written exercises is to allow learners to experience for themselves that they have understood a particular skill and are now ready to apply it in practice. The fifth step is *practice.* Egan has students work in small groups so that they can practise skills with other students. In *feedback,* instructors and students give evaluative comments to reinforce what is done correctly and to correct what was wrong. Finally, in step seven, the *learning experience is assessed. Time is* taken to reflect on the whole process of the training. Steps one to six cover the acquisition of the necessary skills, while step seven is dedicated to working in training groups. Finally, when participants are ready, they get *practice with real clients under supervision.*

Before specific exercises are presented, here is again a brief overview of the model and its skills:

Stage I: The current state of affairs

Clarification of the main problems that call for change

1. Help clients to tell their "story".
2. Help clients to tackle their blind spots and gain new perspectives.
3. Help clients to focus on areas that will bring about significant changes (focus setting).

Some skills for Level I:

- Attentive listening
- Basic empathy
- Enquire/probe
- Summaries
- Advanced empathy
- Information exchange, self-revelation, and immediacy

Level II: The preferred scenario

Helping clients determine what they need and want

1. Help clients unlock a range of possibilities for a better future.
2. Help clients turn possibilities of the preferred scenario into goals.
3. Help clients feel committed to the goals they choose.

Some skills for level II:

- Divergent thinking
- Brainstorming
- Formulation of goals
- Bring about self-commitment

Level III:Strategies for action
Helping clients discover how to achieve what they need and want.

1. Help clients brainstorm a range of strategies to achieve their goals.
2. Help clients to choose action strategies that best fit their needs and resources.
3. Help clients to come up with a plan.

Some skills for level III:

- Assessment of personal skills
- Definition of a strategy
- Balance sheet matrix method
- Additional support

Exercises are intended to provide a link between understanding a skill and actual practice. The following exercises are an abridged version of Egan's (1998) "Counselling Skills Practice Manual".

3.3.1 *Exercises for Level I Skills*

Level I deals with building a cooperative relationship between helper and client and helping the client to focus on key areas. Basic communication skills and stimulation are important throughout the conversation.

Exercise 1
Feedback on attention behaviour

1.	Students should recall the acronym SOLER.	
	S	Squarely face the client
	O	Open posture
	L	Lean towards the client at times to emphasise your attention.
	E	Eye contact without staring.
	R	Relaxed while interacting with clients.
2.	During the training programme, give yourself and other students occasional feedback on the quality of your listening attention using the following checklist:	
	a.	How effectively does the counsellor use posture to signal willingness to work with the client?
	b.	In what ways does the counsellor distract the client?

(continued)

	c.	How does SOLER help the counsellor to work more effectively with the client?
	d.	How naturally does the counsellor behave when he devotes himself to the client?
	e.	What else does the consultant have to do in terms of attention in order to achieve more impact?

Exercise 2
Active listening

1.	Listen carefully to what clients are saying.
2.	Identify key experiences of clients.
3.	Identify key behaviours of clients, what they do, don't do or are ashamed of.
4.	Identify the key emotions associated with these experiences and behaviours.

Example 1
A man, 38 years old, has been told that he will never walk properly again as a result of a bad fall on a building site. He says to you: "Why did this happen to me? I'm still a young guy. I was really careful at work, but a gust of wind knocked me down while I was lifting a plywood panel. What am I going to do? I'll never be able to walk again" (he starts sobbing).
Key experiences of the client:
Key behaviours of the client:
How does the client feel about these experiences and behaviours?

Example 2
A single mother with three children talks to a job counsellor about how she could find a job and get off welfare: "I just never make ends meet. I'm always broke at the end of the week. I can't buy my children decent clothes, and they find it terrible that they can never bring friends to our run-down apartment building. How can I find a job that will free me from this miserable life?
Key experiences of the client:
Key behaviours of the client:
How does the client feel about these experiences and behaviours?

Example 3
A young man in his twenties who had served some time in prison was sent for counselling to help him find a job. He is reluctant to see a counsellor and says: "I don't know what I am doing here. No counsellor has ever helped me. Why don't you give me your easy job and then I'll also bore the clients for a while. I don't want to talk to you. You definitely won't get anything out of me today."
Key experiences of the client:
Key behaviours of the client:
How does the client feel about these experiences and behaviours?

Exercise 3
Show empathy

1.	Identify for yourself the client's key experiences, behaviours, and feelings.
2.	Formulate an empathic response using the following form: You feel . . . (identify the emotion) because . . . (describe the key experiences and/or behaviours that evoke this emotion).
3.	Make empathetic statements (without using the formula).

Example 1
A 59-year-old early retiree says to the counsellor: "Now that I am retired, I spend a lot of time just wandering around the house, which is much too big for me ... (he pauses and looks aimlessly out of the window). When I was working, life offered much more. I knew what to do ... That was quite a difference. Now that I'm comfortably retired ... I just don't know."
Key Experience(s):
Key behaviour(s):
Key feelings/emotions:
Empathic statement (formula):
Your own empathetic statement:

Example 2
A middle-aged man complains about his aged mother: "She uses her old age and arthritis to bully me. She has bullied me all her life. When I counter her, she cries and complains about all her sufferings and pains. (He presses his lips together). I bet she will even manage to make me feel guilty about her death."
Key experience(s):
Key behaviour(s):
Key feelings/emotions:
Empathic statement (formula):
Your own empathetic statement:

Example 3
A first-semester student talks about all the difficulties of getting used to life in the big city and going to school with hundreds of students. Going to university. She comes from a small town far away: "It's so difficult to know what to do. I get invited to parties, but I still feel like a real outsider. I don't wear the right clothes. But, yeah, I'm enjoying university (looks sullen) and soon I'll make friends as close as I had back home."
Key experience(s):
Key behaviour(s):
Key feelings/emotions:
Empathic statement (formula):
Your own empathetic statement:

Exercise 4
Enquire/Probe

1.	Respond with empathy first.
2.	Formulate a follow-up question that might help the client to identify or explore main issues.
3.	Briefly state the reasons for using the probing question.

Example 1
An employee who has trouble with his colleagues says to the HR manager: "I can't take criticism. When people make reprimanding remarks to me or give me negative feedback, I smile and shrug my shoulders, but inside I know I want to get back at those people who criticise me. I'm just waiting for one of them to make a mistake."
An empathetic response:
An exploratory question that might help the client to get to core issues:
The reason for the question:

Example 2
A young man talks to a counsellor about his relationship with his mother: "I feel guilty and depressed as often as my mother calls and tells me how lonely she is. Then I get angry at myself for succumbing so easily to feelings of guilt. My whole day is then spoiled, and at work I am nervous and irritable. But I always give in to it."
An empathic reaction:
An exploratory question that might help the client to get to core issues:
The reason for the question:

Example 3
A law student is talking to the counsellor: "Yesterday I found out that I messed up the law exam. I won't get a second chance. What a bummer! This was my first year in a big city and I couldn't cope with all the distractions. I don't know how to face my parents. They've been paying for my living and now I have to tell them it's all down the drain."
An empathic reaction:
An exploratory question that might help the client to get to core issues:
The reason for the question:

Exercise 5
Summarise

In his Exercise Manual, Egan (1998) suggests the following exercise to help students learn the skill of summarising.

1.	The students are divided into groups of three.
2.	There are three roles in each of these subgroups: Helper, Client and Observer.
3.	The helper spends about 7–8 min counselling the client.
4.	After four minutes, the helper summarises the main points of the interaction. After about eight minutes, the helper should make a second summary.
5.	After each summary, the helper should ask the client to draw his or her conclusion, which in turn leads to the next step.

(continued)

6.	Then the observer and client give feedback to the counsellor on how accurate and helpful the summary was. A summary is helpful if it leads the client to problem clarification, goal setting and action.
7.	The process is repeated until everyone in the group has had a chance to play all three roles.

Exercise 6
Questioning and stimulating a response

General rules

Unproductive mental attitudes and corresponding actions are specifically questioned.

1.	Read the case studies and determine in which area this client could benefit from questioning.
2.	Briefly describe what new perspectives might be helpful.
3.	Share your observations with a fellow student. Record similarities and differences to your suggestions.
4.	Discuss how you would proceed further to help clients question themselves.

Example 1
Daniel is leading a project but is way behind schedule. Talking to his supervisor, he says, "This is the first time I've been a project manager and the others are not used to working with me. The key people from planning and production are delaying everything. They keep saying they have other projects to work on. I know our client wants delivery by the end of the month, but that's his schedule and it's not necessarily realistic. He is pushing so hard. Now it's already uncomfortable to take his phone calls."
What attitudes and corresponding behaviours could be questioned here?
What could helpful new perspectives look like?
What kind of action could such a perspective lead to?

Example 2
A new counsellor - who works locally in a hospital - believes that doctors have no respect for counsellors. She feels bullied because she is new, a woman and a counsellor. When a colleague advises her to confront the doctors, she says: "That would only make things worse. I think it's more important to stand up for my profession by just being myself and helping the clientele as much as I can. I know doctors are mean, but that's a game they play in every hospital. That's the way it's always been. In general, it's not such a big deal."
Which attitudes and corresponding behaviours could be questioned here?
What could helpful new perspectives look like?
What kind of action could such a perspective lead to?

Advanced empathy

Advanced empathy means sharing sound assumptions about the client's experiences, behaviours, and feelings. This skill is only used after a good working relationship has been established.

1.	Approach the client with elementary empathy.
2.	Formulate one or two assumptions about the client's experiences, behaviours and feelings.
3.	Respond with advanced empathy.

Example 1
A student in his first semester of mechanical engineering at a renowned technical university talks about being disappointed with himself and his school performance. His father, a very successful engineer, did not put any pressure on his son to study mechanical engineering. The student says: "I lack the necessary enthusiasm. My grades are okay, maybe not quite as good as they could be, but I know I could be much better. I don't know why my disappointment with the university and the professors weighs so heavily on me. I'm not usually like this. Even as a child, I wanted to be an engineer. I should be happy to be able to study at this good university, but I'm not."
Elementary empathy:
Your assumption and your justification for it:
Advanced empathy:

Example 2
A high school graduate is talking to the counsellor about his study plans. In doing so, he mentions his disappointment at not being chosen as the graduation speaker: "I know I would have liked to have been the valedictorian, but I know you can't rely on something like that. They have chosen Nicole. She will do a good job. She is a good speaker, and she is extremely popular. No one is entitled to be valedictorian. I'd be kidding myself if I thought any differently. I did better than Nicole in school, but I'm not as outgoing or popular as she is."
Elementary Empathy:
Your assumption and your justification for it:
Advanced empathy:

Exercise 7
Giving information

Giving information is the skill of providing clients with information that helps them to see their problem situation more clearly.

1.	Point out possible blind spots of the client in the following examples.
2.	Indicate what information might help the client to gain new perspectives and move to action.

Example 1
A man in his mid-twenties is aware that he drinks too much. Last weekend he had a short blackout after an alcoholic binge. So far he had always managed to hide his addiction. He works alone and has had more sick days than the average person in the company. Most of the time, the alcohol excesses take place on weekends. No one in his family or among his friends has ever been an alcoholic.
What blind spots could this client have?
What information could help this client to develop new perspectives?

Example 2
A high school graduate, whose two older sisters are doctors, discusses her career plans with the counsellor. Her school performance is below average; she is particularly weak in science subjects. She is exceptionally talented artistically but would like to follow in her sisters' footsteps and start studying medicine.
What blind spots could this client have?
What information could help the client to develop new perspectives?

Example 3
Markus can't decide which career path he should take. He did well in secondary school, and he could probably do well in any of the three professions he is considering (IT, banking, chemical engineering). He racks his brain to avoid making the wrong career decision.
What blind spots could this client have?
What information could help this client to develop new perspectives?

Exercise 8
Self-Disclosure

Self-disclosures should help the client to perceive their problem situations more clearly. List two areas where you think you have something to share that could help clients with problems similar to your own.

Area 1	What from this area could you talk about yourself?
Area 2	What from this area could you talk about yourself?

Exercise 9
Immediacy

Immediacy refers to the counsellor's ability to deal directly and appropriately with events and behaviours that affect the counselling relationship.

1.	Offer an immediate response to the situations presented, a response that helps the client to question useless perspectives and actions.
2.	Share your responses with a fellow student and give each other feedback. Together, come up with a more effective immediate response.

Situation 1
A man who has worked in the construction industry on and off for the last ten years has problems getting a new job. Now he comes to see you as a job counsellor. During the first part of the interview, he is cooperative, but in the later stages he becomes quite ornery and even begins to doubt your competence as a counsellor.
Immediate reaction:

Situation 2 A counsellor in her early forties helps a young man to think about his career opportunities. At first the young man works well with the counsellor, they get closer to being able to determine some of the young man's career aspirations as well as his interests and skills more precisely. When the counsellor summarises some of the young client's strengths, he suddenly says: "You are just like my mother, who always tells me I have what it takes to make it."
Immediate reaction:

3.3.2 *Level II Skills Exercises*

Stage II focuses on a better future, the client's preferred scenario. Goal setting and self-commitment of the client are important concerns of this stage.

Exercise 10
Divergent thinking

Divergent thinking is used to help clients develop a vision of a better future.

What do I want?

1)	Write your name in the middle of a page. Then draw radiating lines out to the important social factors in your life (school, family, friends, etc.).
2)	Pick out several social references where you currently have problems or suspect unused opportunities.
3)	Next, write down problems and concerns about each of the identified social factors.
4)	Finally, list possibilities for a better future in these areas. For example, consider the following exploratory lead-ins: – This is what I need... – This is what I want... – These are a few items on my wish list ... – When I'm done, I'll ... – I will then ... – Instead I will ... – I will it only ... – There will then be more of ... – There will then be less of ...
First social field referenced: Problem points, demands, conflicts, opportunities, concerns in connection with this social field of reference:	
Opportunities for a better future in this area:	
Second social field referenced: problem points, demands, conflicts, possibilities, concerns in connection with this social field:	
Opportunities for a better future in this area	

Exercise 11
Brainstorming

Non-judgemental suggestions of what it could look like if everything were better. In other words: What would you like to have instead of what you have now?

1.	Read the case study and assume you are that person. (Do not give advice).
2.	Point out a blind spot that might prevent this person from dealing effectively with the problem situation.
3.	Using brainstorming (in pairs or groups of three), produce a series of possibilities for a better future.
4.	Use the list from the previous exercise ("Divergent Thinking") to help develop possibilities for a preferred scenario.

Example
An employee who has trouble with his colleagues says to the personnel manager: "I can't take criticism. When people reprimand me or give me negative feedback, I smile and shrug. But inside I know I want to get back at those people who criticise me. I'm just waiting for one of them to make a mistake so I can pay them back."
A blind spot is transformed into a future-oriented and new perspective:
A range of possibilities for a better future.

Exercise 12
Formulating goals

Goals should be achievable, formulated as outcomes, specific and flexible, and embedded in an appropriate timeframe.

1.	After reading the case study, identify what good intentions the client might have (e.g.: I need to be more energetic if I am to be a good supervisor in this work group).
2.	State the client's broad (very general) goal (e.g.: I want to be more involved in this group).
3.	Write down a specific goal for this client that is realistic and formulated as an outcome (e.g.: I want to express my thoughts in this group at least once every hour, when appropriate

Example 1
Frank is venting about the stress he faces in his job. He has been working in accounting for a large company for five years. He earns a decent salary, but he is becoming increasingly dissatisfied with the nature of his work. He finds it increasingly undemanding and boring and does not think he has much chance of promotion in this company. Many of his colleagues are much more ambitious than he is.
Establishing a positive intention:
Rough target:
Specific target:

Example 2
Claudia feels that she is not confident enough, especially at work. She thinks she gets distracted too often when she is in the middle of a project. She then gets angry at herself for putting her own work aside to help the person who interrupted her. As a result, she sometimes misses important deadlines and thinks the others consider her to be a "Pushover".
Establishing a positive intention:
Rough target:
Specific target:

Exercise 13
The selection of advisory strategies

The following acronym CRRAVE can help those seeking advice to select strategies:

C	Clarity	Is the procedure clear?
R	Relevance	Is it relevant? Is it purposeful?
R	Realistic	Is it realistic? Can I make it?
A	Appeal	Does sit speak to me?
V	Values	Does it correspond to my values?
E	Effective	Is it effective enough? Does it really help?

Use the following four-step process:

1. Think about possible action strategies for one of your goals.
2. Choose two strategies that seem most important to you.
3. Use the CRRAVE questions to test the validity of each of these strategies.
4. Make a provisional choice.

Selection process for strategy 1 (with short explanations in each case)

C	Clear	
R	Relevant	
R	Realistic	
A	Stimulating/appealing	
V	According to one's own values	
E	Effective	

Selection process for strategy 2 (with short explanations in each case)

C	Clear
R	Relevant
R	Realistic
A	Stimulating/appealing
V	According to one's own values
E	Effective

Exercise 14
Obtain self-commitment

When clients make commitments, they are more likely to achieve their goals.

1.	State the most important goal you set for yourself in the training or a goal a client might set.
2.	Discuss (using the following questions to guide you) this goal with a partner to measure the level of commitment.
	a. What is your current readiness for change in this area?
	b. To what extent do you freely choose this goal?
	c. To what extent do you choose this goal from a range of possibilities?
	d. How much of an incentive do you think this goal is for you personally?
	e. Name everything that makes the destination not appealing to you.
	f. What urges you to choose this destination?
	g. If your goal has been imposed on you in some way, what are you doing to make it your own?
	h. What difficulties do you experience in committing to this goal?
	i. To what extent is it possible that your commitment is not a genuine self-obligation?
	j. What can you do to overcome the obstacles?
	k. What can you do to increase your engagement?
	l. In what ways can the goal be reformulated to make it more appealing?
	m. To what extent is the timetable for achieving this goal insufficient?

(Egan, 1998, p. 137)

3.3.3 *Exercises for Level III Skills*

Level III is about what clients need to do to solve their problems. At this level, the counsellor can use the skills of divergent thinking (Exercise 10) and brainstorming (Exercise 11) to help clients identify different ways to achieve their goals. Other skills that counsellors can use during this level are the focus of the following four exercises.

Exercise 15
Steps in a plan of action

This exercise is designed to help you develop an action plan for each of your action goals.

1.	Specify a goal that you would like to achieve.
2.	Review the strategies you have considered.
3.	Outline the main steps you need to take.
4.	Get feedback from others in your training group.
5.	Revise your plan based on the feedback in terms of (a) The objectives to be achieved (b) The strategies for achieving the goal (c) The most important steps in the plan

Exercise 16
Assessment of personal skills

Sometimes problems develop because clients do not understand how to make sense of certain skills that are needed in life.

Assess each of your skills for yourself in terms of their level and importance.
Next, indicate those skills that, if improved, could help you to manage your worries or problems.
State why such a skill is important to you and what you could do to develop it

Checklist	
Expression	
very high expression of this skill	5
high expression	4
average expression	3
moderate deficiency in this skill	2
major shortfall	1
Importance	
very important	5
important	4
average importance	3
rather unimportant	2
not important at all	1

Learning how to acquire skills	**Expression**	**Importance**
Knowing how to read well		
Knowing how to write comprehensibly		
Basic knowledge of mathematics		
Knowing how to learn and study efficiently		
Understanding something about computers		
Knowing how to use a library		
Knowing how to find information		
Other skills in this area:		

Self-management skills	**Expression**	**Importance**
Know how to plan and set realistic goals		— —
Skills to make decisions		
Skills to solve problems		—
Knowledge of how to give rewards and punishments		—
Knowledge of how to manage once own emotions		
Deferred gratification patterns		—
Self-confidence knowing how to meet one's		
Knowing how to fill one's needs		
Satisfying the needs of others		
Other self-management skills		

Communication skills	**Expression**	**Importance**
The ability to actively listen to others		
The ability to understand others		
Empathy		
Being able to communicate understanding to others		
The ability to question others thoughtfully		
The ability to provide useful information to others		
The ability to speak in front of a group		
Other communication skills		
List the most important skills and how you could develop them:		

Exercise 17
Strategy determination

1.	Ask the following questions if clients have difficulty choosing among possible strategies. *Clarity:* Is the strategy clear? *Relevance:* Is it relevant to my situation and goal? *Realism:* Is it realistic? Can I do it? *Incentive:* Does it excite me? *Values:* Is it compatible with my values? *Effectiveness:* Is it effective enough? Will it get me where I want to go?
2.	Share your findings with a fellow student. What can you learn from the differences?

Case study

A young man in his final year of school is completely undecided about what career direction he wants to take. He has good grades. He prefers more practical learning and would therefore rather go to a technical college than to a university. On the other hand, he thinks it would be better in the long run if he enrolled at university. Use the above criteria to evaluate the following strategy of the young man: "I'll go to university for a year first and if I don't like it, I'll change to a technical college".

Exercise 18
Balance sheet matrix method

The balance matrix can be used to help clients choose both goals and strategies. The balance matrix should not be used in its entirety, but only those parts that can currently help the client.

1.	Choose a personal goal with a partner and brainstorm a set of strategies.
2.	Choose a main strategy or sequence of actions to be studied in more detail.
3.	Identify the significant other and social references affected by your choice.
4.	Explore the possible course of action, using as much of the balance matrix as necessary to make a clear decision.

The decision matrix

	Acceptable to me, because	Not acceptable to me, because
The Self		
Gains for the self		
Losses for the self		
Significant others		
Gains for others		
Losses for others		
Social environment		
Gains for the social environment		
Losses for the social environment		

(Egan, 1998, p. 344)

Exercise 19
Use supporting forces

In this exercise, you identify forces that could help clients to implement their strategies and plans.

1)	Discuss a goal and an implementation plan with a partner. Imagine that you are actually (in real life) trying to implement the steps of the plan.
2)	Identify some forces that could help you achieve your goal. Some examples: a) Pride b) Keeping a promise to oneself c) Trying something new d) Encouragement from the family e) Encouragement from friends f) A pleasant feeling g) Saving money h) Postponing current pleasures
Your examples:	
Which supporting forces from the list are most helpful?	

Exercise 20
My family and I

Dealing with one's own family history plays an important role in most cultures. The following questions should be discussed in the small group:

- What important life events have touched your own family? Tell the story of your family.
- Tell us about the most crucial event in your life and how it influenced you and the work as a counsellor. Was there any multicultural impact?
- How has the family influenced where you are today?
- In the literature, the four essential life roles are defined as loving, learning, working and leisure. How did these roles differ in the different ethnic groups?
- Comment on your culturally specific development and in what way it may have influenced you with regards to your self-perception and the perception of others.

Exercise 21
Your own multicultural worldview

It is undisputed that in North America and Europe, white, male, heterosexual and middle-class people enjoy power and privileges that they are often not even aware of.

Part 1	Discuss the following statements and decide whether you would accept them as "normal".
a.	If I move, I am absolutely sure that I could rent or buy a house in the area of my choice.
b.	When my children have difficulties at school, the teachers always have an open ear for me.
c.	I have never been asked to speak for all the people in my cultural sub-group.
d.	When paying by credit card, my financial reliability was never questioned because of my skin colour.
e.	I can afford what I want, not just what I need to live.

Part 2	It is now assumed that multiculturally oriented counsellors perceive themselves as culturally aware, have knowledge about ethnic groups and have skills that are appropriate for different clients. In a small group, discuss the following questions:
a.	Do you have prejudices against ethnic minorities? Do you expect some cultural sub-groups to have lower levels of education?
b.	Do you have the same attitudes towards homosexuals, women, minorities, and disabled people?
c.	Have you prepared for cultural diversity in your counselling practice?
d.	What knowledge do you have about the ethnic groups in your area?
e.	Which counselling approaches are most appropriate for which minority groups?

Exercise 22
Overcoming obstacles

The following role play serves as an exercise on how to help people who postpone dealing with problems or have difficulties in overcoming obstacles:

Scenario 1:	Roland has difficulties motivating himself to get up early every morning and look for a job. He always finds new excuses for not being active.
Scenario 2:	Sarah informs the counsellor that she will soon be moving to a smaller town where counselling services are not readily available. What advice can be given to Sarah to manage without easily accessible counselling options in the future?

References

Bandura, A. (1969). *Principles of behavior modification*. Holt, Rinehart & Winston.

Brammer. (1973). *The helping relationship: Process and skills*. Prentice-Hall.

Carkhuff, R. (1969). *Helping and human relations* (Vol. 1). *Selection and training*. New York: Holt, Rinehart & Winston.

Carkhuff, R. (1971). *The development of human resources*. Holt, Rinehart & Winston.

Carkhuff, R. (1973). *The art of problem solving*. Human Resources Development Press.

De Bono, E. (1987). *Six thinking hats*. Penguin.

De Bono, E. (1992). *Serious creativity: Using the power of lateral thinking to create new ideas*. Harper Business.

Egan, G. (1975). *The skilled helper*. Brooks/Cole.

Egan, G. (1982). *The skilled helper* (2nd ed.). Brooks/Cole.

Egan, G. (1986). *The skilled helper* (3rd ed.). Brooks/Cole.

Egan, G. (1990). *The skilled helper* (4th ed.). Brooks/Cole.

Egan, G. (1994). *The skilled helper* (5th ed.). Brooks/Cole.

Egan, G. (1998). *The skilled helper* (6th ed.). Brooks/Cole.

Egan, G. (2002a). *Skilled helping around the world*. Thompson Learning.

Egan, G. (2002b). *The skilled helper* (7th ed.). Brooks/Cole.

Egan, G. (2007). *The skilled helper* (8th ed.). Brooks/Cole.

Egan, G. (2010). *The skilled helper* (9th ed.). Cengage Learning Brooks/Cole.

Egan, G. (2018). *The skilled helper – A client centred approach* (2nd ed.). Cengage Learning Brooks/Cole.

Egan, G., Owen, J., & Reese, R. (2013). *Exercises in helping skills: A manual to accompany the skilled helper: A problemmanagement and opportunity-development approach to helping* (10th ed.). Cengage Learning Brooks/Cole.

Eisenberg, W., & Strayer, J. (Eds.). (1987). *Empathy and its development*. Cambridge University Press.

Eysenck, H. J. (1965). The effects of psychotherapy. *International Journal of Psychiatry, 1*, 97–178.

Gaza, G. M., Asbury, F. R., Balzer, F. J., Childers, W. C., Phelps, R. E., & Walters, R. P. (1995). *Human relations development* (5th ed.). Allyn & Bacon.

Gilliland, B. E., James, R. K., & Bowman, J. T. (1989). *Theories and strategies in counseling and psychotherapy*. Prentice Hall PTR.

Goldstein, A. P. (1966). Psychotherapy research by extrapolation from social psychology. *Journal of Counseling Psychology, 13*, 38–45.

Hackney, H., & Nye, S. (1973). *Counseling strategies and objectives*. Prentice-Hall.

Hackney, H., Ivey, A., & Oetting, E. (1970). Attending, island and hiatus behavior: A process conception of counselor and client interaction. *Journal of Counseling Psychology, 17*, 342–346.

Ivey, A. (1971). *Microcounseling: Innovations in interviewing training*. Thomas.

Ivey, A. (1972). *Microcounseling: Interviewing skills manual*. Thomas.

Ivey, A., Ivey, M. B., & Simek-Morgan, L. (1997). *Counseling and psychotherapy: A multicultural perspective* (3rd ed.). Allyn & Bacon.

Ivey, A., D'Andrea, M., Ivey, M., & Simek-Morgan, L. (2002). *Theories of counseling and psychotherapy* (5th ed.). Allyn & Bacon.

Kagan, N. (1973). Can technilogy help us toward reliability in influencing human interaction? *Educational Technology, 13*, 44–51.

Krumboltz, J. D. (Ed.). (1966). *Revolution in counseling: Implications of behavior science*. Houghton Mifflin.

Lazarus, A. A. (1981). *The practice of multimodal therapy*. McGraw-Hill.

Locke, E. A., & Latham, G. P. (1984). *Goal setting: A motivational technique that works*. Prentice Hall.

Maier, N. R. F. (1960). Screening solutions to upgrade quality: A new approach to problem solving under conditions of uncertainty. *Journal of Psychology, 49*, 217–231.

Morrow-Bradley, C., & Elliott, R. (1986). Utilization of psychotherapy research by practicing psychotherapists. *American Psychologist, 41*, 188–197.

Rogers, C. R. (1961). *On becoming a person: A therapist's view of psychotherapy*. Houghton Mifflin.

Rogers, C. R. (1965). *Client-centered therapy: Its current practice, implications and theory*. Houghton Mifflin.

Rogers, C. R. (1980). *A way of being*. Houghton Mifflin.

Rübner, M., & Sprengard, B. (2010). *Handbuch für Berufsberaterinnen und Berufsberater – Beratungskonzeption der Bundesagentur für Arbeit (Bd. 1) (Handbook for career counsellors – Guidance concept of the Federal Employment Agency)*. Nürnberg: Bundesagentur für Arbeit

Schulz, W. E. (1996). *Basic counseling skills*. Human Resources Development Winnipeg.

Skinner, B. F. (1953). *Science and human behavior*. Free Press.

Chapter 4
Solution-Focused Counselling

4.1 Development and Status of the Approach

The development of counselling was influenced by various disciplines, primarily psychology, medicine, and philosophy. Later, the developments of career counselling, test application and mental health care were added, so that the current approaches to counselling emerged from this mixture. A great deal of energy has since been invested in explaining, diagnosing and understanding human nature, but little attention has been paid to problem-solving. Many clients find out that a comprehensive explanation of their problems is not synonymous with a significant improvement in their situation.

In the 1980s and 1990s, brief counselling, especially solution-focused brief counselling, challenged many of the assumptions of earlier theories and models. These earlier models had emphasised that real change was only possible when clients fully understand the true nature of their problems. Closely related to this notion is the assumption that symptoms indicate problems and that every problem has a deep, threatening underlying cause. This may be true for medicine, but hardly for counselling.

O'Hanlon and Weiner-Davis (1989, p. 26) contrasted the solution-oriented views with the central assumptions of the problem-oriented approaches:

1. Symptoms always have deeper causes.
2. Insight is a necessary prerequisite for change or elimination of symptoms.
3. Simply eliminating the symptoms is at best useless or superficial and at worst dangerous or even harmful.
4. Symptoms have an essential function.

Updated translation of chapter 4 from: Handbuch Beratungskompetenz, 4th ed. by Bernd-Joachim Ertelt & William E. Schulz, 2019, Springer Verlag.

B.-J. Ertelt et al., *Counsellor Competencies*,
https://doi.org/10.1007/978-3-030-87413-1_4

5. Many clients are ambivalent about change and are not very receptive to counselling.
6. Real change takes time-short consultations are superficial and short-lived.
7. The focus is on identifying and correcting problems and deficits.

Solution-focused counselling offers new ways of thinking about counselling, because this model focuses on the potentials rather than the weaknesses or limitations of the clients. This counselling approach can be exemplified by this brief story: In 1984, Jim Fry, manager of the Chicago Cubs baseball team, saw his star player watching a recent video about his performance. The player was in a slump, he had been hitting the ball out of bounds for the last three weeks and wanted to analyse his mistakes. Jim Fry then looked for video recordings of successful games and challenged his player to improve his batting by taking his cue from his previous successes.

4.1.1 Influences and Development

The late family therapist, Milton Erickson, is considered one of the pioneers of the solution-focused idea. His counselling work gave many impulses to solution-focused counselling.

One of the cornerstones of Erickson's approach was the consideration of clients' typical behavioural patterns and experiences. In doing so, he not only accepted their representations but also actively included them in his treatment plan. He thus integrated the clients into problem-solving through their language, interests, attitudes, behaviours, symptoms and resistances (O'Hanlon, 1987, p. 24).

Some startling examples will illustrate Erickson's influence on contemporary solution-focused counselling.

Example 1: Counselling integration of the client's interests and motivations

A police officer who retired early for health reasons no longer had any impetus to leave the house. He ate little, drank and smoked. Erickson advised him to buy only one packet of cigarettes at a time and to go to the other side of town. In addition, he should only ever buy his food from a shop that was at least one kilometre away from home but only for one meal at a time. The same applied to drinking; everything was allowed, provided the client always went to an inn at least one kilometre away. In this way, it was possible to connect the client's behavioural patterns by linking his interests with the goal of going out among people again (Rosen, 1982, p. 149).

Example 2: Changing behaviour patterns
An elderly man, whose wife had died, developed pathological insomnia. Although he spent 14–15 hours in bed, he only got an average of two hours of real sleep, the rest of the time he tossed and turned. Erickson found out that the man hated to polish the floorboards in his house because he had to do it by hand and also couldn't stand the smell of wax. Erickson agreed with the client that he should wax every night when he could not sleep. In only two nights the client's condition improved (Haley, 1985, Vol. 1, p. 54).

Solution-focused counsellors, like Erickson, are convinced that it is much easier to redirect a flow than to dam it up completely. Thus, they focus their interventions on the behavioural patterns of their clients as well as on the "channelling" of their behaviours and experiences.

But others also influenced solution-focused brief counselling. These include the work of Bandler and Grinder (1979) on neuro-linguistic programming and the elaboration of clear goals through outcome-oriented techniques (cf. Bandler & Grinder, 1997, 12th ed.). Haley's work (1976) highlighted the importance of "problem negotiation" with the client.

Further influences on modern solution-focused brief counselling came from social constructivism, which focuses on the sense-making of human experience.

The solution-orient counsellor sees his task less in defining the problem, but rather in shaping this cooperative process, taking into account the client's potential and responsibility (Cade & O'Hanlon, 1993; De Jong & Berg, 1998; De Shazer, 1992, 1994, 1997, 6th ed.).

It should be mentioned that the concepts of Narrative therapy according to White and Epston (1990), independently developed in Australia and New Zealand, also focus on promoting the client's own solution approaches by concentrating on the client's resources. In Narrative therapy, the counsellor helps the client to narrate a problem-related view of their own life and then develop alternative narratives. Narrative counselling has influenced various solution-focused counsellors, such as Durant (1995), Hart (1995), Metcalf (1995) and Murphy (1997).

However, the main influence on the development of solution-focused counselling was the founding of the Mental Research Institute (MRI) by Don Jackson in 1958. This institute started a project on brief counselling in 1966. The project leader, Richard Fisch, attempted to solve clients' problems by narrowing the focus of treatment and helping them to change the specific behaviours associated with their problems (Fisch et al., 1982). The emphasis was on treating the presented problem and less on developing self insight in the clients. The problems were understood to be interactional in nature, caused by interpersonal difficulties, rather than coming from within the person.

The counsellors at the MRI thus pursued three goals (Segal, 1991):

1. Finding remedies and methods for a quick, effective relief of the client's complaints.

2. Transforming counselling from a skill to a teachable craft.
3. Exploring changes in human systems.

The MRI counsellors and therapists hypothesised that problems result from mishandling of everyday events and that problems are perpetuated by people's multiple attempts to solve them. The work of the counsellor basically consists of deliberate actions to change ineffective behaviour patterns of the client when interacting with others.

Amatea (1989) and Segal (1991) outlined the counselling process at MRI with the following questions:

1. What are the complaints?
2. What has the client done about it so far?
3. What is the client's goal?
4. What is the client's attitude to his complaints and to the treatment?

After these questions have been answered, the counsellor must interrupt the previous attempts at a solution and give the client new perspectives. Concretely, the counsellor must answer the following questions:

1. What is the new attempt at a solution?
2. What happens to this solution approach when it is rotated 180 degrees?
3. What specific behaviour brings about the change?
4. How can the counsellor make the client aware of this new behaviour?
5. How can you tell from the client that the intervention has been successful?

In the MRI method, the counsellor will first identify the nature of the problem and then identify the ways in which the client has already tried to solve the problem. MRI counsellors suspect that the way clients define and handle their problem often contributes to prolonging it. Therefore, counselling efforts are directed towards innovative approaches to problem-solving through specific cues to the client to look at their problem from different angles.

Steve De Shazer and Insoo Kim Berg co-founded the Brief Family Therapy Center (BFTC) in Milwaukee, Wisconsin in the late 1970s. De Shazer (1985) moved away from work at MRI, where the focus was on researching the causes of the persistence of problems. He turned to ways of solving problems and promoting positive client development. To characterise his change of perspective, he once used the comparison with picking a lock. The key to opening the door is more important than understanding how the lock works. A counsellor does not need to know much about the problem, but more about ways of solving the problem. A counsellor who has the duplicate keys for as many different doors as possible can help best. The following task is often used successfully by solution-oriented counsellors in the first counselling session:

Clients are asked to remember an experience between the first and second appointments that they want to happen again. This exercise is meant to tune

(continued)

the clients into positive things in their existence and to create expectations for corresponding changes in this direction. A vision of positive future changes is a central aspect of solution-oriented counselling. This vision of a positive future is particularly helpful for the long-term unemployed and for poor students who often lack positive future references with possibilities for action.

At a congress on the development of psychotherapy in 1990, the keynote speaker Victor Frankl spoke to an audience of 7000 about his experiences in a Nazi concentration camp in Poland. Several times he had been close to death, for example when he had to go on a march with other prisoners on a winter day in Poland. They were wearing only thin clothes, no socks, and shoes with holes. Frankl was debilitated by malnutrition and mistreatment and got such a coughing fit that he collapsed. Even the beating of the guards could not get him up, although he knew that this meant the end of his life. As he lay on the ground like this, he suddenly imagined that he was not on the snowfield in Poland. Instead, he saw himself giving a lecture on "The Psychology of a Death Camp" to two hundred attentive students in post-war Vienna. He had prepared this lecture during his imprisonment, and it dealt with the psychological factors of dehumanisation. He explained why, in his opinion, some people were able to cope with this experience psychologically and emotionally better than others. When Frankl told his imaginary audience that he no longer had the strength to get up and continue walking, he actually did get up and continued walking. His body straightened up, the guard stopped beating him and he was able to continue walking, slowly at first, but then better and better. Frankl continued his imaginary lecture throughout the work and the march back to the concentration camp. Only there did he collapse in his bunk, but still remembering the brilliant lecture and the subsequent standing ovation in his mind's eye. Almost 50 years later and thousands of miles away in California, Frankl received a rapturous applause for his lecture from an audience of 7000. Frankl had freed himself from his "problem" by developing a vision of the future.

Solution-focused counsellors realise that they are transforming clients' problems into something that is more treatable (O'Hanlon & Weiner-Davis, 1989). Clients of psychoanalytic counselling, for example, leave the first session of counselling with unresolved childhood issues as the centre of their problem. From behaviourist-oriented counselling, clients come away with the definition of a behavioural problem and the mandate to change certain behaviours.

Problems are defined jointly by client and counsellor and appear very differently depending on the counselling theory. Solution-oriented counsellors, therefore, believe that there is no such thing as "*the* problem" in counselling, but rather that there are a large number of ways of looking at a client's situation.

A client complains about his constant depression. On further enquiry, it emerges that he only has these moods at the end of the week. Specific enquiries

(continued)

reveal that the greatest complaints almost always occur only on Sunday afternoons, but that there is hardly any time for them during work or when hanging out with friends. With this new insight into the severity and duration of the problem, the goal of developing alternative plans of action for Sunday afternoons becomes clearer and more achievable.

In the early 1960s, Abraham Maslow stated that psychology and counselling were moving in the wrong direction. Most psychological research was aimed at understanding the nature of emotional, psychological, and behavioural pathologies. Instead, Maslow argued, the focus should be on studying the best and healthiest people to learn more about human life. This changed view of solutions and strengths has already changed much of counselling work.

4.1.2 Research Results

Research findings seem to confirm the success of action-oriented counselling with its solution orientation and full inclusion of clients' potentials. Lambert's (1992) graph summarises three decades of research on what best helps people in counselling (see Fig. 4.1).

- Factors on the part of the clients
  The greatest influence on the success of counselling (40%) comes from the client's talents, strengths, attitudes and positive social background.
- Relationship factors
  As Carl Rogers and other relationship theorists have pointed out, empathy, emotional warmth, respect for the other person and an accepting attitude are of great importance for the success of counselling (30%).
- Expectations
  Hopes and expectations of positive change explain 15% of the success of counselling, as Lambert's (1992) research shows.

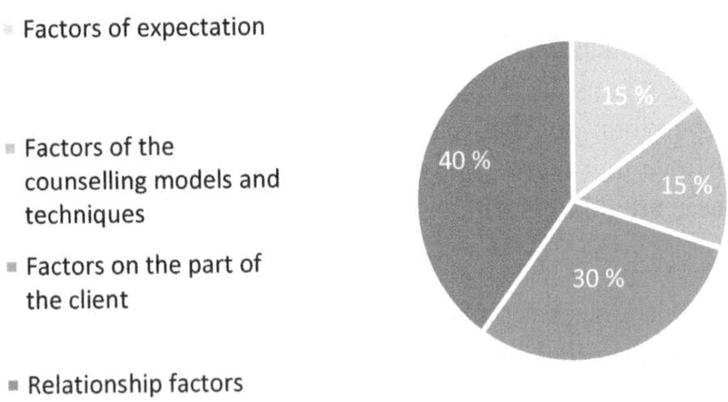

Fig. 4.1 Factors in counselling success

- Method-related factors

  The counsellor's theoretical orientation and counselling techniques also play a 15% role in the success of counselling.

Although the number of counselling theories, models and methods has increased immensely over the last three decades, "results" research has not shown any one of these approaches or compilations of techniques to be consistently better than others. It seems that the similarities among the models explain the counselling changes much better than the specifics of any one model (only 15%).

Solution-focused counselling is strongly influenced by the fact that the client's potentials and the relational level in counselling are of the greatest importance for change (Garfield, 1994; Lambert, 1992). Therefore, solution-focused counsellors encourage the use of the client's own skills, motivations and attitudes in problem-solving. Research (Howard et al., 1986; Lawson, 1994) on positive pre-intervention change shows that desired client progress happens before actual counselling. This should encourage counsellors to see their clients as quite capable of coping with their problem situation themselves and to encourage them to be more self-active.

With regard to the relationship level factors, Patterson (1984) states that there is convincing evidence of the importance of respect, warmth, and genuineness in behaviour for counselling success. These factors lead to higher client engagement in counselling. Orlinsky et al. (1994) reviewed over 1000 studies and concluded that the quality of client involvement in counselling has a strong impact on outcomes. Solution-oriented counsellors use knowledge of this research in their approaches.

Expectations also clearly influence the success of counselling. These factors include both the client's hopes for the counselling and the perception of the counsellor's credibility. The power of hope and expectation has been demonstrated in a number of studies (Frank & Frank, 1991; Snyder et al., 1991). Career counsellors and school guidance counsellors in particular can increase hope in their clients by directing their gaze to the future and to the existing possibilities for improvement, emphasising confidence in clients' potential.

Beutler (1994) came to similar conclusions as Lambert (1992) based on a review of studies. According to his research, 75% of the client's progress results from contextual variables in counselling (environment, constellation, frequency, duration), from the extent of support from the counsellor, and from the client's internal and external resources. Only 10% of the changes can be attributed to the counselling models or techniques.

The research findings also support other core elements of solution-focused counselling. Cultural aspects are important everywhere, but especially in career guidance. The collaborative nature of solution-focused counselling (as opposed to the more directive approaches) reinforces a sense of autonomy and equality in counselling for ethnic minority clients. Ridley (1995, p. 82) emphasises that clients are to be understood from their cultural frame of reference and that they are considered experts on themselves and can set appropriate goals.

Duration is another important factor in counselling, with research showing that short-term counselling (such as solution-focused counselling) is as effective as long-term counselling (Budman & Gurman, 1988; Koss & Shiang, 1994; Orlinsky & Howard, 1986). Similarly, Talmon (1990) stated that 88% of clients from one-time counselling sessions reported improvements in their problems in follow-up surveys after 3 and 12 months.

The practice of school and career guidance needs methods that are easy to implement, easy to handle and time-efficient. Solution-focused counselling meets these requirements, even more so if one starts from the optimistic idea that even very short counselling sessions can bring about significant improvements.

4.1.3 Strengths and Weaknesses of the Model

Research speaks for action-oriented counselling and the comprehensive use of the client's potential. As already shown, short-term counselling seems to be just as effective as long-term counselling. Moreover, a time limit can also signal to the client that they are trusted to manage their own affairs to a certain extent.

In this model, the counsellor is very active and asks a lot of questions. This activity shows both interest and involvement. If someone says: "I don't know what to do with my life, I'm totally at the end". Counsellor reaction to this comment can vary widely. One counsellor may remain silent and thus allow the client to talk more about his or her apparently hopeless situation. Another counsellor may ask questions such as the following:

- "I would like to know more about it. What are some of your symptoms and how long have you had this feeling?" (Confirmation that it must be a serious problem)
- "What made you think you couldn't do anything with your life anymore?"
- (Introduction of certain doubts about the problem situation)
- "What is different from the days when you manage your existence well?"
- (Suggest that there are times when the problem does not occur).

Another reason for the growing popularity of solution-focused counselling may be the zeitgeist. In North America, short-term counselling quickly became the method of choice across the private counselling practice sector. Businesses offer counselling services to their employees but are only willing to pay for a limited number of sessions. But clients also want short-term counselling, and they expect a structured, focused, and problem-solving approach. Career counsellors, career advisors and school counsellors are expected to serve a number of clients every day. This is another reason for using time-limited models such as those offered by solution-focused counselling.

Solution-focused counsellors often use the techniques of "reframing" or imagining a new reality (cf. Bandler & Grinder, 1997, p. 167). Ellis (1996) describes "reinterpretation" as a critical conversation about irrational assumptions clients make about disturbing occurrences. However, by making a reality appear in a different light, counsellors change the subjective perception and behaviour of clients. The classic story of Tom Sawyer offers an example of the ability to reinterpret. As punishment, Tom Sawyer had to paint a fence every Saturday when his friends were allowed to play outside. Tom presented this ordeal to his friends as an opportunity not afforded to every boy. In exchange for payment, he passed on the privilege of painting the fence.

Solution-focused counsellors have also made significant contributions to the issue of client resistance. At Brief Family Therapy Center (BFTC), it is assumed that there is no such thing as client resistance, but that clients are open to change. Clients offer counsellors different ways of cooperation, and it is up to the counsellor to learn from this and to choose the appropriate way of cooperation (see Exercises 1 and 2 at the end of this chapter).

Solution-focused counselling has expanded the counsellor's scope of action with a number of useful intervention techniques. These include the frequently used methods: "wonder-question", "defeating the expert", "paradoxical recipes" and the "random task". These interventions are described in the following chapters.

Perhaps solution-focused counsellors are right in saying that in long-term counselling too much time is spent on extended reflection on feelings and listening to problems. In contrast, counsellors using solution-focused counselling emphasize the need for greater client involvement and the need to use more creative techniques.

However, critics have also pointed out a number of possible shortcomings. For example, there is little or no connection to a theory or at least a conception of generally recognised human needs. Too often symptoms are treated as something to be separated from the client. A somewhat harsh criticism is that the only thing short about brief counselling is the counsellor qualification. But most counsellors are traditionally trained in long-term methods; only with this background can short-term counselling be practised appropriately.

"The counsellor knows best" is the subliminal message when the solution-oriented counsellor gives guidelines. Although counsellors always emphasise the inclusion of the client's potentials, there is an imbalance on the relationship level that can lead to clients not contributing their assessments and skills sufficiently. In such cases, counsellors should remember the following short story:

> Once upon a time there was a man who gave parents lessons on good parenting. He called it "Ten Commandments for Parents". Mothers and fathers who were unsure about their parenting skills came from near and far. The man himself had no family of his own at the time. But one day he got married and had a child. He then changed the title of his lecture to "Five Suggestions for Parents". When the second child came, he changed the title again to "Three Preliminary Suggestions for Parents". But after the third child, he stopped his parenting classes completely (O'Hanlon & Weiner-Davis, 1989, p. 9).

This story is a reminder that no one has final answers or solutions to all human problems.

Ellis (1996, p. 129) has drawn attention to further limitations of solution-focused counselling:

1. Many clients cannot say exactly how they solved their problems so far.
2. Current depression, anxiety or aggression often prevent clients from transferring past solutions, even if they can remember them.
3. Earlier solutions are better than nothing, but not always good for the current situation.
4. Previous solutions work for the time being, but they do not necessarily have a permanent effect.
5. Quick, solution-based "arrangements" may prevent clients from longer-term better solutions. For example, if someone who has a height phobia and only rents a flat on the first floor because of it, he or she is not dealing with the actual causes of the phobia and a long-term solution.

In many areas, there is a need for more than a "quick fix" and for consideration of the underlying forces of a problem. The solution-oriented approach can be very technique-oriented, especially if counsellors see counselling as a repair shop. Then the person is seen like a machine where everything can be made objective and visible. In this case, the recognition and appreciation of the uniqueness of the human being is missed. A lot of humanity is lost in counselling when counsellors do not sufficiently appreciate the individuality of each client.

Another limitation of this model relates specifically to school and career guidance. Solution-focused brief counselling may perhaps reinforce a phenomenon common among young people that can be called "premature closure". When the pressure to make a career choice becomes too strong, there is a real danger that indecision will lead to a hasty and premature commitment, often resulting in young people closing themselves off to further information.

Solution-focused counselling makes too little reference to the process of decision-making and the importance of differentiated information-gathering and evaluation.

The increased popularity of solution-focused (brief) counselling is also underlined by two publications in the German-speaking world: Wolters, Lösungsorientierte Kurzberatung (2015, 4th ed.) and Bamberger, Lösungsorientierte Beratung (2015, 5th ed.). Both works contain case studies and exercises that offer good supplements to our explanations and open up new fields of practice.

4.2 Model of Solution-Focused Counselling

> "If I focus on the problem, it becomes bigger; if I focus on the solution, it becomes more effective" (Alcoholics Anonymous).

Solution-focused counselling appears to be the methodology of the future. Brown (2012, p. 71) counts it among the "postmodern" approaches. It offers immediate reinforcement and rapid counselling assessment. This appears to be very important at a time when there is more and more need for counselling and less time for longer models. Methods of abbreviated, concentrated help are in demand (Carlson & Sperry, 2000; Thompson & Rudolph, 2000, p. 137). This solution-oriented thinking is now also finding its way into other areas, such as medicine (cf. Bamberger, 2015, p. 39).

It was once said of solution-focused counselling that it is "a person-centred stew, fortified for good measure with a dash of cognitive behaviourism" (James & Gilliland, 2003, p. 309). Yet it is among the few theories that look more to the future than to the past or present. The main counselling task is to enable clients to perceive their problems in new ways and with new possibilities.

In the practice of career guidance, career counselling and school counselling, the counsellor usually does not have enough time for a longer, in-depth counselling with appropriate support. Solution-focused counselling is a unique method that offers clients the opportunity to solve problems in a relatively short time. Pupils, students, job seekers, people who are dissatisfied with their jobs and other target groups are encouraged to use their own strengths and potentials. This focus on strengths and the use of the client's own potential is the key to solution-oriented counselling.

The counsellors must radiate the conviction that the client can do better. Recent research supports Rosenthal's (1966) work on the influence of the experimenter's expectations on the outcome of an experiment. Positive or negative biases of the counsellor influence the counselling results. As a result, solution-focused counsellors focus their positive expectations on their clients' strengths and possibilities for action.

Beyond this, however, there are a number of other prerequisites for this form of counselling (Ertelt & Schulz, 1997, p. 182).

4.2.1 Basic Assumptions

1. *Change without deeper self-insights*
   Often too much time is spent on promoting self-insight and not enough time on learning how to make important changes. In fact, knowledge of certain symptoms can be used as an excuse for inaction. So, improvements can also be made without in-depth self-insight.
2. *Client's self goals are motivating*
   When counsellors set goals and take on the role of experts, they take on a heavy burden. They can hardly be trusted to offer viable solutions to all the situations clients face. However, when clients set goals themselves, they become more aware of their capacity for self-activity. For example, in responding to the question of "What needs to be different?", the client is motivated to spend time on ways to get there.
3. *Limitation of the problem analysis*
   It is not necessary to know everything about a problem to be able to help. Some clients find it easier to see a counsellor if they know that they do not have to

explain their problem in great detail. When the problem is talked about in counselling, this aspect expands; when solutions are talked about more, solutions become more likely.

4. *Problems are seen as being normal*

   When counsellors look at the exceptions to the problems, problems seem more normal and more solvable. For example, if a student is sent to the counsellor with a diagnosis of "hyperactive", this phenomenon seems less unusual if the student is said to have too much energy. The counselling session can then focus on the times when the pupil has behaved in a controlled way.

Also, if on certain occasions a young person can hardly contain his anger towards his instructor, the counsellor tries to find similar situations in which the young person remained calm, even though the situation should have provoked anger. The counsellor might ask him to think: "How did you manage to control yourself there?" The aim is to make the young person think of some positive coping mechanisms that he or she was not yet aware of.

5. *Complex problems do not always require complicated solutions*

> *Example*
>
> Some time ago, a daily newspaper carried the headline "Queen of Violets Dead - Hundreds Mourn". The background was as follows:
>
> Years ago, a very depressed elderly woman who no longer enjoyed anything or anyone, came to see a solution-focused counsellor. She was very active in church and devoted to flowers, especially African violets. The counsellor asked the woman to give someone an African violet the next time she went to church. Soon she was giving such violets at every birthday, wedding and funeral. So the woman was quickly integrated and lost her depression, she had become the "violet queen". A very simple solution to a complex situation!

This rule is intended to encourage attempts to make small positive changes and not to wait for "big solutions". Often it is just small progress that has far-reaching effects. For example: A young person tells the counsellor that during the week he has no problems with his vocational training, but on the weekend, he is always so dissatisfied with the programme and he thinks of dropping out. The solution-oriented counsellor immediately targets the "simple solutions" that this student uses during the week to be motivated.

6. *Strengthening self-motivation*

   Often clients are not that motivated to make positive changes in their lives because they do not know exactly what they want. Therefore, the solution-focused counsellor should ask the client the question early on: "Are you willing to do everything possible to improve your situation?" If a client is not quite sure what needs to be improved, the following task can help motivate him: "In the coming week, pay attention to moments when you feel particularly good in your training. Register where you are, who is with you and what you are doing. At our next meeting, tell me which of these moments you want to relive."

7. *Realise that retrospection is not essential for problem-solving*

   To be able to help, you do not necessarily have to know everything about a problem. An understanding teacher told of a pupil who came to her whenever he felt depressed and sad.

   The teacher never asked to talk about the causes and the teacher did not try to pressure the pupil into revealing what his problem was. Rather, she gave him her full attention during the multiple visits and was able to help the student get through his depressive phases better through her rather passive behaviour. Often, respect for a client's privacy reduces resistance and improves the conditions for a helping conversation.

8. *Even small changes can have a lasting impact*

   The "ripple effect" occurs when clients take initial small actions that then trigger larger changes. Instead of counselling in order to get a huge insight, counsellors should rather guide their clients towards small, manageable steps, being aware of the motto: "Even a long journey begins with the first step" (Confucius).

9. *If it goes forward, do not stop; if it does not, move on!*

   Many clients try the same ineffective strategy over and over again. A "no" to the question: "Has this approach helped you so far?" suggests other strategies. "What approach has helped you so far?" is the next important question. This encourages clients to remember the successful ways in the past that could be followed now. This focus is especially important for those seeking advice who have had a lot of problems in school and vocational training. The counsellor quickly directs the counselling session to the "land of opportunity" for the future. Instead of focusing on the "problem zone" of worries, failures and aversions, the counsellor and client talk about overcoming the problems. They focus on successes achieved in the past. They deal with the question "What will happen when the problem has been solved?"

   Moving the client away from the problem, even temporarily, can help them become aware of positive behaviours and see them as goals for a changed life.

10. *The search for exceptions*

    "I'm always so down!" or "Others never do anything for me!" These blanket complaints are typical of clients who find their situation hopeless and see no way out. But no one is depressed 100% of the time. By making it clear to such clients that there is an exception to every problem, counsellors can open up the possibilities for clients to realise that they can control the situation better than they previously believed.

The counsellor asks a counselee who complains of persistent depression: "When do you feel less depressed?" He answers that this is the case from Monday to Friday at work. He also feels fine at the weekend, especially on Saturdays, when he is with his bowling friends. But on Sunday afternoons he starts to mope and become increasingly depressed. The counsellor: "So out of the 168 h in a week, you feel down for six hours on Sunday afternoon. I mean, you should look more at the 162 hours of the week when you hardly notice any depression."

As shown, the goals of solution-focused counselling are directed towards changing the clients' view of the problem in the direction of how they can improve their situation. Focusing on the problem seems to be of little use. Much more meaningful and useful, however, is the cooperation of client and counsellor in the search for and development of possible solutions. The following case study illustrates the process of solution-oriented counselling.

Case study
The highly unmotivated pupil Robert shows very poor performance. He rejects most of his teachers and gets into sharp arguments with his parents when they take him to task for his lack of effort and poor grades. Robert is sent to a solution-focused counsellor. There he drops into the chair, appears sullen and stares at the wall.

Counsellor	Pupil
What would you like to experience at school?	I want to pass the class so that I can get out of school as soon as possible.
What grade point average would you be satisfied with?	At the moment I have hardly any chance of getting through. For me, "sufficient" or "satisfactory" would be enough; I don't even want to have good or very good grades!
Have you ever had an average performance?	Yes, but that was months ago.
Well, what was different then compared to your situation today?	Back then I could work undisturbed in my corner of the classroom, but now everyone talks at cross purposes in class and dawdles around. I do not feel like it anymore either.
Have you tried to achieve a satisfactory performance at least once in a while?	Yes, I have already tried to study more intensively again, and I sat down somewhere else for a day or two.
And what else?	I recently asked the teacher for a detailed explanation. She gave me a very good explanation and I fully understood it at that time.

This little dialogue shows how the counsellor tries to find out behavioural patterns that have helped the student in some way. In the course of the conversation, Robert became less and less negative because the counsellor used Robert's own solutions. The pupil increasingly participated constructively and was encouraged in the further counselling sessions to use the strategies that had already helped him to do better at school.

Murphy (1997, p. 9) emphasises that using the success strategies, attitudes and behaviours that are already part of the client's repertoire prove to be more effective and workable than trying to teach the client new behaviours or to change their attitudes.

4.2.2 Process of Solution-Focused Counselling

Although not all solution-focused counsellors proceed in the same way, there are generally five steps in this method of counselling (Miller, 1993):

Step 1: Both counsellor and client striving to build a good working relationship.
Step 2: Working out clear counselling goals.
Step 3: Orientation of the client towards solutions.
Step 4: Developing solution-focused interventions.
Step 5: Maintaining the goal: How do you help the client to make changes permanent?

Step 1: Establishing a good working atmosphere

> "Tell me something, I forget it. Involve me, and I will understand it"
> (Chinese proverb).

Like many other counselling approaches, the solution-focused model considers a cooperative relationship between counsellor and client to be very important. Counsellors should be open-minded and respectful towards their clients and be willing to listen patiently and empathise with them.

Solution-oriented counsellors consider it helpful for counselling cooperation if they distinguish three types with regard to the client-counsellor relationship:

- The "customer" type
- The "visitor" type
- The "complaining" type

When a jobseeker visits a solution-oriented counsellor in a "customer" attitude, he or she also wants to be treated as a customer:

"Suggest something to me, I want to do it!" or "I hope you have new ideas on how I can find a job!" or "I don't know what else to do. What suggestions do you have for me to find a job again?"

These clients show a willingness to work with the counsellor immediately. They want to discuss concrete alternatives for action as quickly as possible and to be included in the rapidly progressing counselling process.

"Visitor" type clients are those who have been advised by others to see a counsellor. They are often not very motivated and committed. Suggestions for action by the counsellor usually fall on deaf ears with this type. The counsellor can ultimately help them better if s/he realises that the client is only a "visitor". The client's attitude (although negative) must be acknowledged. ("I realise how unpleasant it is for you to have to come to me in order to continue receiving social assistance.").

Although "visitors" among the clients have a negative view of the counselling, the counsellor promotes changes in the client from the beginning with questions like the following: "What do you think we can achieve so that you do not need another counselling appointment with me?"

These clients need a lot of positive and timely reinforcements:

"Although things are not good for you, you came here today!" "I am very impressed how clearly you describe your difficult situation!"

These clients cannot be told what to do. Rather, counsellors must try to renegotiate the counselling goals and make them more attractive.

"Would you be interested in working out a way or two to make your job search more effective?"

Clients of the "complaint type" acknowledge that they have a problem and are willing to talk about it at any time, but they resist taking action to solve the problem. These clients believe that someone else is responsible for change.

Solution-focused counsellors have found that listening, reinforcement and getting the client's opinion work well with this "complaint type". By offering these clients new insights and interpretations, the counsellor leads the "complaining" type client to the first steps of action. It is often helpful to ask such clients to think about something, observe something or predict something related to their problem. Some examples may illustrate this:

"Since you know a lot about unemployment in your city, it would be helpful for me if you reflect on what you think could improve the situation".

"In order for me to help you more effectively, it would be good if you could look at other jobseekers' ways of getting a job".

"Please try to make a prediction every morning about whether you will have a good or bad day in your job search. I am very curious about your predictions!"

Such or similar interventions actively involve the client and lead him/her to a greater willingness to accept action-oriented suggestions.

Murphy (1997, p. 54) has summarised the three types of counsellor–client relationship as follows:

Type	Labelling	Cooperative strategies
Type "Visitor"	Does not perceive a problem or sees it as affecting someone else	Avoiding action-oriented suggestions to the client
	Comes to counselling under duress. Does not engage in solving the problem	Recognition of the client's point of view
		Praise for positive aspects of her or his presentation or viewpoints
		Redefining the problem and the goals so that they seem more attractive and important to the client
		Inclusion of extracurricular or non-professional interests and hobbies
"Complaining" type	Acknowledges the problem and its importance, but is hardly willing to contribute significantly to the solution	Avoiding action-oriented proposals
		Listen and praise
	Sees himself as an "uninvolved bystander" who is relatively helpless to change the problem	Offering new questions and perspectives ("reframe")
		Engaging the clients as problem-solvers and brainstorm possible solutions with them
	Sees responsibility for problem-solving in others	Transferring tasks of observation, reflection, prognosis
Type "Customer"	Acknowledges the problem and its importance; is willing to actively contribute to problem-solving and wants to be involved	Proposal of action-related tasks
		Clarification and utilisation of the client's ideas for problem-solving
		Regular communication with the client about progress in problem-solving and further measures for active participation in the problem-solving process

Exercises 1 and 2 in the following section are meant to contribute to further understanding of this first step of solution-focused counselling.

Step 2: Set well-defined goals for action

"Beginning with the end in mind" (Miller, 1993)

The behavioural sciences, especially the cognitive-behavioural ones, have contributed much to goal setting in guidance. The early formulation of specific goals in the counselling interview helps both counsellors and clients to proceed in a goal-oriented way and provides criteria for evaluating the effectiveness of any intervention.

Solution-oriented counsellors set goals in cooperation with their clients. In doing so, the counsellors steer the process of jointly working out new realities for the clients. Language plays a central role in this process.

The questions used refer to the strengths, potentials, and abilities of the clients.

Example 1: Typical dialogue

Client:	My boss is always shouting at me and giving me the worst jobs. He is so unfair to me; a real jerk!
Counsellor:	You judge him quite harshly? It may be that he is just trying to get more performance out of his staff.
Client:	What do you think?
Counsellor:	You may both have a personality conflict.
Client:	If you say so!

Example 2: Solution-focused dialogue

Client:	My boss is always shouting at me and giving me the worst jobs. He is so unfair to me; a real jerk!
Counsellor:	What all is he doing that you are angry about?
Client:	He talks bad about me in front of others and belittles me. I hate that!
Counsellor:	When did he leave you alone and when did he annoy you last? What were you doing at the time?

Solution-focused counsellors often use "hypothetical language", where questions and comments suggest something without saying it directly. It is used in the goal-setting phase to encourage clients to explore their own possibilities and to raise their expectations of goal achievement. "What would change in your life if you started to make an effort to work every day?" "How would you notice that things were getting a little better between you and your boss?"

The characteristics of the goals in solution-oriented counselling can be summarised with the acronym "MOPS":

M (meaningful)	Of importance to the client "What is to be achieved in the time we are together now?" "What is the most important thing for you to work on first?"
O (observable):	Comprehensible, clear and specific objectives: "What will be different when you are less depressed about your unemployment?" "What will you do differently when you have more self-respect?"
P (positive statements):	Positive statements about something desirable. "What else could you do every day instead of turning on the TV?" "What would you do if you stopped sleeping so late every morning?"
S (small goals):	Small, realistic, achievable goals "What do you see as the first sign of a better relationship with your work colleagues?" "You say you feel at level 3 on a 10 scale. What would level 4 or 5 look like?"

Peller and Walter (1992, p. 125) have designed a useful scheme for the development of goals (also applies to other aspects of the solution-focused counselling process) (see Fig. 4.2). The all-important destination of wishes and complaints versus goals and problems is made first. Then the overview is laid out in terms of frames and the accompanying questions.

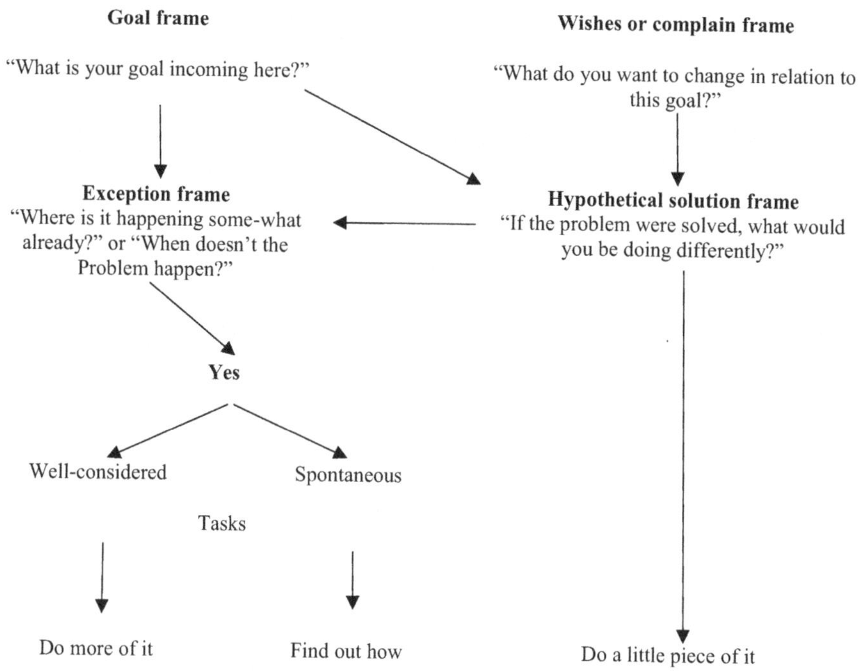

Fig. 4.2 Pathway of constructing solutions

Exercises 3, 4 and 5 aim at improving the formulation of specific, solution-focused goals.

Step 3: Orient the client towards the solution

> "The emphasis should be more on what the patient is currently doing and would like to do in the future than on simply understanding why a long-ago event happened" (Milton Erickson).

Solution-focused counsellors want their clients to focus on the present and future, where opportunities for change exist, rather than dwelling on the past in order to perhaps better understand their problem (insight can lead to blindness). The counselling practice of searching and diagnosing deficiencies in the counselee leads to a listing of what is not possible rather than a focus on the client's strengths and new approaches to solutions (Fig. 4.3).

Problems are often brought up vaguely ("I feel down"); "I am not motivated"; "There are no jobs"). Useful concrete descriptions are obtained by the solution-oriented counsellor by directing the client to the "when", "what", "where" and "who" in describing the problem.

When	"When do the difficulties occur, more in the morning, at midday or in the evening?"
What	"What usually happens immediately before the problem occurs?"
Where	"Do you usually notice the problem at work or at home, in the evenings or at weekends?"
Who	"Who is usually present when the problem occurs?"

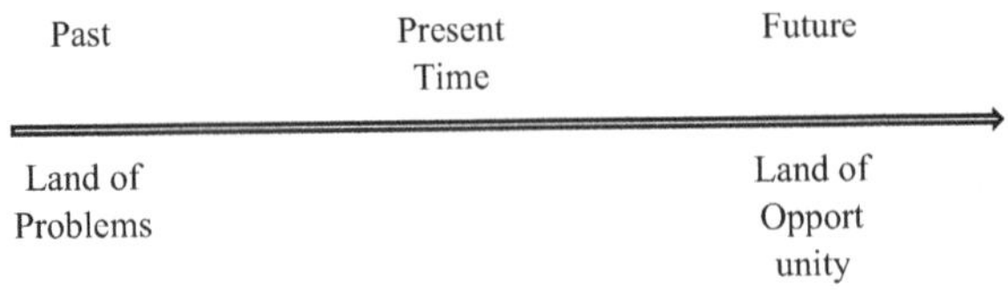

Fig. 4.3 Into the land of opportunity

Murphy (2008) suggests the following strategies and questions for clarifying the problem and guiding clients towards solution-oriented thinking:

Strategy	Description	Useful questions
Problem definition	Achieve an accurate behavioural problem description	If I were to record the problem on video, what would I see and hear? What of what the client does is "irresponsible"?
Clarification of the circumstances surrounding the problem	Achieve a clear description of the structure and context of the problem.	When does the problem typically occur? Who is usually involved? What happens just before the problem? What happens immediately afterwards?
Clarification of the attempted solutions	Achieve a clear description of the attempts to solve problems and their relative effectiveness	What have you done so far to solve the problem? What effects did you achieve in the process? What have others suggested to you? Which of the solutions you have tried has been the most effective?
Clarification of the client's position	Assess the client's opinion of the problem and its solution	What do you think caused the problem? What do you think could improve the situation? How strongly do you feel about the problem, please rate it on a scale of 10 (1 = lowest, 10 = maximum concern) How committed are you to solving this problem?

The orientation of clients towards solutions begins as soon as counselling starts. In their effort to build a cooperative relationship with clients, counsellors show great non-judgemental interest in everything clients have to say, from their sporting interests, to the weather, to art objects, to what brought them to counselling. The language used by solution-oriented counsellors is also channelled in productive ways.

So when clients use negative labels to describe their situation, these descriptions are transformed into actions. For example, to a student who says they have a "school phobia", the counsellor might respond, "So you didn't go to school the other day". Or if clients say they are depressed, counsellors might reply, "Did anyone, when you were not discouraged, tell you that?"

Most sessions in solution-focused counselling start with the question: "What brings you here?"

After the clients have had a chance to talk about their problems, the counsellors ask a series of questions in order to find exceptions to the problem. Some examples follow:

1. "*How does your day go differently if you don't stay at home and your unemployment doesn't make you depressed?*"

   This question asks clients to recognise the connection between times when they do something different and times when they do what they normally do. This question makes the clients see the positive sides of taking action in their lives.
2. "*How do you manage that?*"

   What the counsellor wants to do with this kind of question is to find out from what the clients have done what was worth the effort in the past when dealing with their situations. This question encourages the clients and makes them understand that they should take credit for every step in the right direction, even if the success is small and rare.
3. "*Have there been times when you got along well with your colleagues at work?*"

   Solution-focused counsellors want their clients to focus on getting along and not on the discord with colleagues. When clients say they never got along with their colleagues, counsellors try to find out the best of the bad times. ("When are the arguments with colleagues less strong?").
4. "*How is this different from the way you normally spoke to your boss?*"

   Many clients do not recognise any progress they have made, so this question makes it clear that movement towards the goal has taken place. The answer to the question often allows counsellors to reinforce the positive.
5. "*Assuming our joint work is successful.*

   What will be different in your life that will tell you that the counselling was successful?"
6. "*Where are you today on a scale of 1 to 10 (where 1 means your situation is at its worst and 10 means it is at its best)?*"

   Questions 5 and 6 are often used to set realistic, achievable goals. They can also be used as a baseline against which future progress can be measured. Scaled questions, such as the latter question, can also be used to assess the client's readiness to move towards the set goals.
7. "*Have you ever had this problem before? (If yes) How did you solve it then? What would you have to do to make it work again?*" Counsellors want clients to use their own resources. This builds up the clients as they become aware that they have dealt with a similar problem before. This questioning also allows counsellor and client to work out together what needs to be done to successfully use a previous solution again. Murphy (1997) uses the "5 E" method to find exceptions:

Elicit	exceptions
Explore	conditions and circumstances surrounding the exceptions.
Expand	encourage the client to find more exceptions
Evaluate	help the client evaluate progress
Enhance	with focused collaboration, help clients to continue to make desired changes.

Exercises 6, 7, 8, 9 and 10 in the next section are specifically designed to help counsellors learn more about solution-focused questioning and, in particular, asking questions to detect exceptions.

Step 4: Develop solution-focused interventions

"Counselling is often about tipping over the first domino" (Milton Erickson).
"If you only have a hammer as a tool, everything looks like a nail" (Abraham Maslow).

Step 4 is mainly about designing interventions that make clients change. The exercises in Sect. 4.3 will help counsellors to understand this process. Many solution-focused counsellors take a short break of 5–10 min before beginning this next phase of solution-focused counselling.

Initially, the "pause" was used for a counselling team to deliberate about the client. Now the pause is used as a "thinking break", but it also puts the clients in a very receptive mood to hear the "instructions". The clients consider the communication after the break as important and binding.

The structure of the message or instruction and the nature of the task for the client emerge from the nature of the client-counsellor relationship that has emerged by the end of the conversation. As long as clients still feel like visitors without a real problem, the main goal is to get them to attend further sessions. For these clients, therefore, the communication should include praise for something they are doing that is good for them and encourage them to continue counselling. A few examples:

- "It sounds like you have a very good handle on the situation with your boss".
- "I'm really pleasantly surprised by all their efforts to find work, despite the fact that jobs are really scarce at the moment".
- "Your resolution not to be late for school next week is really good. It shows that you are making an effort to improve your relationship with the teachers".

A single mother with three teenage children was having great difficulty making ends meet on her low wage, and there was little prospect of escaping her work impasse. The children did not help at all with the housework and spent their free time with friends. The mother complained and moaned a lot and did not really expect any change or solution. At the end of the "visitor" type interview, the counsellor praised her for her great caring towards the children and her ability to describe their difficult lot so well. She was also praised by the counsellor for her willingness to seek outside help.

It is important that praise from counsellors is sincere and based on the information gained in the session. Praise empowers clients by highlighting and acknowledging what they have already done to solve their problems. Praise makes clients receptive to further steps; clients regain hope.

Clients of the "complaint type", who are usually good at describing goals, should be praised for being able to describe what they want. But since they are not yet anxious to take steps to solve the problem, counsellors often give these clients tasks that require them to observe something positive. A few examples:

- "How will you know when we no longer need to meet? What will happen then?"
- "Suppose tonight, while you were sleeping, a miracle happened, and your problem was solved. By what events would you recognise that a miracle happened? What would you do differently then? What would be the first little change that you would notice?"
- "What will it be like when you no longer have the problem? What will you do then?"
- "How will your life be different then? Who will be the first to notice? What will he or she say then? How will you respond?"

To a client who is afraid of a job interview:

- "What will it be like once you have a good interview behind you? How will you feel then? Who (besides you) will notice the confidence you feel? How will your friends or family react when you tell them about your good interview?"

Often, when talking to a "complainant" type, counsellors try to gently modify the complaint pattern. For example: A client says his goal is not to be depressed, but he does not do much about it. He is asked to schedule his depression for a certain time every evening instead of waiting for it to occur randomly.

If the conversation is with a "client type", where the client is ready and willing to act immediately, the counsellors give distinctly action-oriented tasks. This is usually done in conjunction with an observation task, asking clients to look for changes in the way they complete their tasks. The following examples are typical:

Use of exceptions
A student who was not doing well in school and who was not getting along with other students was told by a solution-focused counsellor to put out a list of all the things the student would like to continue doing in the next week. This task asked the student to think about exceptions to the general views s/he had of her or his depressing life. When the student returned a week later, the list contained a number of exceptions to the idea that nothing was right in her or his life. The details of the positive exceptions were examined closely, and the student was encouraged to continue with these positive exceptions.

Tackling ingrained patterns of behaviour

Solution-focused counsellors often try to change the personal or even interpersonal patterns in which the client's problem or complaint is embedded.

One unemployed client made little effort to find a job but complained to his wife about how bad his day had been and what a "broken government" they had, a government that would allow their country to have double-digit unemployment. She then told him that maybe he should try a little harder and he would feel better. As usual, there was then an argument. The solution-oriented counsellor suggested to the woman that she record her husband and discuss the recording together in a few weeks. Two weeks later, the wife had nothing to bring to the counsellor because, she explained, that every time she turned on the recorder when her husband started to complain, he refused to talk. But the experiment succeeded when the wife told her husband that she needed the recording for the counsellor. Soon things improved so much that no further consultation with the counsellor was needed. The wife also noticed that whenever she turned on the recorder, she spoke more deliberately and clearly because she knew the counsellor would listen to the tape.

When behavioural patterns of whining and complaining are broken, this small change often "makes all the dominoes fall down".

The task of the first session

Solution-focused counsellors found that the following task worked effectively with a large number of clients with different problems:

> I want you to observe from now until our next meeting, what is happening at work that you would like to continue to happen.

Clients far too rarely expect the counsellor to ask them what is working well and then are surprised to find that quite a lot is going well after all. Moreover, since they are not asked to do something new, clients are quite receptive to continuing something they are already doing. Almost always, the extra effort of what they are already doing is exactly what is needed to solve the problem.

Use of paradoxical techniques

The use of paradoxical techniques is widespread in solution-oriented counselling. Paradoxical techniques are used to find a positive side directly or indirectly to the client's worries and needs. Paradoxical techniques can be used:

1. To help clients see symptoms and problems more positively.
2. To change the typical thinking or behavioural patterns of a client.
3. To increase client motivation to solve the problems.

Typical types of paradoxical interventions include prescribing the symptom that the client has, or even instructing the client to relapse for a certain period of time. The client's problems are given a positive connotation.

"But what you are experiencing in your family is very unpleasant. I believe that if you change something (the client is currently at home, not looking for work and drinking too much), it will only get worse with your family, which is already so dysfunctional. What you do is best". The hoped-for reaction to this paradoxical intervention would be something like: "The devil take me if I go on like this and become a scapegoat for my crazy family".

New versions

For Watzlawick et al. (1974, p. 95), "reframing" consists of "changing the conceptual and/or emotional background or point of view as referents for the experience of a situation [and] setting another framework that fits the 'facts' of that very concrete situation just as well or even better; thereby, completely changing its meaning".

A gloomy labour market, for example, can be presented more positively by pointing out that in Toronto or Vancouver hundreds of people get new or different jobs every day. Recasting helps clients to perceive their problems differently and puts problems in a new perspective, so that motivation, skills and other resources are "elicited" from the clients.

Change what we do and how we do it

Another technique of solution-focused counsellors is to encourage clients to do something completely different. O'Hanlon (1987) gives a number of examples that have been helpful for school counsellors.

- In a situation where parents constantly remind students to do their homework, parents are encouraged to limit the frequency of their reminders to six arbitrary times per week.
- *Changing the intensity of the problem pattern*
  If the teacher reprimands the pupils loudly, s/he should be encouraged to whisper her or his reprimands to the pupils.
- *Changing the time of the problem pattern*
  In a situation where students (or others) argue several times a day, the counsellor might suggest that they have a single round of arguments/discussions weekly.
- *Reversing the pattern of behaviour*
  When a parent and a young person often argue and the young person ends up stamping her or his foot angrily and leaving the room saying "you just don't understand me", the counsellor suggests that the young person first leaves the room in a rage, then comes back in and talks about the situation.

Webb (1999, p. 214) suggests summarising the content in the client's own words at the end of the first session in order to plant new ideas for solutions in the client. These messages consist of

1. Compliments
2. Connections
3. Homework

The compliments can refer to risk-taking, courage, perseverance, attitudes, sensitivity, understanding and creativity. The "Connection" statements link compliments to the counselling outcomes desired by the client and the tasks to be tackled.

Counsellors will not always have a particular intervention ready, but they may suggest, as a last resort, that the client should behave differently than others expect. Often clients develop quite creative strategies as a result.

Step 5: Stick to the goal

"It's easy to give up smoking, I've done it hundreds of times" (Mark Twain).

Exercises 16 and 17 in Sect. 4.3 deal with the issues of closure and goal maintenance. Counsellors want to help clients hold on to any positive changes they have made during and after counselling. Miller (1993) suggests that the second and subsequent sessions begin with the counsellor asking the client a series of key questions:

- Ask for positive changes.
  - "So, what happened last week, if you had your way, should continue to happen?"
  - "Which was better?"
  - "What successful actions have you done this week?"
  - "How did you manage? What was helpful?"
- Ask for details of the positive changes.
  - "How did you do it? How did you know you were doing the right thing? How did this change help?"
  - "How did it affect your day when you interviewed with several employers for a job?"
  - "What do you need to keep these changes going?"
  - "What incidents at work were helpful?"
- Make sure that the client notices the positive changes. The counsellor strongly encourages the client in the efforts they have made so far.
  - "Tell me again what all went well!"
  - "What else was better?"
  - "I am really impressed with the changes you have brought about."
  - "What else needs to be done before we know that counselling is no longer necessary?"
  - The solution-focused counselling process looks at each session as if it were the last. This helps counsellors and clients stay fixed on specific goals and savour every success. A complete resolution of all aspects of a problem is not necessary. The main thing is that clients are on a more positive trajectory and clearly understand how, where and when they are succeeding.

The following case serves to demonstrate the five-step procedure of solution-oriented counselling:

The "Klaus case"

Klaus is a 17-year-old athletic young man in his last year at school. Unlike other years, this year he is not doing well in some subjects, he is depressed and rebellious at home. He stays out late at night with friends instead of studying or staying home. At the urging of the teachers and his family, Klaus reluctantly goes to see the school counsellor.

Most school counsellors would start their counselling by looking at Klaus' school reports, his performance in tests and his evaluations by teachers. They might ask about problems with the family and look for reasons why the problems occur at home and at school. Instead, this solution-oriented counsellor turned his attention elsewhere and tried to rethink Klaus' situation. After establishing a cooperative relationship with Klaus, the solution-oriented counsellor looked for exceptions when the problems did not occur.

The counsellor started to look more for competencies instead of exploring what Klaus was doing wrong. The counsellor was interested in Klaus' views and solutions to his family and school problems because he knew that in order to count on his cooperation, he would have to ally himself with him firmly against the problem. The counsellor also knew that Klaus was quite capable of good academic performance in most areas, as he had done quite well in school until recently. But now, all that was left of any successes were his performances in sports.

The counsellor asked questions to set goals.

Counsellor	How will you know when things are better for you?
Klaus:	I don't know. I think school is better when my family and teachers are no longer breathing down my neck.
Counsellor	Klaus, take me back to a time when school was better for you and your relationship with your parents was fine.
Klaus:	Last year. I passed in all subjects.
Counsellor	How did you do that?
Klaus:	I don't know. I did my classwork and just handed it in, that was good enough.
Counsellor	You now pass some subjects and not others?
Klaus:	Exactly!
Counsellor	Tell me in which one you do well and what your secret is to pass these subjects

Klaus became more and more involved in the conversation and began to talk about other ways and means he had used in the past to achieve success. He also talked about his current strategies that he was now using to pursue his goal. He mentioned that in the past he had received much more praise from his mother for his homework and good academic performance.

After this first counselling session, Klaus was given a simple task.

(continued)

Counsellor: Klaus, I want you to notice when you are doing well in school, especially in the subjects you are good at, and pay attention to how you do that.

By offering a task to remember when the problem was less troublesome, Klaus is more likely to feel relief and more competent. The ability to gain independence from a problem strengthens self-esteem and motivates change.

These exceptions to Klaus' problem offered hints for solutions. Later, not only Klaus, but also his teachers and parents were given tasks. They were all told to provide encouragement to Klaus for what had worked before. By telling Klaus, "Since you've done this before, I'm sure you can do it again," others boost his confidence and reduce his fear of taking a risk.

The five-step solution-focused counselling process has been used extensively to help clients with a variety of problems, ranging from job dissatisfaction and job loss to conflicts among colleagues or in peer group. This process challenges the counsellor to rethink the notion that a problem must be thoroughly explored before change is possible.

In a very similar way, Bamberger (2015, p. 84) recommends dividing the solution-focused counselling process into six phases.

Phase 1: "Synchronisation"

The problem analysis should not be in the foreground, as it is often accompanied by a depressing retrospective and a speculative search for causes, which is rather counterproductive for a solution orientation.

Synchronisation includes situational, emotional, and conceptual coordination processes between counsellor and client, solution-oriented problem analysis, agreement on cooperation and solution motivation.

Phase 2: "Solution vision"

This phase includes the solution-oriented central question, solution tendencies even before counselling, the identification of exceptions, hypothetical solutions and the redefinition of problems ("reframing").

Phase 3: "Solution prescription"

This phase is about getting the client to engage emotionally and cognitively in a solution path. The trusting working relationship with the counsellor ("rapport") plays a decisive role here. A constructive pause between solution vision and solution prescription can also be helpful. After such a pause, the counsellor should actively encourage the client to continue striving for the solution by using positive connotations in the conversation.

A well-known method is the technique of "homework" assignments between counselling sessions. At the end of this phase of counselling, action planning has begun.

Phase 4: "Solution support"
This phase serves to follow up with the client through various communication channels. These communications (letters, emails, tweets) can help to deepen and confirm support for solutions.

Phase 5: "Evaluation"
This phase serves to identify improvements and to analyse possible obstacles and resource bottlenecks for the client. It also checks whether there have been any changes in the "target prescription".

Phase 6: "Securing solutions and the end of counselling"
This phase is about preparing for the time after the active counselling phases:

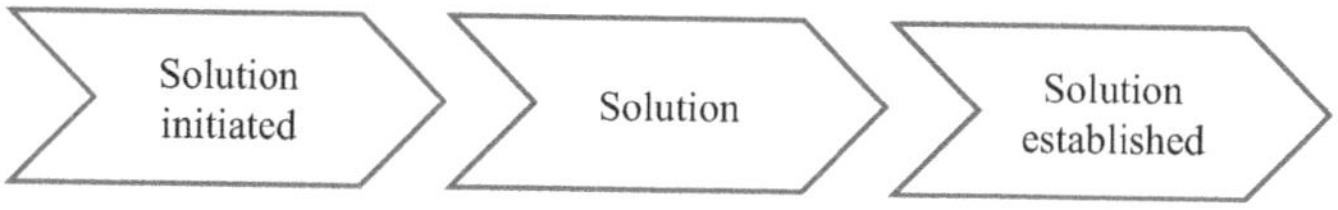

The parting phase for "post-counselling" should consist of an offer to help with any changes. (cf. Bamberger, 2015, p. 218):

- The "follow-up interview" is about the offer for an interview after two or three months.
- The "maybe-talk" raises the prospect of possibilities.
- In the "option talk", the client receives a talk voucher.
- The "success interview" is a follow-up interview after 6 months.

4.3 Exercises for Skill Development

Exercises for counsellors
Ivey and Egan have both developed a whole series of exercises for learning their model and the skills and techniques. There is no comparable collection of exercises on solution-focused counselling; therefore, we have developed exercises to help the reader understand solution-focused counselling. Before we present the 17 exercises in this chapter, we will take a brief look at the five-step process (Miller, 1993).

1. Step: Work with the client to build an effective relationship
2. Step: Set clear counselling goals
3. Step: Orient the client towards solutions
4. Step: Set solution-oriented interventions
5. Step: Stick to the counselling goals

Exercise 1

Types of counsellor–client relationship

Solution-oriented counsellors speak of three types of counsellor–client relationship:

(a) Client type—is willing to set goals and take action.
(b) Visitor type—is hardly aware that there is a problem and is therefore not willing to set goals.
(c) Complaint type-talks a whole lot about the problem, may talk about vague goals but is not ready to act.

1.	Discuss examples of each client type in small groups.
2.	Discuss methods for how counsellors could help the visitor and complaint types to become more "clients".
3.	Give a few examples of linguistic presuppositions (turns of phrase that anticipate change and resolution) that a change-oriented relationship would develop. Example: "What will be different when you spend more time looking for work?
4.	Roleplay counsellor and client (in pairs) scenes where each of the client types are used (client, visitor, complainant).

Exercise 2
Counsellor–client relationship

1. *"Visitor" type relationship* By the end of the counselling session, client and counsellor have not clearly stated a complaint or a goal. The client may not see a reason to change.
2. For the entire session, the counsellor has listened while the client has offered a lot of information about the problem. The client is not yet ready to become active.
3. By the end of the session, counsellor and client have set action-oriented goals and the client expresses a willingness to act to bring about a solution.

Discuss the following with a partner:

a.	Name a previous client who did not clearly state either the problem or the goal.
b.	How would you get this client to focus more on solutions?
c.	"Complaint-type" clients go on and on about the details of their problems. Discuss clients from your practice who know their problem but are unwilling to take steps to bring about a solution.
d.	How do you get this type of client to set goals and take action? "Client-type" clients are ready to act. Is there a danger of rushing into work too quickly?
e.	"Customer-type" clients are ready to act. Is there a danger of rushing into work too quickly?

Exercise 3
Setting counselling goals

1. Role play a situation where the student complains about a perceived unfair teacher. Set goals.
2. Evaluate the effectiveness of your goals by discussing the following indicators for specific, solution-focused counselling goals.

a.	Significant for the client e.g.: "I want you to stop the teacher from always picking on me".
b.	Small rather than big goals e.g.: "What would be the first sign for the teacher that you are serious about improving?"
c.	Identifiable, specific goals e.g.: "What will you do differently?" "What will the teacher do differently?"
d.	Presence vs. absence of something positive e.g.: "Paying attention" instead of "An end to disruptive behaviour"
e.	A beginning rather than an end e.g.: "Build on setting solutions in motion rather than struggling to put an end to old, unproductive patterns."
f.	Realistic and feasible for the client e.g.: "As a first step, you are to keep a record of what works".
g.	Expected to involve hard work e.g.: "You are right, solving this problem will involve hard work".

Exercise 4
Solution Language

1. In groups of two, one being the client and the other the counsellor, start a series of What is your problem?
   (a) What do you want to happen as a result of counselling?
   (b) What is the other person doing or not doing that you see as a problem?
   (c) What do you hope to achieve with the counselling? Are the answers different?

How does the client feel about the questions asked?

2. Exchange ideas with a partner. Each of you thinks of a problem you sometimes have. Ask yourself what would be different if the problem disappeared completely. How would you know that the problem had disappeared? What would be different in your life? What is different if the problem has partly disappeared? What could you do to make the problem disappear even more?

Exercise 5
"Future pull"

A positive vision of the future can be a great help in the endeavour to create a better present.

1)	Think of a situation where you were reluctant to make a change.
2)	Consider each of the following questions as they pertain to the situation. a) What is the goal of your existence? b) What is your vision of your preferred future? c) What dreams did you have for your life? d) What circumstances pushed you to do something? e) What makes you really happy? f) What is holding you back from realising your vision or achieving your goals? g) What steps have you *not* taken to make your vision come true? h) What would people who are admired by you do if they would have to "realise your dream"?

Exercise 6
Six useful questions

In groups of two or three, write down several examples of the following types of questions.

1.	Goal setting questions, e.g.: "How will you know when the problem is solved?"
2.	Questions to find exceptions e.g.: "Are there times in your life that you enjoy or where you have fun? What is different about these times?"
3.	Hypothetical questions e.g.: "Assuming the problem is solved, what is different?"
4.	Scaling questions e.g.: "On a scale of 1 to 10, where would you place yourself today? (10 means you will do anything to solve these problems and 1 means you are not sure)".
5.	Questions on life skills e.g.: "How do you manage to get yourself up for work every day?"
6.	Questions about readiness for change e.g.: "What new things will you do together when your relationship with each other is better?"

Exercise 7
Find exceptions

1)	To practise the use of exceptions in developing action plans for clients, complete the following questionnaire as you think a teacher would (consider a real or hypothetical situation).
2)	Write down statements you would tell clients that would encourage them to do more of the exceptions.
3)	Write down the interests, talents or social supports the client has to cope with the problem.

Exercise 8
Strategies to detect exceptions

John saw his friend Bob looking for something under the streetlamp in front of his house. John asked, "What are you doing?" "Looking for my keys", Bob replied. John helped find the keys and crawled on all fours. A little while later John asked, "Where exactly did you drop the keys?"

"Further over there", Bob replied, pointing across the road. "Then why on earth are you looking here?" "Because the light is so much better," said Bob.

Even if "the light is better" on familiar terrain, the keys or solutions are perhaps best found by paying attention to exceptions.

A	Some exemplary questions to detect exceptions	
	1)	When is your problem less or less noticeable in everyday life?
	2)	Of all your school subjects, which is the most bearable?
	3)	Tell me about a test or a piece of work that was a little better than usual. What was different about the way you prepared?

B	Think of a problem you have. Next, think about when the problem is not so noticeable. Ask yourself the following questions:	
	1)	What was different about those times?
	2)	What do I do differently in these situations in the way I approach, think about and react to the situation or the people involved in it?
	3)	What can I do to make this happen more often or in other situations?

Exercise 9
The "miracle" question

Miracles, crystal balls and videotapes are three useful techniques to help clients create a better future and show ways to take action.

Miracle question

Suppose the next night, while you are sleeping, a miracle happens, and your problem is solved. How could you tell? What would be different? What differences will you notice in the morning and how will you know that a miracle has happened? What differences will others (friends, family, teachers, counsellors) notice?

1. Think of a problem situation, apply the miracle question, and answer each question.
2. What "solutions" emerge for your situation?

____
____
____
____
____

Crystal ball

Look into a crystal ball (imaginary or real) and imagine that you have arrived at a perfect solution to your problem. Describe in detail how you arrived at a perfect solution. Comment on the impact of your solution on the future.

1. The future has a greater influence on the present than the past. How can images of the future affect the present?

____
____
____
____
____

2. Can the details of how you arrived at a perfect solution serve as a template for future action on one of your own problems? Explain.

____
____
____
____

Descriptions for a screenplay

Just like the "crystal ball" and "miracle question", screenplays help clients to create a future with perspectives. It is useful to describe things as one would like them to be.

1. Give a video description of your future. For example, assume that a few weeks have passed, and your problem is solved. If others were to watch a videotape of your life in the near future when your problem is solved, what would you do on that videotape that would show that things are better?

____
____
____
____
____

2. What actions suggest themselves after viewing the video tape of your "Future" for the present?

____
____
____
____

Exercise 10
"When things are better"

Questionnaire

____________________ ____________________

Student Teacher(s)

____

Date

The above student and I would like your help to find out more about times and situations when the student in your class is doing better. This could help us to improve the situation by building on something the student is already doing successfully.

1. Please list what the student is currently doing or has done (even if only rarely) to do well in class.

____
____
____
____
____

2. Describe specific times and situations in your class where the student did a little (or a lot) better than usual.

____
____
____
____
____

3. What do you think we could build on first (based on what you have listed) to improve the pupil's performance in the class?

____
____
____
____

4. Please note anything else that would help the student and me to deal with his/her school problems.

____
____
____
____

Exercise 11
Using our own strengths

Many people who have survived horrific experiences emerge stronger and as radiant victors. The famous personalities that come to mind cover a wide human spectrum, from Oprah Winfrey to Mahatma Gandhi to Viktor Frankl.

1. Consider a difficult situation you had in the past. How did you get through it?

2. When was the moment there for you to turn this difficult situation around so that it no longer had a negative impact on your life?

3. Describe as precisely as possible how you managed this.

Exercise 12
Task of the first session

Some tasks can be used in solution-focused counselling for clients with multiple complaints and grievances (example from De Shazer, 1985, p. 137). I want you to observe from now until our next meeting, in such a way that you can describe it to me next time, what is happening in your family (or school or job search or life, etc.) and what you want to continue to happen.

1. Develop one or two practice tasks for the first session that might deal with situations, problems or complaints you will face as a counsellor.

2. Compare and discuss your assignments with other members of your learning group.

Exercise 13
Use client resources

Outcome-based research has shown that almost half of the success of any counselling service results from the personal strengths, talents, resources, beliefs and social supports that clients bring to counselling.

1. Talk to a group of high school students and ask them what works best when adults (teachers, parents, others) try to help you. What does not work very well?

___
___
___
___

2. Ask these students about the main problems in their school and how they would improve the situation. What do you think of the students' ideas?

___
___
___
___

3. Think about how you could methodically incorporate student factors such as good grades, outstanding sporting or musical achievements, special talents, the ability to work hard, an interest in people, a sense of humour, and so on.

___
___
___

4. Ask students about things in their lives that they would like to continue to happen. Ask students what they have done and are currently doing to make these things actually happen.

___
___
___
___

Exercise 14
Making counselling effective in terms of time

Temporary counselling is a tool that should not be underestimated for counsellors in school and career guidance.

Although this cartoon exaggerates the short duration of compact counselling, it helps to draw attention to the importance of the time factor in counselling.

Consider the following questions and comments:

1. Consider what causes clients to see their counsellor over a long period of time in more traditional approaches to counselling.

____
____
____
____

2. Have you ever had short-term counselling sessions that seemed to produce very good results? What was different about these sessions?

____
____
____
____

3. If each counselling session is seen as possibly the first and last, counsellor and client work more efficiently. Comment on this.

____
____
____
____

4. Two essential tasks of brief counselling are:

a) Change of perspective.

b) Change of action and action.

Can the deconstruction of client stories (change of perspective) be done in one or two sessions? Explain.

____
____
____
____

Exercise 15
Additional skills for solution-focused counsellors

In groups of two or three, write down and discuss examples of the following three skills that solution-focused counsellors often use.

1. Direct/Indirect praise e.g.: "I like the fact that you spent a lot of time looking for a job last week."

____
____
____

2. Restatements e.g.: "On the other hand, you could also say that only one of the ten employers I went to was rough with me."

____
____
____
____

3. Set tasks e.g.: "We recommend that you do more of the 'exception'." Or "Do the easiest part of the 'miracle'."

____
____
____
____

Exercise 16
The solution-focused procedure

The solution-focused process described in detail in Sect. 4.2 consists of five steps.

To help you as aspiring counsellors think through each main step, consider the following questions and comments about each step after you have conducted a solution-focused conversation.

1. Establishing a cooperative, functioning relationship
   (a) Did you use the client's language?
   (b) Have you encouraged the client to teach you about themselves?
   (c) Did you help the client to focus on the future?
   (d) Did you work with the client throughout the interview?
2. Set well-considered treatment goals
   (a) Has your objective been formulated in specific, behavioural terms?
   (b) Were the target steps small, positive and significant?
   (c) Have client resources been identified?
3. Orientation of the client towards the solution
   (a) Have you asked the client how he managed to cope with difficult situations in the past?
   (b) Did you ask the client what he would do if he did not change?
   (c) Did your conversation with the client mainly revolve around solutions rather than problems?

4. Develop solution-oriented interventions
   (a) Have you asked the client how he managed to cope with difficult situations in the past?
   (b) Did you ask the client what he would do if he did not change?
   (c) Did your conversation with the client mainly revolve around solutions rather than problems?
5. Helping clients to stick to change
   (a) Did you assess the counselling progress through scaling questions or otherwise?
   (b) Have you offered the client a follow-up contract?
   (c) Did you use the target you set as a guideline for a conclusion?
   (d) How did you empower your client to keep doing "what works"?

Exercise 17
Final letter

Pick a client situation where considerable improvement has occurred and write a short follow-up letter to the client accordingly.

____
____
____
____
____
____

Pattern (after Murphy, 1997, p. 180) Dear . . . .

I would like to congratulate you on the progress you have made. I would like to know more about how you did it. This helps me with other people with the same kind of problems you had before.

I would like to meet with you to celebrate your success and learn more about what you have done to bring about these changes. Please think about what you have done to improve the situation and what you intend to do to keep the good situation stable. I will make an appointment with you next week.

Congratulations! Yours sincerely, Counsellor

References

Amatea, E. S. (1989). *Brief strategic intervention for school behavior problems*. Jossey-Bass.

Bamberger, G. G. (2015). *Lösungsorientierte Beratung* [Solution-oriented counselling] (5th ed.). Beltz.

Bandler, R., & Grinder, J. (1979). *Frogs into princes*. Real People Press.

Bandler, R., & Grinder, J. (1997). *Neue Wege der Kurzzeit-Therapie. Neurolinguistische Programme* [New ways of short-term therapy, neurolinguistics programmes] (2nd ed.). Jungfermann.

Beutler, L. (1994). *What psychotherapy outcome research can teach us in the age of managed care.* Oregon Psychological Association, Spring 1994 Workshop.

Brown, D. (2012). *Career information, career counseling, and career development* (10th ed.). Pearson Education.

Budman, S. H., & Gurman, A. S. (1988). *Theory and practice of brief therapy.* Guilford Press.

Cade, B., & O'Hanlon, W. H. (1993). *A brief guide to brief therapy.* Norton.

Carlson, J., & Sperry, L. (Eds.). (2000). *Brief therapy with individuals and couples.* Phoenix.

De Jong, P., & Berg, I. K. (1998). *Interviewing for solutions.* Brooks/Cole.

De Shazer, S. (1985). *Keys to solution in brief therapy.* Norton.

De Shazer, S. (1992). *Der Dreh, überraschende Wendungen und Lösungen in der Kurzzeittherapie* [The twist, surprising turns and solutions in short-term therapy] (2nd ed.). Carl-Auer-Systeme.

De Shazer, S. (1994). *Words were originally magic.* Norton.

De Shazer, S. (1997). *Wege der erfolgreichen Kurztherapie* [Ways of successful brief therapy] (6th ed.). Klett-Cotta.

Durant, M. (1995). *Creative strategies for school problems. Solutions for psychologists and teachers.* Norton.

Ellis, A. (1996). *Better, deeper, and more enduring brief therapy.* Brunner/Mazel.

Ertelt, B.-J., & Schulz, W. E. (1997). *Beratung in Bildung und Beruf* [Guidance in education and occupation]. Rosenberger.

Fisch, R., Weakland, J. H., & Segal, L. (1982). *Tactics of change. Doing therapy briefly.* Jossey-Bass.

Frank, J. D., & Frank, J. B. (1991). *Persuasion and healing* (3rd ed.). Johns Hopkins Press.

Garfield, S. L. (1994). Research on client variables in psychotherapy. In A. E. Bergin & S. L. Garfield (Eds.), *Handbook of psychotherapy and behavior change* (pp. 190–228). Wiley.

Haley, J. (1976). *Problem solving therapy.* Harper & Row.

Haley, J. (1985). In M. D. Milton Erickson (Ed.), *Conversations with* (Vol. 1). Triangle.

Hart, B. (1995). Re-authoring the stories we work by situating the narrative approach in the presence of the family of therapists. *Australian and New Zealand Journal of Family Therapy, 16*, 181–189.

Howard, K., Kopta, M., Krause, M., & Orlinsky, D. (1986). The dose-effect relationship in psychotherapy. *American Psychologist, 41*, 149–164.

James, R., & Gilliland, B. (2003). *Counseling and psychotherapy* (5th ed.). Allyn & Bacon.

Koss, M. P., & Shiang, J. (1994). In A. E. Bergin & S. L. Garfield (Eds.), *Handbook of psychotherapy and behavior change (664–700).* Wiley.

Lambert, M. J. (1992). *Implications of outcome research for psychotherapy integration* (pp. 94–129). Basic Books.

Lawson, D. (1994). Identifying pretreatment change. *Journal of Counseling and Development, 72*, 244–248.

Metcalf, L. (1995). *Counseling toward solutions.* Center for Applied Research in Education.

Miller, S. (1993). *From problem to solution: The solution-focused brief therapy approach.* Brief Family Therapy Center.

Murphy, J. (1997). *Solution-focused counseling in middle and high school.* American Counseling Association.

O'Hanlon, W. (1987). *Taproots. Underlying principles of Milton Erickson's therapy and hypnosis.* Norton.

O'Hanlon, W., & Weiner-Davis, M. (1989). *In search of solutions.* Norton.

Orlinsky, D. E., Grawe, K., & Parks, B. K. (1994). Process and outcome in psychotherapy. In A. E. Bergin & S. L. Garfield (Eds.), *Handbook of psychotherapy and behavior change* (pp. 270–376). Wiley.

Orlinsky, D. E., & Howard, K. I. (1986). Process and outcome in psychotherapy. In S. L. Garfield & A. E. Bergin (Eds.), *Handbook of psychotherapy and behavior change* (3rd ed., pp. 311–381). Wiley.

Patterson, C. H. (1984). Empathy, warmth and genuineness in psychotherapy: A review of reviews. *Psychotherapy, 21*, 431–438.
Peller, J. L., & Walter, J. E. (1992). *Becoming solution-focused in brief therapy*. Brunner/Mazel.
Ridley, C. R. (1995). *Overcoming unintentional racism in counseling and therapy: A practitioners guide to intentional intervention*. Sage.
Rosen, S. (1982). *My voice will go with you*. Norton.
Rosenthal, R. (1966). *Experimenter effects in behavioral research*. Apple-ton-Century-Crofts.
Segal, L. (1991). Brief therapy: The MRI approach. In A. S. Gurman & D. P. Kniskern (Eds.), *Handbook of family therapy* (Vol. 2, pp. 171–199). Brunner/Mazel.
Snyder, C. R., Irving, L. M., & Anderson, J. R. (1991). Hope and health. In C. R. Snyder & D. R. Forsyth (Eds.), *Handbook of social and clinical psychology: The health perspective* (pp. 28–305). Pergamon.
Talmon, M. (1990). *Single-session therapy: Maximizing the effect of the first (and often only) therapeutic encounter*. Jossey-Bass.
Thompson, C. L., & Rudolph, L. B. (2000). *Counseling children* (5th ed.). Wadsworth/Thompson Learning.
Watzlawick, P., Weakland, J., & Fisch, R. (1974). *Change: Principles of problem formulation and problem resolution*. Norton.
Webb, W. (1999). *Solutioning: Solution-focused interventions for counsellors*. Accelerated Development.
White, M., & Epston, D. (1990). *Narrative means to therapeutic ends*. Norton.
Wolters, U. (2015). *Lösungsorientierte Kurzberatung – Was auf schnellem Wege Nutzen bringt. Eine Einführung in das Thema lösungsorientierte Kurzberatung mit Praxisorientierung und Beispielsituationen* [Solution-oriented brief counselling – What brings benefits in a quick way. An introduction to the topic of solution-oriented brief counselling with practical orientation and example situations] (4th ed.). Springer Gabler.

Chapter 5
The Integrative Model of Ertelt and Schulz: Information Structural Methodology (ISM)

5.1 Development and Status of the ISM Approach

Our ISM model focuses on individual decision-making processes and use of knowledge that is particularly useful in career decision counselling. Before introducing the ISM specifically, various key factors of ISM, such as decision-making, knowledge of information and client characteristics, will be examined.

From the beginning, one specific feature of ISM was its close orientation towards career guidance and information in schools, as well as in training and employment centres and in personnel development. This latter field, personnel development, has been somewhat neglected, although ongoing efforts are continuing to be made by some writers (Bamberg et al., 2006; Ertelt et al., 2012; Frey et al., 2016; Ivey, 1998; Rosenberger, 2002).

In these publications, it was made clear that ISM is a critical part of the rational decision-making and problem-solving models. ISM takes greater account of individual decision-making logic (heuristics), limited information absorption and processing possibilities, open-endedness (limited or no guarantee of a solution) as well as emotions and conflicts in the decision-making process.

ISM is therefore not oriented towards how one should make professional decisions and solve problems, but how the individual decision-making process takes place and how counsellors can help with this process in a counselling relationship (cf. Brown et al., 1990, p. 396).

In the first period of development, these ideas were transferred to occupation-related information activities for employees and employers (Ertelt & Feckler, 1979) as well as to career education in schools (Ertelt, 1982).

Updated translation of chapter 5 from: Handbuch Beratungskompetenz, 4th ed. by Bernd-Joachim Ertelt & William E. Schulz, 2019, Springer Verlag.

B.-J. Ertelt et al., *Counsellor Competencies*,
https://doi.org/10.1007/978-3-030-87413-1_5

This application to individual career guidance in Germany began in the early 1970s as part of the first academic training of vocational guidance staff by the Federal Employment Service in conjunction with the University of Mannheim.

The basis was a specially designed model of microcounselling, followed by practice with real clients and supervisor feedback. Later work with microcounselling was enhanced by adding valued work done by Allen Ivey and others (Ertelt, 1975; Ertelt & Schulz, 1985; Ivey & Authier, 1983, 1985; Trinemeier & Ertelt, 1978).

The development and application of ISM has been and is being accompanied by empirical studies that focus on the following key areas:

- Studies on information management in institutions and in career guidance media
- Studies on the further development of the methods used in "Distance Counselling"; namely, counselling by telephone, video-conferencing, and the internet
- Analysis of the links between career and labour market-related information in counselling and placement, as a basis for optimising existing media and for further developing demand-oriented information systems
- Investigation of interdependencies between decision-relevant character and personality traits (career interests, self-assessed transferable competencies, coping strategies, heuristics and self-efficacy)
- Development of computer-assisted counselling with Artificial Intelligence (AI)

In order to clarify the fields of application of ISM, selected empirical studies are presented below, the characteristics of each are first outlined in order to understand them. A detailed description of this methodology and its relations to other approaches will follow in the next chapter. Professional problem situations require the individual to make decisions that are often of existential importance and therefore involve strong emotional participation. To solve problems, actions are required whose consequences can seldom be clearly estimated because the individual's forecasting capacity is limited and the procurement of information requires a high level of personal commitment. "Real" problems are characterised by the fact that the previous routine programs for solving them are no longer applicable and therefore require innovative solutions. Innovative activities need to be developed.

To do this, the individual needs information about alternative actions, their chances of realisation and their promise of satisfaction. In order to evaluate alternatives, criterion information is necessary. Criterion is derived from the individual's own interests, motivations and preferences.

The individual decision rules (*prescriptive information*) determine which and *how* much factual and valuative information is to be combined in problem-solving and decision-making. Sampson et al. (1999) stated that "Generic Information Processing Skills" are controlled by meta-cognitions.

Professional problems and decisions are usually complex in nature, and so can therefore be characterised as "poorly-defined situations". Rarely is there only one "right" solution and a clearly predictable conclusion or even a guarantee of a solution for a certain course of action.

Such decision-making processes are usually accompanied by strong emotional involvement, such as problem-solving pressure, information stress, fear of irreversible wrong decisions due to incomplete information, and doubts as to whether the chosen alternative is actually the right one (cf. Peterson et al., 1996, p. 428).

The counselling process is understood as a *simulation of imagined cognitive-affective information processing procedures in the client* within the framework of a learning process oriented towards the counselling goal. Of central importance for counselling information management is therefore the question of how much information the individual needs to be able to make an appropriate decision. However, opinions differ, depending on whether the helper is guided by the normative idea that the client must be led to a rational decision or whether the helper thinks in terms of the client's actual problem-solving behaviour.

In the case of a demand for rational professional choices and decisions, advisory information management would have to ensure that people:

- Know all the alternatives for action open to them and their contributions to the individual goals ("offers of satisfaction")
- Have sufficient evaluation criteria to assess each of these alternatives, so that a preference scale close to the (subjective) benefit emerges, and
- Always choose the alternative that is not surpassed by any other in this order of preference.

The limitations of the individual's capacity to absorb and process information, reactions to information overload (information stress), individual conflicts and emotions as well as the influence of coincidences or "favourable opportunities", are largely neglected in these prescriptive models of decision-making (Ertelt, 1992, p. 95; Holling et al., 2000, p. 10).

Therefore, these approaches are only suitable to a limited extent as a basis for counselling help with career problems, although a large number of national and international programmes for career and course guidance and counselling are still based on them (Holling et al., 2000, p. 28).

The descriptive models of human decision-making, which are oriented towards individual information needs and behaviour, seem more appropriate to the professional-ethical norms of counselling, i.e. they "pick up" the client where he is in his problem-solving process. This is based on the idea of heuristic decision-making behaviour, in which the individual uses a tentative approach and simplification strategies to gradually improve the problem solution (incrementalism), so that the intellectual processing possibilities are not exceeded.

Lindblom (1964, 1965 in: Kirsch, 1977) characterised this behaviour on the basis of six features:

1. The individual strives for only small improvements to the current problem situation, so that the previous horizon of experience and knowledge is not exceeded and an evaluation of the approach remains possible.
2. The individual only includes a few alternatives as hypotheses for a solution in his or her calculations.
3. The consequences of these alternatives are only measured against a few criteria.
4. The problem is not fixed definitively so that the definition can adapt to the new information in each case.
5. The individual does not have the expectation of completely concluding a complex decision problem. This makes the neglect of important aspects seem "less alarming".

6. Individuals seldom strive for long-term goals; rather, they see their problems more in the elimination of current grievances.

From the point of view of heuristic models, a problem solution can be described as "rational" if a conscious deliberative process has taken place, even with the unification of the decision problem (Guichard & Huteau, 2001, p. 98).

In this context, the concept of "*bounded rationality*" originally developed by H. A. Simon should be reflected. According to Gigerenzer and Selten (2002, p. 4), the models based on this concept primarily describe the heuristic decision-making process and the environmental factors under which these heuristics are successful or failures.

This approach challenges the fiction of optimisation strategies that make unrealistic demands on the individual in terms of knowledge, time, diligence or other conditions in order to cope with problems. But by no means are decisions under bounded rationality to be called irrational just because they do not correspond to the norms of perfect rationality. Thus, behaviour that is directed more towards the realistic adjustment of demands than towards maximising utility would certainly be called rational in colloquial language (Selten, 2002, p. 15; Gigerenzer, 2004, p. 64).

According to Keller and Katsikopoulos (2015, p. 4), psychological heuristics are formal models for decision-making and problem-solving that are based on core psychological skills (e.g. recognising behavioural patterns or retrieving information from memory), and they do not use all available information and are easy to understand, apply and explain. They can be divided into "lexicograhic models", which are also called "fast and frugal decision trees" for classification problems according to certain categories. A second "family of heuristics" is formed by the linear "tallying models ... for multi-attribute choice, classification and forecasting, where the weights of all attributes are set to 1" (Keller & Katsopoulos, 2015, p. 9). In contrast to the lexicographic models, other models feel that any attribute can be compensated by any other attribute.

In most theoretical approaches, professional guidelines and practical advice, counsellors and those seeking advice are confronted with demands for a rational or as rational as possible approach to solving professional problems. The action-guiding subjective theories of the counsellors are largely neglected (Ertelt et al., 2017, p. 119).

Klein (2002, p. 109) lists the optimisation conditions for the decision-making process usually presented in the decision-making literature:

1. The goals must be well-defined, i.e. described in precisely measurable terms.
2. The decision-maker's assessments must be stable.
3. The decision-making situation must be stable.
4. The task is limited to choosing between options.
5. The number of alternatives developed must be exhaustive.
6. The optimal alternative can be chosen in a reasonable time and with reasonable effort.
7. The options must be carefully weighed against each other.

8. The decision-maker must pursue a strategy of balancing.
9. The assessment of probabilities must be consistent and accurate.
10. The scenarios for predicting possible failures must be comprehensive and realistic.
11. The evaluation of each individual scenario must be done very carefully (Herr et al., 2004, p. 182).

Professional decisions and problem-solving in counselling practice are definitely limited when restricted to the above-mentioned boundaries, since emotional aspects are largely limited (Nestmann et al., 2007, p. 26; Dauwalder, 2007, p. 15).

From a counselling point of view, it seems necessary to focus on the limited cognitive possibilities of people, their emotions and the conditions under which they sometimes have to make very far-reaching decisions. This is where the so-called "simple heuristics" come into focus, i.e. generalisations and rules that people use when making decisions that have to be made under limited time, limited knowledge and limited processing capacity.

Simple decision heuristics are characterised by speed and simplicity, by "frugality" in terms of the amount of information activity and by focusing on the essentials.

In addition to taking into account the limited human processing capacity and motivation, the success of such heuristics is based on their adaptability to real decision environments, the so-called "ecological rationality" (Dieckmann & Krauss, 2005, p. 190).

In contrast to the rational models, which largely neglect conflicts and emotions, the ideas on decisions under bounded rationality assume an intensive interaction of cognitions and emotions. Mellers et al. (2002, p. 267) distinguish between background emotions, task-related emotions and anticipated emotions.

Background emotions influence the way certain stimuli are perceived and the search strategies (heuristics) for information and alternatives. Thus, positive emotions, such as satisfaction, joy or pride, can limit the search for alternatives, while fears or anger make people more likely to look for ways out.

Task-related emotions arise, for example, when one option does not stand out clearly from the others and thus its choice cannot be justified. Feelings of defensive avoidance, panic or hyperactivity can also be observed when making important decisions under time pressure.

With regard to the influence of *anticipated emotions on* decisions, the studies show a mixed picture. In some cases, the possible consequences of the outcome are hardly predictable, in others, the consequences are clearer. If there are serious doubts the corresponding alternative is avoided.

But avoiding disadvantages cannot be the sole emotional basis for decisions. Rather, some people are more likely to be guided by what gives them short-term pleasure and joy, consciously ignoring negative long-term consequences. Thus, simple emotion-based heuristics can be both appropriate and maladaptive, depending on the context and consequences.

In his study on decision-making in career choice, Hellberg (2005, p. 254) distinguishes three central motivational present feelings in decision-making processes.

The feeling of *pleasure/unpleasure* arises in connection with the imagination of the future job content and working environment against the background of the best possible satisfaction of needs.

The feeling of *inner resistance* arises from such imaginary aspects that result from possible negative consequences of the considered occupation. However, these do not refer to the occupation itself, but to the "motivational boundary conditions" in the examining of the occupation.

The emotional arousal named as *good/bad feeling* refers to imagination contents, whether the job-specific demands and the performances demanded by the integration into the everyday working life seem manageable.

However, the structural information methodology (SIM) not only takes into account the content dimension of advisory information (factual knowledge, value knowledge, process knowledge) and the individual heuristics as well as their limitations, but also the dependence of information needs on *the phases and stages of problem-solving.*

To assess these process-dependent information needs, the following decision phases and stages can be distinguished (Kirsch, 1977, p. 72):

If an individual is only at the *beginning of a problem-solving process,* s/he needs information to define the problem and to motivate her or him to act as actively as possible. This would be possible by comparing the current situation with a target situation that calls for action. The target situation can have a positive colouring, e.g. professional advancement, higher job security, or a negative colouring, e.g. impending unemployment, professional disadvantages.

If a person seeking advice is already at the *stage of searching for information*, counselling assistance must focus on the accuracy of this search process. This requires knowledge of information possibilities that serve to "vitalise" the demand and the utilisation of data sources. Information brochures have proven to be a particularly efficient aid in this regard, as they provide problem-oriented information on the information that can be retrieved.

The stage of *forming and evaluating alternatives* includes a wide range of factual, evaluative and prescriptive information about possible solutions and their consequences for the individual. The criteria for evaluating the respective alternatives, including the chances and ways of realisation, must become clear. Lexical lists are—according to the heuristic decision-making behaviour shown above—relatively ineffective and should therefore be avoided.

In the *decision-making phase* with the final selection of an alternative course of action and personal commitment, the person seeking advice needs informational support that provides him or her with information about his or her own decision-making ability, conflicts of choice, possibilities of realisation and the expected consequences of the decision.

In the personal determination of a solution, individual conflicts can arise, especially in the case of subjectively important decisions, which in extreme cases lead to indecision. The more torn an individual feels between alternatives of similar value, the less subjective certainty the individual has about the correctness of a possible decision.

However, with the increasing importance of the decision and experienced conflict strength, the desire for information increases, which in turn positively influences the individual's search for information.

Another counselling service in the decision-making phase is aimed at counselling seekers who fear that they are restricting themselves too early. After that, resistance to a final decision grows to the extent that it reduces the subjectively perceived room for manoeuvre and the closer the time comes when the decision becomes binding. Information that enables the person seeking advice to recognise his or her real room for manoeuvre and to assess the individual and social costs of not making a decision or of seeking further information is of prime importance here.

Descriptive and interpretive information is needed to prepare for the *decision-making phase.*

Descriptive information serves as an orientation aid by clarifying structures, requirements, difficulties and opportunities of the chosen alternative. In this way, the counsellor makes transparent the range of expectations that the decision opens up for the person seeking advice. The counsellor should be able to define the tolerance limits within which the decision is still perceived as satisfactory or at what point the decision should be changed.

The individual needs the interpretive information to cope with negatively perceived conclusions, to explain the causes of failures and to meaningfully reduce "cognitive dissonance". Many a decision made full of hope (e.g. to further qualify professionally) fails in implementation due to difficulties that would have been actively overcome with appropriate preparatory interpretation (Ertelt & Schulz, 1985, p. 173; Walsh, 1990, p. 270).

The following is an overview of the results of selected empirical studies that incorporate the ISM approach.

5.1.1 Need for Information in Individual Career Counselling

In an earlier study (Mauch, 1986), 62 career decision-making counselling sessions (with adolescents and adults) were analytically examined for client deficits with regard to factual, valuative and prescriptive (process-related) information or premises.

Six problem types were identified. There were "pure" types (63%), and a number of mixed types (37%). Each problem type is characterised by a specific deficit in factual knowledge (knowledge about alternatives and their "satisfaction offers"), evaluative knowledge (criteria) and problem knowledge (decision heuristics of the individual).

1. C-type

   The criteria deficit type (35.5%) was assigned to clients who had alternative courses of action but were unable to weigh them due to a lack of evaluation criteria and therefore had not yet reached a decision.

2. R-type

   Clients with deficits in realisation information (32%) had already committed to an alternative. Criteria were also sufficient, so that the evaluation of the alternatives had already led to a personal commitment. What was needed was information for the realisation of the decision.
3. A-type

   The alternative deficit type (11%) included clients who had none or insufficient ideas about possible alternative courses of action. However, they had criteria for defining the solution space (e.g. professional expectations, interests, dislikes) and knowledge about the further course of action in solving the problem (prescriptive premises).
4. O-type

   The orientation type (10%) was assigned to clients who are reorienting themselves after a break in the previous life continuum (e.g. leaving school, unemployment, accident, divorce). For this purpose, alternatives are sought and the solution space is redefined with the help of criteria. In addition, new methods of resolution must be sought.
5. I-type

   Clients of the insecurity type (6.5%) did not have sufficient occupational alternatives, their interests were extremely diverse and partly contradictory, and they also showed uncertainty about how to proceed with problem-solving.
6. P-type

   The prescriptive deficit type (5%) included clients who were uncertain about their approach to problem solving or those who hoped that counselling would confirm that they had made the right decision.

For more than a third (37%) of the information deficits identified in the counselling interviews, the corrections were difficult to manage. This may serve as a warning against a too quick typification or labelling of the clients' concerns. In addition, the affective area was only taken into account indirectly, e.g. via the problem pressure and the degree of inner involvement of the client.

5.1.2 Investigation into the Linking of Decision-Relevant Information in Counselling

In another study (Hick, 1992) with the same decision-theoretical background, the focus was now on the linking of factual, valuative and prescriptive information during the interaction processes of problem-solving counselling.

For the analysis of cognitive processes in individual problem solving, three main procedures come into consideration (Gallhofer & Saris, 1989, p. 99): "Cognitive Mapping" (CM), "Empirical decision analysis" (EDA) and "Multiple path to choice" (MPC).

A modified thinking structure analysis (CM) was used. Cognitive mapping focuses on the problem definition phase and examines the assumptions and evaluations that play a role in explaining events. The "cognitive land-map", i.e. the cognitive structure of a person is viewed as a flow chart from these valuations. This modification refers above all to the temporal sequence of problem-solving, which the ideal-typical phase structure does not do justice to in reality.

The results show that the linking of factual, evaluative and prescriptive information can be represented as a process in a network with various circuits and islands. In this way, the client's decisions and the counsellor's statements about the results become just as visible in their development as the content of conversations that have no connection to the overall context.

Furthermore, the great importance of prescriptive premises for the course of the conversation becomes apparent. Clients who have a high proportion of this information already describe their concerns in a very differentiated way in the initial phase, so that their problem situation can be defined with only minimal verbal encouragement.

Clients with a high proportion of prescriptive information also tend to paraphrase more, i.e. they repeatedly describe the problem in slightly different words and are thus able to point out the individual facets in the interaction with the counsellor without a greater shift in emphasis.

In the further course of the conversation, these clients not only ask more specific questions but can also better memorise new information through independent summaries and repetitions, so that they can refer back to it later. This should result in a further increase in decision-making competence.

In addition, there were counselling sessions in which the client apparently deliberately described his concerns in very general terms and without his direct involvement. This non-committal nature indicates that the client is hoping for trends rather than binding answers. When the counsellor tries to activate the client and concretise the problem, the chances of a successful conversation is far greater.

In other cases, the clients narrowed down their concerns to individual questions, with the risk that these aspects could not later be put back into the overall context. This phenomenon of "islands of conversation" points either to an unsystematic "hypervigilant" decision-making style (cf. Janis & Mann, 1977, p. 196) or to the shielding of the strong hierarchisation of decision-relevant premises already undertaken.

Based on the presentation of the "problem cycles" in the counselling interview, two typical heuristics of the clients could be identified. In one case, there is a strong preference for a certain alternative course of action that is relatively resistant to external constraints. At the same time, however, the criteria cited for this are only general in character. If one now tries to concretise the criteria with regard to the alternative, there is the danger that the client is not yet able to make these references and "encapsulates" himself or herself. On the other hand, s/he may repeatedly introduce other evaluations ("vagrancy of the criteria").

In the other heuristic, the client is guided in the problem-solving process primarily by limiting conditions, such as the labour market situation, poor report card grades, seemingly outdated personal qualifications, or lack of work experience. With this "restriction heuristic", one's own abilities and interests take a back seat. The clients in question often ask for different career options without the counsellor having the opportunity to assess the clients.

These results suggest that *clients with deficits in prescriptive decision-making premises* deserve special attention when designing professional information and counselling processes. This is because these premises determine the scope and linkage of alternatives and evaluations (criteria) in the decision-making process. They comprise both the individual decision logic and the decision-relevant metacognitions of self-control. Peterson et al. (1996, p. 438) divide these metacognitions into "self-talk" (e.g. positive: "I trust that I will make the right career decision", negative: "I am guaranteed to always make the wrong choice"), "self-awareness", i.e. the self-perception and classification of the decision-making process.

"Self-talk" as a basis for the appropriate reaction to it (e.g. "I am appalled that I am not able to make a good career decision!") and "monitoring and control", i.e. assessing the appropriateness of the preliminary approach and the amount of information on the respective steps of problem-solving (e.g. "I need to seek professional advice to solve my problem" or "There is no point in continuing to search for information about future opportunities in this profession because the forecasts are too speculative!").

5.1.3 Career Information Expectations and Structures in Individual Counselling

In a larger study accompanying innovation on the vocational materials "Ausbildungsberufe im Urteil der Betriebe" (Recognised Training Occupations in the Opinion of Companies) by the Institute for Employment Research of the German Federal Employment Agency (IAB) (Seidel, 1995), further aspects of demand-oriented information for vocational decision-making processes were investigated. Among other aspects, the study was about the connections among clients' participation in the counselling interview, their information expectations and their subjective appreciation of career information offers.

The focus was on two aspects; namely, the need for information regarding the development of person-related and job-related decision-making premises.

The study took place in 70 employment agencies (employment counselling and career counselling) and included a standardised interview with the client before the individual counselling, an observation of the conversation, a standardised interview with the client, and an interview with the counsellor after the counselling. A total of 135 counselling sessions were evaluated.

Selected results are presented below (Ertelt et al., 1997).

The basic prerequisite for the attention and absorption of information in counselling is the inner participation of the client. The most important determinant is the importance the client attaches to the conversation.

Over 95% considered the upcoming counselling to be "fairly important" or "very important". However, there are clear differences between adults (employment counselling) and young people (career counselling) with regard to the category "very important": Employment counselling: 69.3%, career counselling: 45%. For many clients in employment counselling, the counselling interview is of existential importance because financial questions of further training and retraining are discussed. This effect, however, is mainly due to women who expect help with their professional problems from employment counselling.

There are also differences between AB and BB clients in terms of their stage in the decision-making process. A good fifth (21%) of clients in employment counselling are still at the beginning stages of decision-making, more so than the career counselees at 15%.

In contrast, 50% of the career counselling clients were at the stage where they placed themselves as being ready to consider career alternatives (i.e. they have already narrowed down their solution space).

Further analysis of the data showed that 15% of the employment counsellees were in the decision phase and 17% of career counselling clients were in the decision phase. Employment clients in the post-decision and realisation phase constituted 25% of all clients, while career counselling clients made up 18% of this phase.

The large segments of those who have already made up their minds and come for counselling provide important indications for information management, which, in addition to preparing the decision, must also take into account confirming or overcoming the decision and realising it.

In order to capture the dimensions of information demand, the content-related expectations of the clients were analyzed. Four factors emerged (explaining 67% variance):

Factor 1 represents criterion information for the evaluation of occupational alternatives

- Advantages and disadvantages of certain professions
- Opportunities and risks of certain professions on the labour market
- Where do your own professional strengths lie?

Factor 2 combines requests for information on defining personal professional problem situations, on how to proceed and on possible obstacles in training and employment.

Factor 3 includes requests for information on occupational flexibility, mobility and corresponding assistance from the employment agency.

Factor 4 bundles requests for information to confirm personal decisions and to help realise them.

The analysis showed that the need for information before the interview is determined by gender, the type of guidance (career guidance for young people and employment guidance for adults) and the stage in the decision-making process:

- Female clients seek information on problem definition more than male clients (Factor 2).
- Clients who have not yet decided expect more criterion information for the evaluation of alternatives than those who have already decided (Factor 1).
- Those who have decided, on the other hand, want more information to confirm and realise their decision (Factor 4).
- Adults ask more than young people for information on job mobility and financial assistance from the employment agency (Factor 3).

The next part of the study consisted of examining to what extent the medium at hand (MatAB expert survey)[1] was able to cover these information expectations with the various topics, i.e. to what extent it is demand-oriented.

It turned out that the clients' wishes represented in Factors 1–3 could be covered well, but not those bundled in Factor 4. The research during and after counselling revealed a number of other clues important for information management. For example, adults showed far more than expected genuine career choice behaviour with regard to training occupations. Consequently, differences in information and counselling methodology between career guidance and employment counselling can hardly be justified. This also does not seem necessary because the results also indicate that young people already think very intensively about the future labour market and the necessary vocational flexibility during their initial career choice and before completing vocational training. They, therefore, feel satisfied that they are now in a vocational transition stage. Further results showed that counselling very often reflects the individual's decision-making process, but it should not be overlooked that it was precisely the state of vacillation between occupational alternatives that could not be overcome in 60% of the cases. It does not necessarily have to be considered a step backwards if 33% of the clients who had already made up their minds went back to the stage of dealing with alternatives.

Critical to demand-oriented information activity is the fact that the counsellors only vaguely recognise in which phase of the problem-solving process their clients are. It would be expected that the clients' self-assessment would be more in line with the counsellor's assessment.

This means that the basic conditions for effective demand-oriented information management in guidance are often missing.

[1] In the autumn of 1993, about 6500 company experts were surveyed on 94 recognised training occupations as part of a representative study. The results form the basis for "Materialien" (MatAB) No. 2.2/1994.

5.1.4 Information Needs and Media Use Among Clients and Employees Using the Counselling Services of the German Federal Employment Agency (BA)

Within the framework of an evaluation study on the use of media in the BA's counselling services (Seidel, 1997), it was possible to further differentiate the decision-theoretical model with regards to counselling information management.

The following selected results are based on the statements of 1053 clients, 1068 counsellors, 244 teachers and 251 employers. These standardised interviews were collected in the Fall of 1996.

The clients' expectations of counselling at the employment agency or of a visit to a Career Information Centre (BIZ) indicated a high level of commitment. Almost 90% of the clients described this visit as "fairly important" (48%) or "very important" (40%). There were differences, depending on the decision-making phase. Clients who expected help with realisation described the visit to the employment agency/BIZ as important significantly more often.

With regard to the status of the decision-making process, around 17% of the clients were still at the beginning (Stage 1), a third already had alternatives but were still weighing alternatives against each other (Stage 2). Around 23% had decided but would like to further secure their decision (Stage 3). Nearly 25% expected help in realising their decision (Stage 4).

With regard to the main sources of information used, friends/acquaintances and family played a special role, as has already been shown in previous studies. These sources are followed in importance by the BIZ and newspapers/magazines, and somewhat with publications from the employment agency, career guidance centres and schools.

But here, too, there are differences in preferences depending on the stage in the decision-making process:

Friends/acquaintances	Stages	1–4, especially 2
Family (parents/spouse)	Stages	1–3
information centre	Stages	2 and 3
Job counselling	Stage	4
Vocational guidance	Stages	3 and 2
School/Teacher/Higher Education	Stage	3
Writings from BA	Stages	2 and 3, also 4
Newspapers	Stage	4

The answers to the question about the most important topics for clients strongly reflect current economic conditions. The top rankings were "Conditions in the training places market or labour market in certain occupations", "Prerequisites and requirements for training/further training/occupation", "Financial assistance for training/further training, unemployment or taking up employment".

Interest in training, internships or working abroad ranked last among the topics offered.

Overall, 9 out of 13 topics listed were described by the clients as fairly to very important; an indication of the great need for different types of information. This is probably due to differing views of the problem.

For this research study, the correlations between the status in the problem-solving process and the demand for vocational information (as represented in the selected media of the BA) were made visible by means of discriminant analysis.

1. Clients in *the problem definition phase* wanted information about prerequisites and requirements for training, further education or a new occupation, about the income situation in certain occupations, about financial assistance from the employment agency and about important aspects of choosing a career or changing careers.
2. Clients who are *wavering between career alternatives* asked for information about the content and requirements of vocational training or university studies. In addition, training or working abroad also played a role.
3. Clients who *already know exactly what they want to do professionally* appreciated information about training/working abroad, about prestige and career opportunities of certain professions, about working conditions and about labour market developments in certain professions.
4. Clients who come to counselling with the *wish for realisation information* wanted information about other institutions that provide information, about counselling and placement services offered by the employment agency, about financial assistance for training and further education, and about ending unemployment.

For the design of the interface between supply and demand of decision-relevant information, the study provided further important trends. All respondent groups pointed to the need for *personal assistance* in the use of the media offered. This demand can be interpreted as a reaction to the abundance of differentiated information offered. It is difficult for the individual user to keep track of all this information. As a result, there is a desire for networked and regionalised systems that can be adapted to individual questions and search habits.

5.1.5 Use of Media and the Employment Agency's Careers Information Centre (BIZ) by Clients of the German Job Placement and Employment Counselling Service

The empirical study commissioned by the Regional Employment Office of Baden-Württemberg was intended to record empirically the opinions of clients in job placement and counselling services about media equipment and self-information facilities. An overview of the results is presented below (Ertelt & Hesse, 1999).

1. There are statistically relevant differences between customers who do and do not visit the BIZ:

   - BIZ visitors are more interested in questions of further education, information on specific professions, knowledge about their own strengths and weaknesses and activities abroad.
   - Non-BIZ visitors are more interested in financial assistance from the employment agency.

2. With regard to the status of problem-solving, it can clearly be observed that the BIZ visitors fluctuate more often between occupational alternatives. They obviously hope for more information on the evaluation (criteria) of the alternatives they are considering. Among the non-BIZ visitors, however, those who have already made a decision and therefore need help in realising it, slightly outnumber those who have not made a decision.
3. With regard to the way in which their vocational questions are answered, the non-BIZ visitors prefer a personal conversation in the employment agency, want significantly less written material and also want to use the information possibilities significantly less in the future. A similarly negative picture emerges with regard to answering questions via the internet and computer. However, it must be realised that both groups only appreciate the internet and computer to a small extent for answering their vocational questions.
4. BIZ visitors have a significantly higher level of education. A number of other characteristics are related to educational attainment that indicates a risk group: dealing with information systems is less attractive for Hauptschule (lowest general school, 9 years) students (with or without a diploma) than for clients with Realschule or Gymnasium completion. This corresponds to the results of other studies as well. BIZ visitors are on average much younger (29 years) than non-BIZ visitors (37 years). In the trainees and student groups, there are hardly any who do not go to the BIZ (91 % and 95 %, respectively).

   Only a few clients who are unemployed, or have been or are housewives, go to the BIZ.
5. The assessment of the individual stage in the decision-making process also proves to be an important tool for identifying different information needs among customers. The strongest differentiation exists with regards to specific information on occupations. This information is needed above all by those seeking advice who want to evaluate alternatives. Specific information on certain occupations is less important for those seeking advice who want to confirm a decision they have already made. Less important for them is the information on job search/application/introduction and on their own professional strengths and weaknesses. Regardless of the decision stage, clarifying the professional future is most important for all.
6. The evaluation of the *age distribution* at the decision-making levels yields an interesting result. While the younger visitors predominate at Stage 2 (weighing up the alternatives), the older clients are more strongly represented at Stage 3 (realisation assistance after the decision has been made). Older people, therefore, tend

to come to the employment agency with more decisive ideas. It is also noticeable that the *need for personal counselling* becomes stronger with increasing age.

The distribution of clients according to the decision-making levels (degree of decision-making) is influence by their level of education. It is worth noting that secondary school pupils (with or without a diploma) are highly represented at level 1 "Don't know yet what to do with my career". On average, visitors with a secondary school or grammar school diploma come to the BIZ in an already advanced problem-solving stage.

Visitors with a secondary school education prefer the personal interview at the employment agency more than others. The higher the level of education, the more likely it is for clients to have access to an internet connection (there is a particularly clear correlation here).

7. When looking at the decision-making status according to occupational status, the statements made under point 7 stand out more strongly.

   Those with a lower occupational status are more often at the beginning of the problem-solving process, whereas those with a higher occupational status are in more advanced decision-making phases. It seems understandable that a relatively large group among the unemployed are still at the beginning of the problem-solving process, i.e. they need more guidance (problem definitions).

Overall, a stronger use of *self-information* can be assessed positively on the basis of this study. However, in order to optimise this self-information, it is absolutely necessary to take the following characteristics into account; namely, age, general education degree, vocational qualification and current status of the profession. Independent of this, the individual status in the decision-making or problem-solving process proves to be a key variable. Counsellors must concentrate on the differentiation of the information offered and on the information guidance systems.

The results clearly show that a self-information system must always be combined with *personal counselling services.* Such a networked system is invaluable for helping special target groups in the labour market (Ertelt & Muswieck, 2000), but is equally of value for highly involved, professional users of information services (see also Ertelt et al., 2004).

5.1.6 Individual Decision-Making Strategies for Professional Decisions

In an explorative study, Wegmann (2005) investigated the procedures underlying individual career decisions. With the help of open interviews, which were conducted using the methodology of the biographic narrative of the narrative interview, the decision-making processes of five people (over 28 years of age) were explored in their career choices.

The following list shows the decision strategies discussed in the literature and on which the evaluation was based. They can be classified according to three characteristics:

1. Search rules for alternatives and/or their attributes
2. Stop rules for establishing the search
3. Decision rules for choosing an alternative
   (Gigerenzer & Selten, 2002, p. 8).

Search, stop and decision rules of the individual decision strategies

Examples of heuristics	1. Search rule	2. Stop rule	3. Decision rule
Optimisation	No search rule, since perfect knowledge of all possible alternatives and attributes is assumed	No stop rule, as no search has to be carried out	Values of the attributes weighted by relevance are summed up. Decision in favour of the alternative whose attributes achieve the highest value
Sub-optimisation	No explicit search rule	The search is stopped as soon as its effort exceeds the benefit of the decision optimisation	Values of the attributes weighted by relevance are summed up. Decision in favour of the alternative whose attributes achieve the highest value
"Satisfaction"	Search rule according to the random principle	The search will be stopped as soon as an alternative is available. "Satisfaction level" corresponds to	Decision in favour of the first alternative, which corresponds to the "satisfaction level"
Incrementalism	Search for alternatives that deviate only slightly from the initial state	Search is terminated when an alternative is found that represents an improvement on the initial situation	Decision in favour of an alternative that differs only slightly from the initial situation but represents an improvement
"Minimalist" heuristic	Random search for a relevant attribute in which the alternatives differ	The search ends as soon as an attribute is found in which the alternatives differ	Decision in favour of the known alternative. If neither or both are known, decision in favour of the alternative with the higher value on the selected attribute

Search, stop and decision rules of the individual decision strategies			
"Take the last" heuristic	Search for an attribute that has ended the search in a past decision situation	The search ends as soon as an attribute is found in which the alternatives differ	Decision in favour of the alternative with the higher value on the selected attribute
"Take the best" heuristic	Search for an attribute that has the strongest deciding power	Search is terminated as soon as an attribute is found in which the alternatives differ	Decision in favour of the alternative with the higher value on the selected attribute
Availability heuristics	Search is determined by the ease with which information can be retrieved from memory or generated	No explicit stop rule	Decision is determined by the ease with which information can be retrieved or generated from memory
Representation heuristic	No explicit search rule	No explicit stop rule	Decision based on the assumed correspondence ("representativeness" between an object to be assessed and a certain population)
Anchoring/ adaptation heuristics	The search is based on a starting value or situation	No explicit stop rule	Decision is oriented towards an initial value or situation (anchor)

(Wegmann, 2005, p. 25)

The results show that the simplest decision strategies, namely heuristics and the incrementalism strategy, are by far the most common. Of the total of 31 assignable strategies, only one decision showed a tendency towards the optimisation strategy, i.e. rational behaviour.

None of the respondents used the same behavioural pattern across all decisions in their careers, but they usually used three to four different patterns. However, no particular rule can be identified in the changes in strategies over time either.

The following criteria proved to be particularly relevant in professional decision-making (ordered by frequency of mention):

1. Pre-qualification or decisive previous experience
2. Desire to earn money or secure a living
3. Family influence
4. Leisure activities
5. Interest or pleasure in the respective activity
6. Local proximity of the place of training or work or the place of study
7. Friends influence
8. Inner wish or long-cherished dream

Wegmann (2005, p. 109) draws the hypothetical conclusion from the results of the study that with increasing age, the willingness to accept more radical breaks and greater efforts in order to realise a career aspiration increases. With increasing experience and personal maturity, career decision factors tend to move away from extrinsic to intrinsic motivations.

Particularly important for career guidance are the behaviours at the externally set decision points, such as graduation from school and career choice. The interviews showed that the interviewees did not seem prepared for these transitions despite their predictability, because the decisions were characterised by great uncertainty and easy influence.

Methodologically similar studies (Trisoglio-Wanka, 2008; Wresch, 2008) indicated that at the beginning of a career, i.e. when choosing a profession for the first time, the satisficing strategy predominates and that the majority of respondents rely on imitating social role models (especially parents) along the lines of "one-reason-decision-making".

As the career progresses, once a satisfactory path has been taken, incremental strategies emerge. Respondents opt for options that successively bring them closer to their actual goals.

Overall, strong evidence has so far been found for behavioural patterns similar to patterns identified in Krumboltz's (2003) "Happenstance Approach" (Krumboltz & Lewin, 2004; Mitchell et al., 1999).

This approach emphasises the use of unplanned favourable events and aims to help individuals move towards the goal of a satisfying life rather than focusing on rational decisions.

Based on these patterns, the following five counselling steps are suggested:

1. Make it clear to the person seeking advice that coincidences are a normal and necessary phenomenon in career choice and development.
2. Support those seeking advice in identifying what could enrich their professional life.
3. Use the positive experiences of those seeking advice with unplanned events as a basis for recommendations for action.
4. In future, support those seeking advice to recognise and make use of favourable coincidences.
5. Enable those seeking advice to identify such perceptions and external obstacles that hinder the implementation of constructive courses of action.

It would seem seems to be crucial that rationally oriented theories are put into a wider perspective in the further development of the science of counselling, considering the growing importance of counselling in education, occupation and employment (Schiersmann, 2007, p. 150; Ruppert & Ertelt, 2007).

5.1.7 Individual Migration Decisions

In a qualitative study, Seyffer (2015) investigated the individual decision-making processes in final transnational migration (in this case from Poland to Germany).

Special interest was paid to the heuristics used and their dependence on biographical and socio-economic conditions. It turned out that individual decision-making was only systematically carried out in the sense of an optimisation strategy in exceptional cases. The vast majority of the interviewees acted according to a satisfaction strategy; namely, taking the best minimalist affect or even any available heuristic.

The reason for migration and the phase in the life cycle as well as gender played a role in the (conscious or rather unconscious) choice of approach.

With regard to the important question of the constancy of individual decision-making strategies, Seyffer (2015, p. 123) came to the conclusion that people "... who have used a decision-making strategy several times over the course of time ... always (use) it in similar situations under comparable conditions and, especially, if the result of the previous decision was satisfactory".

It is predominantly the female respondents who included emotions and the wishes of others in the decision-making process. These were expressed through the more frequent use of affect heuristics or affectively shaped "one reason decisions" (ibid., 123).

However, the strongest conditioning factor for the choice of heuristic applied was the individually named reason for migration. These reasons controlled the intensity of the information search as well as the weighting of the criteria.

The survey results also reflect that heuristic decision-making strategies do not lead to subjectively worse results than the more rationally oriented approaches. In this context, it was not overlooked that the insufficient informational preparation for migration led to difficulties in linguistic adaptation, occupational disadvantages and cognitive dissonance (cf. Seyffer, 2015, p. 125).

Women were apparently more burdened by these factors, while men seemed to find it much easier to reduce dissonance. Women also expressed a need for change more often in the retrospective view of their migration decision (Seyffer, 2015, p. 117).

5.1.8 Current Research on Professional Decision-Making Behaviour

Based on a differentiated literature review on the further development of an instrument to survey occupational decision-making behaviour, Tittel (2019) drew up a number of hypothetical statements.

Thus, following a qualitative study by Klevenow and Weber (2016, p. 482), it became clear that the decision-making process was apparently not characterised by one heuristic, but by a "mix" of interwoven heuristic behaviours (cf. also Seyffer, 2015, p. 29).

In the analysis tool on professional decision-making behaviour developed by Tittel (2019, p. 91), heuristics are regarded as multidimensional constructs.

According to Gigerenzer and Todd (1999, p. 16), the description of heuristics is possible with the help of three building blocks, the search rules, the stop rules and the decision rules. Tittel used the search and decision rules as the basis for item construction, which was measured using a 4-point scale ("Does not apply at all" to "Fully applies") in relation to personal career choice.

Heuristics with sample items:

- *Intuitive decision-making behaviour*

  Gut feeling: "I listened to my gut feeling"

- *Rational decision-making behaviour*

  1. "I try to get to know every professional field".
  2. "I have collected little information" (coded negative).
  3. "I have informed myself about many different professions and career alternatives".
  4. "I am eliminating different professions step by step".
  5. "I weigh all alternatives carefully and decide on the profession/career alternative that best fulfills all my wishes".

- *Satisfaction heuristic*

  "I choose the profession that first met my wishes when I searched for information".

- *Incrementalism*

  1. "I am looking for occupational alternatives that can bring about at least a small improvement in my life situation".
  2. "I am looking for jobs that are only slightly different from my current state".

- *Recognition heuristics*

  1. "I have read up on professions I have heard of".
  2. "I have informed myself about popular professions".

- *Take-the-First-Heuristic*

  1. "My first idea is ultimately also my favourite".
  2. Information search is done "just go for it".

- *Take-the-Best Heuristic*

  "I choose the profession that meets the criterion that is most important to me"

- *Social imitation*

  1. "I have informed myself about occupational alternatives that important role models practise or have recommended to me".
  2. "I have excluded professions that others have advised me against".

- *Happenstances*

  "I choose to take advantage of a favourable opportunity that has come my way".

However, the use of heuristic principles can also lead to errors and cognitive biases.

In contrast to the idea that the use of heuristic principles will lead to errors and cognitive biases (originally put forward by Kahnemann (2012), is the view of Gigerenzer and Todd (1999) that an "ecologically rational" heuristic adapted to the environment will lead to a realistic decision and that any additional supply of information will reduce the quality of the decision ("less-is-more effect").

In our view, a very important analysis result for guidance marketing relates to the dependence of the choice of decision strategy on individual involvement. The higher the involvement, the more consciously the individual deals with the problem (Braun & Benz, 2015; Petty & Cacioppo, 1986).

According to Tittel (2019), the conclusions drawn from Braun and Benz (2015) that intuitive and conscious decision-making processes can be combined and thus lead to more satisfactory results than purely intuitive processes, once again confirms the advantage of conscious reflection on heuristics and intuitions in a counselling process.

Concerning the SIM described in the following chapter, it should be emphasised that the science-based analysis of individual heuristics by the counsellors in the sense of "cognitive empathy" (Ertelt & Ruppert, 2011) forms the prerequisite for the sensitive adaptation of decision-relevant information to the internal conditions of the counselee. With regard to information and its weighting, ethical aspects of professional counselling must be taken into account. In the possible rejection of the client's wish to support the transformation of information into premises through evaluative statements, we see the ethics of counselling violated just as much as through a well-meaning oversupply of seemingly neutral data in the erroneous assumption that counselling seekers could somehow develop decision-relevant information or even premises from it. Against the background of the explanations on heuristics, this would certainly be unprofessionally interpreted "help for self-help".

Another area of research in the field of career guidance that has received too little attention so far, in our view, concerns the interdependence of important influencing factors with decision-making behaviour, especially career interests, self-assessed transferable competences, coping strategies, self-efficacy beliefs, involvement or even experiences of unemployment and burn-out.

We endorsed the research done by Brown (2012, p. 151) on the connections between self-efficacy, decision-making behaviour and professional interests.

In the research environment of the German University of Applied Labour Studies of the Federal Employment Agency (HdBA), a number of target group-related studies on the multifactorial interaction of career-relevant personality variables have recently been identified.

In an empirical study on the connection between occupational interests, transferable competences and decision-making heuristics, Holder (2016) was able to show significant connections between occupational interests (measured according to the

MZZ test by Noworol, 2013) and decision-making heuristics on the basis of a survey of students in pre-secondary level II classes ($n = 322$).

There are also highly significant correlations between occupational interests and interdisciplinary social and methodological competences. This has lead to the conclusion that self-assessed competences and interests reinforce each other.

The study highlights the particular importance of interest group classification in identifying possible interdependencies with heuristics, involvement, feelings of reactance and commitment (Holder, 2016, p. 69).

Interdependencies between occupational interests, generic competences, coping strategies and occupational decision-making behaviour among young unemployed people ($n = 53$) were the subject of a pilot study by J. Schulz (2017). Coping strategies could be mapped as independent variables in two clusters. Cluster 1 showed relatively weak values in relation to actional and cognitive coping strategies. Cluster 2, on the other hand, showed significantly higher values on both scales and can be characterised as "strong in confrontation".

With regard to occupational interests (according to the MZZ test by Noworol, 2013), the test persons in Cluster 2 have significantly higher values in all areas. This also applies to performance orientation as part of the transferable competences (measured with the smk72 according to Frey & Balzer, 2007).

Very important for guidance practice is the result that the members of both clusters differ significantly in their decision-making behaviour. Whereas those from the highly engaged Cluster 2 approach the career choice and decision-making process systematically (incrementally) in manageable steps and thus come close to the optimisation heuristic, those from Cluster 1 take larger steps, act without a conscious or recurring pattern, and often avoid a systematic information activity.

However, this behaviour could also be related to the fact that the majority of respondents from Cluster 1 state that they already know exactly what they want to do professionally and do not need any further help. In contrast, those from cluster 2 are still in the middle of the career decision-making process.

In a methodologically similar empirical study of young jobseekers ($n = 106$), Baldamus (2018) was able to demonstrate very differentiated interdependence between the personality variables already mentioned.

Of particular interest for counselling-supported employment services and employment-oriented case management is the influence of the duration of unemployment on these variables.

It can be seen that young jobseekers with strong expressions of their occupational interests have a shorter duration of unemployment, while those with the highest average unemployment, have weaker expressions in almost all interest dimensions.

A similar picture emerges with regard to transferable competences. Respondents with particularly high levels have a significantly lower duration of unemployment. Baldamus (2018, p. 80) derived consequences for action from this result: "If competences are formed in the social environment, emphasis should be given to supporting young unemployed [people] even more in carrying out internships, holiday jobs or social work already in the lower grades of school".

Against this background, it does not seem surprising that there is also a significant correlation between the development of coping strategies and the duration of unemployment. It is to be feared that even after a relatively short period of unemployment, the coping strategies of the individual diminish.

The inclusion of decision-making behaviour provides further important insights. For example, the duration of unemployment is significantly lower for those who dealt with it before entering the labour market than for those who did not prepare.

Critical for adequate behaviour is also the finding that people who have been unemployed for a long time tend to look for the causes for their current occupational situation within themselves (internal attribution), while those who have been unemployed for a short time tend to attribute it externally. In addition, the longer the unemployment, the more difficult it seems to be to develop career perspectives and to find the motivation to change. Counselling help here could refer to the interests and enjoyment of the occupational activity. These feelings were strongest when respondents first chose a career.

Interdependence research related to other target groups with a focus on counselling-related decision-making and problem-solving behaviour is being intensively pursued.

5.2 The Information Structural Methodology (ISM)

The role of guidance professionals in many career-related guidance systems for young people and adults is influenced by a number of specific conditions: limited counselling time, low contact frequency, often only one-session counselling, high existential problem pressure (especially in the transition processes from school to vocational training, as well as frictions in the career pathway), high expectations regarding the diagnostic, vocational, labour market and mediation competences of the counsellor. In addition, counsellors often have responsibilities in the area of financial support for education and training, in ending unemployment, in mobility and in promotion processes.

It follows that professional counsellors have to combine different and sometimes conflicting role requirements in order to meet the internationally customary ethical guidelines and the legal-institutional framework conditions of a specific field of activity.

Counselling theories provide different answers to this question, and the reality is that counselling is too diverse to be dealt with by only one particular approach.

Corey (2013), after evaluating various empirical studies for clinical and general counselling work, predicted an increasing convergence and integration of theoretical orientations and stated that a trend towards "creative synthesis, arbitrary integration and systematic eclecticism" was emerging.

Hofer and Papastefanou (1996, p. 52) hold the following problems responsible for the poor application of scientific theories in educational-psychological counselling practice:

1. For important problem areas, there are still *no validated theories;* many of the approaches suffer from *complexity deficiencies,* i.e. they hardly provide concrete decision rules for the procedure. Thus, counsellors often have to make up their mind based on various other similar theoretical models, or develop their own model based on trial and error.
2. Trained counselling practitioners in particular often consider new research findings to be trivial because they seem to suggest procedures that are self-evident and have been known for a long time. Conversely, people tend to reject new knowledge that contradicts their own convictions and do not part with knowledge even though it has never been seriously tested for practical suitability.
3. However, even if new scientific findings are adopted into the knowledge system, this does not guarantee that they will be translated into counselling action. Reasons for this resistance for change include: contradictions to the counsellor's own conception of guidance, lack of appropriate working conditions or insufficient counsellor training.
4. Ultimately, problems arise from the *incongruence between the language of theory and the language of practice.* This is clearly shown when it is not possible to make certain theory-led procedures understandable to the client.

Overall, it can be assumed that the majority of counselling practitioners are implicitly or explicitly guided by theories or counselling models and also see their work as scientifically based. However, the defining constructs are predominantly generalised theories about problems and their causes as well as corresponding approaches, such as those suggested by client-centred, behaviour-analytical, or systems-theoretical concepts (Ertelt et al., 2015; Highly recommended here is the practice-related overview of the career theories and models edited by Arthur et al. 2019).

According to Hofer and Papastefanou (1996, p. 54), counselling practice could be more theoretically sound "if future counsellors acquire the broadest possible overview knowledge during their studies, become familiar with the language of science and practise applying theories taught by lecturers to their (personal) practice".

Overall, it can be assumed that the eclectic counselling methodology will become an independent field of development for career counselling as well (Crites, 1981, p. 168; cf. Gibson & Mitchell, 1990, p. 139).

The ISM is an *eclectic approach for career decision counselling*. It is descriptive in nature, i.e. it does not describe how to solve professional problems, but is oriented towards the clients' *actual* decision-making behaviour. The ISM model focuses on the individual decision-making process, its phases and stages of information processing, as well as the emotions accompanying the stages.

ISM, like all other approaches, must be measured by the contributions it can make to counselling action in concrete problem situations. In order to cope with the various sub-processes, the counselling practitioner needs special knowledge for each area of knowledge (cf. Hofer & Papastefanou, 1996, p. 25):

1. *Goal knowledge* includes normative considerations that serve to structure and classify problems formulated by the client. With the setting of a target situation to be achieved through counselling, a first target decision has already been made.

   Accordingly, norm-referenced thinking is required when the general goal ("Helping people to help themselves") is to be implemented on a case-specific basis. Particularly in career counselling, it is important to practise a relationship appropriate to the person and situation between actively helping and letting the client find his or her own way.

   Thus, a responsible choice of means cannot be used without societal considerations, because not every approach that promises effectiveness can be accepted in counselling.

   Ethical guidelines of large national and international counselling associations serve as an important aid for locating one's own counselling activities (cf. Ertelt & Schulz, 1997, p. 365 and p. 407; cf. Schulz, 2000).
2. *Diagnostic knowledge,* especially in relation to determining the nature and extent of individual information deficits in decision-making processes, plays an important role in ISM.

   In the phase of problem definition, this knowledge serves to determine the exact concern as well as the actual-target discrepancy between the current state and the expectation of success (treatment-preparatory diagnostics).

   In the counselling process, information is needed about the respective state and progress of the person seeking counselling. This requires treatment-accompanying diagnostics or progress diagnostics or formal evaluation.

   The treatment-final diagnostic (summative evaluation) serves to determine the intervention effects of possible other consequences and the degree of goal achievement.
3. *Object knowledge* consists of theoretically sound knowledge about the problems of those seeking advice and about possible causes.

   This knowledge gives the counsellor clues for the precise conceptual classification of the problems, the targeted search for possible determinants, and the effects that can be achieved with the client and the corresponding procedure. Object knowledge for ISM includes sound knowledge of decision theory, learning psychology, motivational psychology and developmental psychology.
4. *Operational knowledge* includes knowledge of procedures and their effectiveness for solving the problem. Most of the overarching counselling concepts that can be used for career guidance can be traced back to three directions; namely, humanistic, behavioural and systems theory. It should be noted that these approaches were, originally, primarily therapeutic approaches and their transfer to career guidance should therefore be examined very critically. The goal of *humanistic counselling* is to increase self-acceptance and to mobilise resources for self-development. According to Rogers (1972), the necessary counselling influence is adequately defined by empathetic understanding, positive regard and authenticity in behaviour. Through this "non-directive" basic attitude, clients are helped by helping themselves.

The core of *behaviourally oriented counselling* is the process of relearning, whereby maladaptive behaviour is to be transformed into adapted behaviour (psycho-education). ISM considers itself a psycho-educational concept within cognitive-behavioural approaches. In the sense of inter-actionist approaches, the person seeking advice is regarded as a self-responsible individual who actively helps to shape his or her career. The system-theoretical approaches consider it more promising to not only concentrate on the individual but to start with the system as a whole and to include the reference persons as "important others". This is one of the reasons why systematic methods are so widely used in family therapy but are also gaining importance for career counselling. Empirical studies have long shown that parents, relatives and friends play a central role in career choice. However, the social environment also plays a decisive role in coping with career problems later on; for example, in the case of unemployment or mobility issues.

Therefore, it goes without saying that ISM includes systemic aspects in a way that is appropriate for the individual and the problem situation.

5. Specialist counselling with the *introduction of solution knowledge* requires the counsellor to have differentiated knowledge about educational opportunities, labour market processes, career developments, counselling and placement opportunities, financial assistance and the corresponding legal regulations.

   Counselling information management includes client-related collection, processing, selection and dissemination of problem-solving data. It is important to take into account the individual's capacity to absorb and process data, as well as her or his diagnostic and prognostic knowledge about the interaction between personality traits and the recommended measures (cf. Ertelt, 2001, p. 1385).

As an eclectic approach, ISM must be based on a consistent theoretical foundation on the one hand, but on the other hand, it must also do justice to different forms of counselling. Today, "distance counselling" by telephone or social media (Offer et al., 2001; Flederman & Watts, 2014, p. 481; Gati & Tal, 2008, p. 178) as well as computer-assisted counselling systems (CACG) (Harris-Bowlsbey, 2013; Gore et al., 2013, p. 522; Brown, 2012, p. 197) are joining the "classic" face-to-face counselling.

Thus, in an earlier study (Metzler-Burren, 2001), different counselling theories were compared in terms of their usefulness for career counselling by telephone. Factors that were evaluated included according to the aspects of communication, relationship level, counselling skills, career choice concepts and decision models.

It turned out that only the ISM was effective in all five areas and could therefore form the theoretical basis of a European pilot project on distance counselling (within the framework of the EU programme LEONARDO DA VINCI) (Ertelt & Muswieck, 2001).

5.2.1 The Counselling Process with ISM

In ISM, the counselling process is understood in the sense of a simulation of imagined cognitive-affective information processing procedures in the client, within the framework of a learning process oriented towards the counselling goal. The client increasingly becomes a learner who learns about information knowledge.

The extent of the knowledge information deficits is determined together with the counsellor and adjusted according to the progress of the counselling.

A prerequisite is the counsellor's ability to assess the client in terms of how he or she is affected by a problem or a decision-making task, by previous personal heuristics, and by the stage in which the client is in the problem-solving process. Also assessed are the corresponding deficits that the client may have with regards to factual, evaluative and prescriptive premises.

Because ISM is not only about solving career problems, but also about the longer-term improvement of the client's decision-making competence with future career problems, the counsellor's approach must be transparent. This transparency also refers to the agreement on goals and the evaluation of success during counselling.

The necessary knowledge for success, i.e. knowledge of clients' problems and possible causes, as well as operational knowledge, i.e. knowledge of procedures and their effectiveness for problem-solving, has already been outlined in the previous section. This knowledge is further differentiated in counselling and expanded to include an approach related to ISM, namely "cognitive information processing in career problem solving and decision making" (CIP). According to Walsh (1990, p. 270), all approaches to career guidance implicitly or explicitly include stage models. The model on which ISM is based assumes that individual decision-making and problem-solving processes can be divided ideally into a pre-decision phase, a final phase and a post-decision phase, each with its own characteristics and information activities.

The phases are each characterised by specific objectives, emotions and combinations of the following information (decision stages):

Factual knowledge includes information about possible alternatives and their ("Satisfaction offers") realisation paths and chances of success. Comprehensive and qualified help in the area of factual information for career guidance is offered by the "Information System Education and Career" of the Federal Employment Agency (http://infobub.arbeitsagentur.de/). Within this online offer, the two databases BERUFENET and KURSNET are particularly worth mentioning.

BERUFENET offers a brief description of each occupation with the most important information at a glance, as well as detailed information on tasks, training, legal regulations and sources of information.

Tasks/Activities

- Working conditions
- Workplaces/industries
- Work equipment
- Access to employment (access occupations, application, selection procedure)

- Specialisations
- Further education
- Starting a business, opportunities for self-employment
- Alternatives/Job-Family
- Suitability/Interests
- Competences
- Earnings/Income

Training contents/procedure/completion

- Duration of training
- Training conditions
- Training locations/industries
- International
- Access requirements
- Suitability/Interests
- Financial Aspects
- Perspectives
- Review/Outlook
- Alternatives

Legal regulations

- Laws/regulations
- Equivalence of vocational qualifications in Europe
- Crediting of school-based basic vocational training years towards the training period

Sources of information

- Information services of a Federal Employment Agency
- Information from ministries, associations, and organisations
- Trade Journals
- Selection of books/media available in bookshops
- Professional/interest associations, employer/employee organisations
- Using job search help in BERUFENET and KURSNET (German)

The special focus of KURSNET is on continuing career education and training. With more than four million entries (International, European, and Binational), KURSNET is the most comprehensive database of its kind. The uniform presentation enables the direct comparison of several events.

In our view, the internationally recognised US Occupational Information Network (O*Net) is an extremely helpful instrument for differentiated clarification of occupation-related factual knowledge (cf. Ertelt & Frey, 2019, p. 313; Hanna et al., 2019, p. 581). The occupations are described using two dimensions of content descriptions:

The Worker-oriented ones include "Worker Characteristics" (Abilities, Occupational Interests, Work Values, Work Styles), "Worker Requirements" (Skills,

Knowledge, Education) and "Experience Requirements" (Experience and Training, Skills, Entry Requirements, Licensing).

The Job-oriented information includes "Occupational Requirements" (Work Activities, Organisational Context, Work Context), "Workface Characteristics" (Labour Market Information, Occupational Outlook) and "Occupation-Specific Information" (Title-Description, Alternative Titles, Tasks, Tools and Technology).

A key strength of O*Net is its orientation towards occupational reality through data collection from employees, occupational experts and labour analysts.

The multilingual Classification of European Skills, Competences, Qualifications and Occupations developed by the European Commission is particularly suitable for transnational career guidance and placement: "ESCO connects people with occupational vacancies ..." (European Commission, 2017). It provides specific information on knowledge, skills, competences, and qualifications for almost 3000 occupations (not "jobs"). It also provides job titles in the 26 ESCO languages and links to other major international and national classification systems.

Valuing knowledge comprises criteria that have developed from ideas on self in comparison to the perceived professional-social environment. Examples of clients' evaluative premises are:

- Interests and values in relation to school, education, employment
- Dissatisfaction with the current professional situation
- Self-assessed vocational information level
- Subjective ability
- Confidence in one's own ability to learn
- Expression of performance orientation
- Upward orientation
- Future perspective and ability to postpone satisfaction of needs in favour of longer-term goals ("deferred gratification pattern") Power orientation, prestige orientation
- Enjoyment orientation, leisure orientation
- Safety orientation
- Social orientation, human orientation

The personality typological approach of John Holland (1997) provides important information on individual professional orientations from which assessment criteria result. Here, six types are distinguished: the realistic, the explorative, the artistic, the social, the entrepreneurial and the conventional type (Ertelt & Frey, 2013, p. 276).

Personally binding problem-solving strategies show the individual the way in which factual knowledge and value knowledge are to be combined to solve problems. Examples of prescriptive premises are:

- Previous career information behaviour
- Information level
- Behaviour in existentially important decisions and personal decision-making (more rational, more incremental in the sense of step-by-step improvement, more random, more routine-oriented) (Ertelt & Schulz, 1997, p. 234)

- Independence in decision-making ("personal control")
- Reaction to obstacles to decision-making (frustration tolerance)
- Self-efficacy in decision-making behaviour (Brown, 2012, p. 151)

This prescriptive information includes subjectively significant rules of problem-solving, such as perception of the importance of a decision situation, realistic determination of the necessary steps, careful examination of previous experiences in similar situations, development of various alternatives, collection of information about these alternatives, weighting of the alternatives on the basis of criteria and weeding out of unattractive alternatives (Mitchell & Krumboltz, 1996, p. 173).

Only the information included by the individual in a particular problem situation is called "decision premises".

A "real" decision-making and problem-solving process begins when the individual is confronted with a new situation that has existential significance for him or her and can only be transformed from a current to a desired state through innovative action. That is, problematic situations are characterised by the fact that they cannot be solved by routine programmes or proven algorithms of action.

If clients are at the *beginning of his problem solving,* they need information to define the situation that is challenging for them. This relates to the description of their initial state, the type and level of the resolution required, the final state to be achieved, the processes to transform the initial state into the final state and the effort required for this.

A "non-operational" problem definition can emerge when the description remains vague or ambiguous, so that it does not allow a reliable evaluation of a solution hypothesis as to whether it meets the requirements of the problem definition. The solution space thus has "open constraints" and thus makes the search for and examination of satisfactory alternatives more difficult (Kirsch, 1977, p. 149).

At the stage of *generating alternative courses of action, it* is not so much a matter of naming many possibilities, but rather of specifically working out alternatives with a view to the framework conditions of the problem definition. The information must make the consequences of the individual paths for the person transparent and adapt flexibly to the individual search heuristics.

At the stage of *evaluating solution hypotheses,* information is needed to raise awareness of relevant criteria that can be used to assess the instrumental significance of an alternative for client goals. Valuative premises are fed by interests, motivations, perceived abilities, influences of "important others", requirements in education and occupation, perceived conditions on the training and labour market conditions.

In the *decision-making phase* where a final choice of an alternative and a personally binding commitment to this course of action is needed, the client needs informational support that provides him/her with information about his/her own decision-making ability, conflicts of choice, fear of making an irreversible commitment too early, chances and problems of realisation and the expected consequences. In this phase, in the case of existentially important decisions, precisely because a revision of the decision seems possible, if at all, and only at considerable personal cost, there are more or less major conflicts, which in extreme cases lead to pathological indecisiveness.

Therefore, information is required on the exact description of the client's scope of action, on possible (also negative) decisions or how to cope with them, and on the disadvantages of avoiding or delaying the decision. A special counselling challenge is the desire for evaluative and guiding information typical for this decision phase as well as the motivation to delay the final decision. This is especially true when the subjective leeway is reduced and the time at which the decision becomes binding is approaching.

The *post-decision phase* is characterised by the realisation of the decision and the control phase with an evaluation of the result and, if necessary, correction of the decision with a renewed decision-making process.

Depending on the decision, the client needs sound knowledge of education, training or job opportunities, application strategies and recruitment procedures.

Characteristic of the post-decision phase is dissonance experiences due to subjectively perceived deviations between the decisions reached and those actually expected.

Descriptive and *interpretive information is* needed to cope with negative deviations that have already occurred, usually coupled with feelings of more or less strong regret about the decision, or to prepare counsellors for such experiences.

Descriptive information serves as an orientation aid by clarifying structures, requirements, difficulties, and opportunities of the chosen age group. In this way, the counsellor makes the space transparent that is opened up to the client by his decision. This should enable clients to define their tolerance limits (frustration tolerance) within which the consequences are still perceived as satisfactory, or at what point the decision has to be changed or reversed.

The individual needs interpretive information to classify the experiences in the new environment. Particularly important, for example, after entering vocational training or a new job, is information that is oriented towards the client's attribution patterns (causal attribution) for success or failure.

In a similar way to the ISM, Peterson et al. (1996, p. 444, 2002, p. 312) and Sampson et al. (1999, p. 3) use their approach, the "Cognitive Information Processing Approach (CIP)", to identify the processes involved in occupational problem solving and decision-making. The focus is on the extent to which career counselling can enable clients to acquire knowledge about their own personality, occupations and decision-making skills in order to make effective and responsible career decisions now and in the future.

A problem is defined in CIP theory as a perceived distance between the current state and a desired state in working life. To solve the problem, the individual must gather information and acquire cognitive strategies for action. The result of this process is a choice that has a reasonable probability of narrowing the gap between the current and desired state. Decision making involves translating the choice made into specific action steps.

The knowledge elements that an individual needs for problem-solving and decision-making can be depicted in the "pyramid of information domains" (cf. Sampson et al., 1999, p. 3; cf. Peterson et al., 1996, p. 445, Peterson et al., 2002, p. 320; Osborn 2019, pp. 733).

The basic prerequisite for appropriate career decisions is self-awareness with regard to the values, interests, skills to be taken into account, as well as preferences regarding working conditions and family involvement ("Self-Knowledge")

In the ISM, the *valuative premises* result from knowledge about the client's own person or self-concept.

Career knowledge includes not only knowledge about the contents and requirements of the occupations under discussion, but also about the types of employment opportunities and working conditions, including application and recruitment procedures, used by specific companies ("Option Knowledge").

In ISM, this vocational knowledge is part of the *factual* information from which the *factual premises* develop.

For an informed and careful career choice the individual needs "Decision-Making skills" as well as "Metacognitions" for the evaluation process: "Thinking about my Decision Making".

In ISM these dimensions are part of the prescriptive premises (personally binding heuristics).

Prescriptive premises and Heuristics (ISM)
Metacognitions Higher-level knowledge for monitoring and control in problem solving Thinking about my decision making
Decision-Making-Skills Decision-making and problem-solving skills and abilities Knowing how I make decisions

Valuative premises (ISM)	***Factual premises (ISM)***
Self-Knowledge Knowledge of one's own person (self-concept): values, interests, skills, preferences, influence of the family Knowing about myself	**Options/Occupations Knowledge** Vocational knowledge: Job titles, classification criteria, requirements, rewards, job opportunities, etc. Knowing about my options/occupations

For the design of the professional decision-making and problem-solving process, the CIP approach puts decision-making skills into a sequence of five activities in a cycle form, the so-called "CASVE Cycle" (Sampson et al., 1996, p. 8, 1999, p. 7; Peterson et al., 1996, p. 435).

The CASVE Cycle helps to identify the necessary information in the process of professional problem-solving.

1. *Communication phase (C):* In a given situation, the individual becomes aware, through cues from within (e.g. fears, ambitions) or without (e.g. requests from significant others, dismissal, opportunities for promotion, completion of education), that decisions need to be made. Recognising a gap between the current state and a desired future state motivates problem-solving.
2. *Analysis phase (A):* Based on knowledge about oneself (values, interests, skills, career preferences, family situation) and knowledge about career opportunities, the client analyses the gap between the actual and target state and identifies the problem components. In this phase, the client can also be encouraged to reflect on his or her previous professional decision-making behaviour.

   However, it is precisely in the integration of knowledge about oneself and about occupations that fundamental problems arise, due to the structural differences between the two areas of knowledge. Counselling help is required here, especially with regard to working through the clients' experiences of the interaction of their personality with certain occupational environmental factors (cf. Holling et al., 2000, p. 19).
3. *Synthesis phase (S):* Here possible solutions are worked out (elaboration) and then reduced to a few realistic possibilities (crystallisation). The counselling goal at this stage must be to not forget any important options for the client, but also to ensure that in this phase of final selection, not too many possible solutions get in the way of a decision.
4. *Valuing phase (V):* Each viable alternative is evaluated in terms of its contribution to transforming the current professional situation into a desired future situation.

   This also includes an assessment of the chances of realisation as well as the individual cost-benefit ratio, also taking into account the opinion of important reference persons of the client.

   he results of this phase are the formation of a ranking, a preliminary decision on a certain solution and a commitment to implement it.
5. *Execution phase (E):* In this phase, an execution plan is defined with intermediate objectives and the activities required to achieve them, as well as their implementation.

In a final step, the result of this problem-solving process is compared with the initial situation in the communication phase. In particular, there is a critical review of whether the measures taken were able to positively reduce the gap between the current and the desired future professional situation.

The top level of information in decision-making processes is formed by *metacognitions,* which serve to monitor, guide and correct the lower-order functions (in the pyramid). This includes information intake, processing and use, as well as the implementation of cognitive strategies for problem-solving (CASVE Cycle).

The basic metacognitions include self-talk, ego-awareness, self-observation and self-control.

Self-talk is clients' quick, silent conversation with themselves about their ability to solve a specific task. Positive self-talk helps clients to keep going in the face of difficulties, to actively seek information, to pursue a viable career decision, to make more use of the opinion of key caregivers and to seek professional help. Negative self-talk prevents clients from recognising and highlighting their strengths, actively applying for jobs and effectively presenting themselves.

Effective *self-awareness* involves paying attention to the interaction between thinking, feeling and behaviour, specifically the paralysing effect of negative job-related self-talk, the need for further information and the state of the decision-making process. A strong ego-awareness helps clients to concentrate on problem-solving and to ward off disturbing external influences. This is necessary, for example, if the client is advised by others to take the next best job rather than think about it intensively, or to break off a longer qualified training because the career opportunities seem unclear.

Self-monitoring and *self-control* mean that the individual can carry out the problem-solving and decision-making process purposefully. This includes assessing when a step can be completed, when new information needs to be obtained, and when help needs to be sought.

It is therefore more or less the quality control of the CASVE Cycle.

Based on the CIP theory, Sampson et al. (1996) developed a test inventory to diagnose and modify dysfunctional thinking in career decisions. This Career Thoughts Inventory (CTI) provides both an overall measure and subscores for three aspects of dysfunctional thinking: namely, confusion in the decision-making process, fear of final commitment to an alternative, and conflict due to lack of balance between self-perception and the influences of significant others.

A study using CTI (Saunders, 2000, p. 288) showed that incoherence in occupational matters is related to a weakly developed occupational identity in connection with unhelpful activity-related thoughts. In this constellation, there are serious disabilities in relation to the cognitive information processes in problem-solving.

Conversely, a person with a strong professional identity and without dysfunctional professional thoughts can very quickly regain appropriate resolve in problem situations, such as job loss.

In the ISM, the *prescriptive premises* include both the CASVE Cycle and the metacognitions. The overall view of both approaches shows strong parallels that definitely lead to synergy effects in practical application. However, in terms of the ISM's orientation towards individual decision heuristics, attention must be paid to the more *normative character of the CIP approach. From the ISM* point of view, the CASVE Cycle can be seen more as a diagnostic tool for determining the status of the problem-solving process than as a model for advisory procedures.

For the advisory implementation of their CASVE Cycle, Peterson et al. (2002, p. 337) propose a procedure in seven steps:

Step 1: Initial interview to develop qualitative information about the context and nature of the professional problem and problem space.

Step 2: Preparatory assessment focuses on determining the individual's readiness for problem-solving and decision-making.

Step 3: Problem definition and root cause analysis leads counsellor and client to a first understanding of the problem in terms of a gap between professional indecision and desired state of decision.
Step 4: Counsellor and client jointly formulate the counselling goals to strive for. Agreeing on concrete goals sets a framework of expectations for both and promotes the development of a good working relationship.
Step 5: The collaborative development of an individual learning plan involves the use of resources and activities to help the client solve their problem.
Step 6: The counsellor supports the client's implementation of the individual learning plan with information, reinforcement, advice on how to proceed with problem-solving and preparation for future experiences.
Step 7: Summative evaluation and generalisation serve to review the progress made in achieving the objectives and in transferring the approach to future professional problem-solving.

5.2.2 The Prescriptive Model PIC for Career Guidance

For Gati et al. (2019, p. 120), six dimensions are crucial for an appropriate career decision: extensive information search, internal locus of control, low tendency to procrastinate, faster decisions on a final choice, low dependence on others and few needs to please others.

However, the limited cognitive abilities of individuals limit their decision making in many ways, and given the range of options available, pose the danger of "information overload" (p. 119).

Therefore, the fundamental question of suitable decision-making models arises for counselling. Gati et al. (2019, p. 122) distinguish between (a) normative, (b) descriptive and (c) prescriptive models.

Re (a) According to these models:

1. Each alternative is evaluated as to its usefulness for the client's own goals and preferences,
2. Each alternative is evaluated according to the estimated probability of achieving the desired result.

Normative models describe the behaviour of a perfectly rational decision-maker and assume that the advantages of an alternative can compensate for its disadvantages. Therefore, normative models are also called "compensatory models". But these normative approaches often prove to be irrelevant for normal decision-making behaviour and effective counselling.

Re (b) The descriptive models examine how people actually make their decisions and focus on the gap between the ideal behaviour of choosing the best option and an appropriate option that is often not optimal.

Another well-researched decision-making characteristic concerns heuristics and subjective judgements in individual decisions.

Since descriptive models cannot provide a reference point for reasoned decisions, they too—like normative views—are not suitable for career guidance.

Re (c) While the normative models focus on the analysis of the factors of a rational decision and the descriptive models on the actual decision-making behaviour, the prescriptive interventions attempt to bridge the gap between the normative ideal and individual behaviour. In doing so, the prescriptively oriented interventions must also exhibit characteristics of normative views.

The counselling prescriptive model "PIC" developed by Gati et al. (2019, p. 126) has three phases: "Prescreening", "In-depth Exploration" and "Choice". It aims to provide a systematic process to make better career decisions rather than striving for a fully rational approach.

"Prescreening" entails the pre-selection of possible vocational alternatives according to individual preferences and competencies.

The "sequential elimination process" relates to the most important job-related aspects and their individual weighting, according to three criteria: the importance of each characteristic, the most important characteristic and the best way to express it.

"In-depth exploration" means the in-depth engagement with these alternatives so that a manageable number of suitable and feasible courses of action emerge.

"Choice" means the final selection of one alternative through detailed comparisons with the others. Because of the remaining uncertainties regarding realisation, it is highly recommended to also keep an eye on the other alternatives, based on their ranking.

In this way, the PIC model integrates the normative and descriptive approaches by guiding the complex career choice process into clearly defined steps towards a ranking of alternatives that are best suited for the individual. But implementation is not easy and requires the support of a counsellor or a computer system.

Regarding the latter, according to Gati et al. (2019, p. 137), most computer-assisted career guidance systems (CACGs) aim to support but by no means replace the professional career counsellor in the guidance process. It has been proven that these systems are most effective when they are used by a counsellor.

In our view, this approach underlines the expert role of the counsellor about job-related information and at the same time opens perspectives for the further development of AI-supported CACGs. The consideration of individual heuristics in the construction of consistent solution spaces based on valuative premises (criteria) appears to be of central importance. AI could make significant progress here in terms of advisory assistance in the consistency checks of individual preferences and competences as well as the chances of realisation.

A special challenge arises with regards to the linking of certain information systems about professions, courses of study, further training opportunities, available options, and labour market developments. The essential thing is to support the counsellor in selecting and prioritising client information, by means of AI (artificial intelligence), to prevent an "information overload" for the person seeking advice.

5.2.3 Practical Design of the Counselling Process

ISM is descriptive in that it does not specify how to decide (like the normative models) but is oriented towards the client's decision-making behaviour. However, the following steps are recommended for implementation in counselling practice, whereby the ISM also acquires a prescriptive character much like that of Gati et al. (cf. Ertelt & Schulz, 1997, p. 248):

Step 1: Definition of the situation and operationalisation of the problem

- Encourage comprehensive problem description by the client.
- Differentiate individual problem areas.
- Assess the status of the problem-solving or decision-making process and make it transparent.
- Carry out a first global information gap analysis, related to the stage in the decision-making process.
- Determining the client's problem pressure and involvement in problem-solving, taking into account the reference systems that are important for him/her.

Step 2: Definition of possible counselling goals

- Stimulate the client to describe the goal in terms of transforming the present situation (perceived as unsatisfactory) into a future situation (perceived as worth striving for) (legitimize through personal experience).
- Introduce possible goals from a counselling point of view (legitimize through personal experience). Other factors include the client's problem-solving ability, the necessary counselling effort (especially time), the counsellor's professional competence, possible ethical and legal concerns, and market conditions.

Step 3: Negotiate and conclude a counselling agreement— a "counselling contract"—with, if possible, a written definition of the priority in the processing of the counselling goals.

- What should be discussed today?
- What is the subject of follow-up consultations?
- Which goals or intermediate goals cannot be achieved efficiently in guidance and should therefore be the subject of other activities (e.g., use of self-information systems, media for self-assessment and decision support, programmes on job search strategies)?

Step 4: Fine-tuning of the process planning and implementation of the counselling contract.

- Precise definition of goals and tasks for today's counselling based on the counselling agreement (counselling contract).
- Differentiated information deficit analysis in relation to the specific guidance problem.
- Joint determination of information needs.

Step 5: Diagnostic phase

Elaboration or completion of missing, unstructured or incomplete decision-making premises.

- Factual knowledge: Occupational information on training and activities (such as work requirements, working conditions, job content, income, career opportunities, job security), personal perspectives (suitability from a psychological and occupational health perspective), access requirements, training conditions and labour market.
- Value knowledge: Values, interests, abilities, and skills, cultural, imprinting, influences by important others, and imprinting by professional experiences. The main theories of career choice and development, such as the personality typology approach (J. Holland), the developmental psychology approach (D. Super) and (especially for career counselling of professionals) the theory of work adjustment (R. Dawis) offer important aids for hypothesising in valuative premises. Super) and (especially for career counselling of working persons) the theory of work adjustment (R. Dawis) (cf. Brown and Brooks (eds.) 1994, 1996; Ertelt & Schulz, 1997; Schulz, 2014; for a comprehensive grounding in German-speaking countries: Nestmann et al. (eds.) (2013).
- Prescriptive premises: Decision-making style, information behaviour, previous experiences with similar problem-solving, decision-making fears, dys-functional thinking in decision-making and problem-solving processes, and experiences of conflict.

Diagnosis in ISM does not at all mean the comprehensive clarification of the above-mentioned premise areas, but rather the identification and reduction of the client's specific information deficits. In this respect, there are methodological parallels here to solution-focused counselling.

Step 6: Elaboration and weighting of alternative courses of action to achieve the objectives agreed to in the counselling contract

Next, an examination of the extent to which the client can personally commit to an alternative (commitment) is dealt with. Attention should be paid to feelings of reactance and phenomena of indecisiveness. If a viable decision has been made, agreements on the realisation are to be made, if possible, based on concrete written plans. It is then particularly important to prepare for the post-decision conflicts, especially if it was a far-reaching decision under information uncertainty.

According to Siebert et al. (2020, p. 1183), skilled decision-making behaviour in generating alternatives is the key to effective decision-making. Four proactive cognitive skills; namely, "systematic identification of objectives", "systematic identification of alternatives", "systematic search for information", and "using a decision radar" (Siebert et al., 2020, p. 1173), play a role in their interdependence with the two general personality traits "striving for improvement" and "taking the initiative". "By actively and systematically developing decision alternatives that are aligned with personal goals, proactive decision-makers increase their odds of achieving desired outcomes; that increase contributes in turn to the positive self-evaluations of their life . . ." (Siebert et al., 2020, p. 1181).

Counselling support consists of helping to construct "solution spaces" that are as closed and consistent as possible on the basis of criteria ("constraints"), so that counsellors can assess which alternatives fit into these spaces and are thus perceived as satisfactory by the client. According to Hofstedt and Löffler (2021, p. 715), the term *constraint* refers to "... a linguistic concept for the declarative description of conditions and relations between variables or objects with the aim of efficiently modelling and solving problems about which only incomplete information is available".

Methods supported by Artificial Intelligence (AI) could bring significant progress in the definition of such solution spaces and their transformation into action spaces; namely, assistance in the interaction of interests and competences, consistency checks of the "constraints", realisation aids and success probabilities of the individual alternatives.

Step 7: Evaluation of the counselling and preparation for the post-decision phase

Counselling must be accompanied by an evaluative analysis that includes the following aspects (cf. Ertelt, 2000, p. 4734 f.; cf. for the overall classification: Nationales Forum Beratung in Bildung, Beruf und Beschäftigung (nfb), Forschungsgruppe Beratungsqualität am Institut der Universität Heidelberg, 2014).

- *Input evaluation*: quality of clarification of concerns and consideration of the client's personality traits and problem background
- *Goal evaluation*: scope and differentiation of the counselling goals, appropriateness of the goals to the person and the case, joint formulation and agreement of the goals, conformity with professional, ethical, and legal-institutional norms.
- *Process evaluation*: Assessment of the methodology, the intermediate results, the Involvement of the stakeholders and transparency of counselling
- *Output evaluation:* Evaluation of the results of guidance according to quality criteria (cf. Kinnier, in: Ertelt & Schulz, 1997, p. 236.; cf. Ertelt, 2000, p. 4731).
- *Transfer evaluation*: Determining the extent to which the clients have used the counselling results want to and are able to implement.
- *Resource evaluation*: Assessment of the efficient use of human and material resources in counselling as well as the adequacy of the framework conditions (time, space, disturbances, etc.).

Each of these steps requires specific counselling skills, which are assigned to the counselling tasks within the framework of ISM in the following. These skills are to be integrated into the basic qualitative characteristics of counselling: above all empathy, attention to positive approaches with the client, respect for the individual and emotional warmth, concreteness of statements, immediacy, and authenticity.

These qualitative aspects of counselling do not exclude the use of directive behaviour such as: directing hints, pointing out logical consequences, confrontation in case of discrepancies in the client's statements or negotiation of the counselling contract (cf. Peavy, 1981, p. 190); (for a more detailed description of counselling skills cf. Ertelt & Schulz, 1997, p. 238 and the literature cited therein; cf. also Horan, 1979, p. 198; Ivey, 1983, p. 169; Ertelt & Schulz, 1985, p. 180; Ivey & Authier, 1985; Rübner & Sprengard, 2010).

These are the counselling skills that are suggested for the five (ideal-typical) steps of a decision-making process. These steps are also to be used in counsellee training programs.

1. Problem definition and goal setting
   - Verbal and non-verbal encouragement to speak
   - Positive expectations
   - Open and closed questions
   - Paraphrases
   - Reflection of the feelings
   - Cognitive restructuring
   - Socratic dialogue
2. Development of alternatives
   - Brainstorming
   - Other methods of creative thinking (partial change method, chessboard method, checklist method, similarity method, verbal reinforcement and positive expectation, modelling).
3. Weighting of the alternatives
   - Concreteness
   - Confrontation technique
   - Comparison schema for the evaluation of alternatives and their consequences
   - Structuring
   - Reinforcement
4. Decision and personal commitment to an alternative
   - Positive challenge
   - Encouragement to act
   - Technique of logical consequences
   - Concluding a contract for trading
   - Forms of collective problem-solving (bargaining, persuasion, forced consent)
   - Interpretation of feelings of reactance
5. Preparation for disappointment in the post-decision phase
   - Self-affirmation techniques
   - Roleplay with role reversal
   - Assigning homework
   - Demonstrating techniques to reduce cognitive dissonance
   - Modelling

The most important task in heuristic-information-structural counselling is to create transparency: only if the client "understands" the counselling at all times, but especially in the diagnostic phases, can he or she cooperate, correct, and learn in a self-responsible way. And only then can the counsellor, with appropriate communication, recognise the changes in the client's factual, evaluative, and prescriptive premises.

5.3 Case Studies and Exercises for Developing Counsellor Competencies

The following case studies and exercises serve to exemplify the application of ISM in education, training, and employment. It is important to note that ISM is an eclectic approach that combines aspects of different guidance theories. The exercises, however, focus on the specifics of ISM, without claiming to be able to provide satisfactory counselling for every career problem with this methodology. The case studies should be continued in role-plays and continuously incorporated into the ISM schema.

Case Study 1
Mrs. Susanne Stein is 34 years old, married, a qualified office clerk and mother of two children. Her son (11 years old) has just started secondary school and her daughter (6 years old) has started primary school in her hometown. After her secondary school leaving certificate, Mrs Stein worked in a craft business.

She trained as an office clerk and worked there as a commercial employee for three years after graduation. However, she has not been gainfully employed for about 11 years. Due to her son's speech impediment, she has contact with various social and therapeutic professions.

Susanne Stein makes statements in the following order during the initial phase of counselling:

- "Now that both children are in school, I want to go back to work at least half-time so that I don't lose touch with working life in the long term, but also because of the contacts and mental challenges at work".
- "Through the experiences in the past years in connection with my son's speech disorder, I would like to change to a therapeutic profession. However, I am completely unsure about the training requirements that will surely be necessary. I don't know if I can do it, especially since the exams are supposed to be so difficult!"
- "I have hardly heard about a therapeutic career and about training. On the one hand I don't really know where to learn about it, and on the other hand, I don't like to talk to others about it until I have more details and have made up my mind".
- "Mainly because my vocational training was so long ago and my past experience has nothing to do with my current wishes, I'm just unsure about whether I can get through a long training programme. I must not embarrass myself in any case, especially not in front of my husband's colleagues and employees. My husband

has a good position in the company. We have a terraced house in the new development area, where many of the company's employees live."

Analysis of decision-relevant information

To help in the counselling with Mrs. Stein, the following schema is recommended. This schema should be filled out during counselling, together with the client. In this way, both keep track of the situation and can monitor the progress of the counselling.

The connections between the types of information can be made visible with arrows, so that an initial overview of the client's cognitive structure is created. An additional column is used to indicate accompanying emotions.

To facilitate the analysis, counsellors should use episodes as a guide, i.e., self-contained units of meaning that refer to only *one* category of information (alternative, evaluation, procedure). Since the order of the utterances can also be important, the episodes should be numbered consecutively. In this example, the background information is treated as an episode.

Factual knowledge/alternatives (factual information or premises)	Valuation knowledge, justifications (valuative information or premises)	Process knowledge (prescriptive information or premises)	Emotions
Biographical data: – 34 years, married. – Two children – (6 & 11 years) – Trained as an office clerk after finishing secondary school. – Worked for a company for another 3 years in this profession. – Unemployed for the past 11 years. 3. Current professional preference: therapeutic profession	1. Re-entry into working life (at least half-time) because of – Reduced childcare requirements. – Wanting a working life. – A need for social contacts – Wanting a mental challenge 4. Anxiety over her lack of knowledge about training requirements and subsequent examinations Negative evaluation of her own career aspirations. 7. Lack of criteria for assessing her own	2. Due to the son's speech impediment, contacts and experience with therapeutic professions. 5. So far, no systematic search for information because of her ignorance of the – Sources of information – Procedures – Looking for information has been largely unsystematic	Fear of adequate performance and of losing confidence due to her lack of knowledge and training in the therapeutic profession. Uncertainty about the information on therapeutic professions. Fear of negative opinions of important others

(continued)

Factual knowledge/alternatives (factual information or premises)	Valuation knowledge, justifications (valuative information or premises)	Process knowledge (prescriptive information or premises)	Emotions
	potential because vocational training and school were so long ago. 8. The opinion of the social environment ("colleagues, employees") plays an important role as a criterion for the decision.		

Counselling summary of the preliminary information structure analysis

(1) Due to the reduced care requirements for her children, the client is thinking about re-entering the workforce. The income situation does not seem to play a role here, but the desire not to move too far away from gainful employment, to have more social contacts and to experience new mental challenges does.

(2) and (3) As a solution hypothesis (preliminary stage for an alternative), the client brings in an unspecified therapeutic profession. Her former job as an office clerk is obviously no longer an option. This means that within the (non-operational) solution space defined in (1), only the solution hypothesis "therapeutic profession" is felt to be satisfactory.

(4) A lack of professional knowledge of the therapeutic occupational field tends to result in assessments that hinder her pursuit of the desired occupation due to fears of not being able to meet the requirements of the training and passing examinations.

(5), (6) and (8) However, these fears have not led to self-active information-seeking behaviour in the past. Rather, her present condition (lack of knowledge of information sources and procedures) points to deficits in the prescriptive premises; these being reinforced by the fact that she obviously tends towards an internal decision-making style (tendency to decide largely without interaction with others) (cf. on this Johnson, in: Ertelt & Schulz, 1997, p. 235; cf. Ertelt, 1992, p. 100). The fear of negative evaluation (in case of failure) by the environment should be noted. This negative evaluation indicates a limited independence in decision-making ("personal control") (8).

(7) The client does not yet have reliable criteria for assessing her own potential regarding the training requirements in therapeutic professions. Orientation towards the previous training is not possible due to differences in content and the time gap.

Status in the problem-solving and decision-making process

The client has a (still too general) hypothesis for a solution and wants to relate it to her potential from the point of view of training requirements. This process is accompanied by emotions, which are mainly fed by the fear of embarrassing herself by failing in front of "important others" and thereby also damaging her husband professionally.

It seems important to first attempt to concretise the solution hypothesis "therapeutic professional field" to such an extent that it is possible to create examples to define professions for her. This would help her to prepare for the second step, which focuses on criteria for assessing her potential for training in a concrete position in the therapeutic profession. For the necessary information activity, the client's rather unsystematic internal decision-making style must be considered. At least in the first phase, more solution knowledge must be provided by the counsellor regarding information sources and procedures. This could be done in the form of "homework".

Case Study 2

An employee at the operational level in a company asks for a meeting with the personnel developer and explains his request as follows (story: has already been prepared for content analysis):

1.	"I have been working in my current position for 3 years now and
2.	I am very satisfied with the job and
3.	probably my supervisor is too.
4.	I would like to move on now,
5.	As a group or team leader, for example, and
6.	also take on more responsibility
7.	as well as have greater creative freedom.
8.	Of course, there are also financial reasons,
9.	but they are not in the foreground. I will not conceal the fact that
10.	prestige inside and outside the company is a motivation.
11.	I am prepared to take part in possibly necessary further training, for instance
12.	in personnel management or
13.	Computer-aided work organization
14.	with company support.
15.	However, I have not yet obtained any information or taken any initiatives.
16.	I wanted to wait for our conversation first, which I hope will give me some clues on how to proceed. I would like to add,
17.	that my family, especially my wife, would not only encourage me in my professional goals, but also fully support me in all corresponding activities.
18.	However, they would also be disappointed if it did not work out,
19.	I feel a bit under pressure there."

Assign the statements (only the numbers) to the schema for problem/decision analysis within the framework of ISM. Duplicate assignment of numbers should only occur in exceptional cases.

Factual knowled ge and alter-natives	Valuation knowledge Criteria	Process knowledge Prescriptions (heuristics)	Emotions

You can then compare your answers with the solution suggestions (presented after Case Study 9).

Case Study 3
Mr Johannes Ziegler is 29 years old and single. After graduating from high school, he completed a seven-week training course as a flight attendant (steward) with an airline. Afterwards, he worked for about 9 years with an airline service. Due to the airline bankruptcy, he is now unemployed; he has intensively investigated career alternatives and now wants to become an insurance salesman. He makes the following statements about his new career direction:

- "What do I have to consider now? I am not sure if I will be accepted for training by an employer at my age?"
- "How is the vocational school organized, am I in a 'special' class or do I have to sit with young apprentices?"
- "Do I have to go to vocational school at all? I'm no longer of school age, but would attending vocational school still be advisable?"
- "And, above all, how can I finance the whole thing, because I have hardly any savings?"
- "Would you rather advise me to do a shortened apprenticeship if that is what the training company offers?"

Exercise

1. Classification of the statements in the information structure schema.

Factual knowledge and alter-natives	Valuation knowl-edge Criteria	Process knowledge Prescrip-tions (heuristics)	Emotions

2. Determination of the stages in the decision-making and problem-solving processes as well as the specific information deficits (paying attention to emotions, if needed).
3. Outline of the further advisory procedures to reduce the information deficit that Ziegler has.

Case Study 4
Tilmann Schirmer is 18 years old and has a secondary school diploma. He is currently in his second year of training as a chemical technician in a large chemical company. He makes the following statements about his concerns:

- “Maybe it’s hard to understand, but I’m thinking of dropping out of my training program”.
- “Sure, my friends are envious of my apprenticeship and my later work opportunities in the company”.
- “Sure, I will lose some money while I am in training and even more so before I begin working for the company in the future”.
- “But somehow it’s not my world now. I can’t say anything concrete, but my overall feeling is very negative. Maybe I didn’t think it through very carefully at the time when I first chose my career”.

Exercise

1. Classification of the comments in the information structure schema

Factual knowledge and alter-natives	Valuation knowledge Criteria	Process knowledge Prescriptions (heuristics)	Emotions

2. Determination of the stages in the decision-making and problem-solving process as well as the specific information deficits (discussion of emotions, if applicable).
3. Formulate hypotheses to clarify the statement “Somehow this is not my world now!” using selected theories of career development. Note: Particular attention should be paid to D. Super’s career development approach and the work adjustment approach by R. Dawis (in: Brown and Brooks 1994, 1996). Furthermore, the phenomenon of cognitive dissonance after decisions must be taken into account.

Case Study 5

Susanne Schottköfer has just started the 10th grade of the Realschule. She makes the following statements about her concerns:

- “Hotel management would definitely be a good profession for me, everything about it interests me.”
- “But my mother is right too, these working hours!”
- “I would like to have a real family life like my parents have but later on; but that doesn’t fit in with working in such a profession!”
- “I’m just not getting anywhere now; I should have applied for an apprenticeship long ago!”

Exercise

1. Classification of the utterances in the information structure schema.

Factual knowledge and alter-natives	Valuation knowledge Criteria	Process knowledge Prescriptions (heuristics)	Emotions

2. Determination of the status in the decision-making and problem-solving process as well as the specific information deficits (if applicable, identifying any emotional conflicts).
3. Outlining the approach to reducing information deficits

Case Study 6
Erwin Bauer, a 9th-grade secondary school student, comes to the vocational counselling centre on the advice of his class teacher. He expresses himself as follows:

- "My class teacher thinks it's high time to start thinking about what to do after school".
- "We have been to the career information centre with the class before, but I haven't given much thought to what I want to be".
- "I have an idea. My uncle is a lorry driver for a large trucking company here, and I would like that too. My uncle thinks that if I must work in a trucking company, then I should learn about the office work in the trucking company. But I don't know enough about that".
- "Maybe I'll still go to school, but that would be a last resort, in case I don't get an apprenticeship".
- "I don't think working just like that, without training, is anything; besides, my parents won't go along with it!"

Exercise

1. Classification of the statements in the information structure schema.

Factual knowledge and alter-natives	Valuation knowledge Criteria	Process knowledge Prescriptions (heuristics)	Emotions

2. Determination of the status in the decision-making and problem-solving process as well as the specific information deficits (if applicable, identifying any emotions).
3. Outlining the approach to reducing information deficits

Case Study 7
Achim Weber, a graduate engineer for a process and plant engineering company, 35 years old, married, two children, has worked in the company for 5 years. In the appraisal *interview for the* personnel department, he is asked to assess himself based on concrete examples and facts. He expresses himself as follows:

- "I am satisfied with my current area of responsibility; I master most of my work routinely. However, I sometimes find it boring, also I see the danger of becoming one-dimensional".
- "The other day, a new colleague arrived, fresh from her studies. She commented that there are new things in my field; that's when I became a bit apprehensive and thoughtful".

- "My particular strengths lie in absolute adherence to deadlines; this is possible where I am now working. I can't do it any other way, because otherwise the business would come to a standstill. I can also deal well with my colleagues and staff, only sometimes they want to solve the problems differently and think they can reach their goal faster that way".
- "My inclinations are more towards expanding my responsibilities, for example, working at other facilities at new locations, there would also be a new challenge in terms of new social contacts. But for the time being, while my children are still small, we're pretty much tied to one place at the moment. Also, we are remodelling our house".
- "My present development aspirations are in the direction of training and development.

  I would like to broaden my competences, especially in terms of cooperation with other departments. For that, I would have to complete a more demanding further training course".

The assessments of his superiors are as follows:

- The employee does his work very accurately and on time; however, he often shows very rigid behaviour.
- His rigidity is the cause of many disagreements with colleagues and employees; these disagreements must then be cleared up by the supervisor. As a rule, however, the employee's suggestions are well-founded and very helpful.
- An assignment to another location would be very positive from an operational point of view, also because there are already corresponding work requirements. However, Weber has so far reacted rather negatively to a transfer because of his family situation.
- One cannot get rid of the feeling that the employee has competitive fears; namely, that others might excel him in his absence.
- Other development opportunities are not foreseeable in the short and medium term, for both operational reasons and for reasons that lie with Weber.
- The employee is currently difficult to replace in his field of work.

  Even if he had extensive further training, this additional training could not be readily accommodated by our company.

Exercise

1. Classification of the statements in the information structure schema.

Factual knowledge and alter-natives	Valuation knowl-edge Criteria	Process knowledge Prescrip-tions (heuristics)	Emotions

2. Determine the status of the problem-solving process and the specific manifestation of the problem or possible conflicts.
3. Outline the approach to reduce the deficits in the three types of information as well as possible emotional conflicts.

Case Study 8

Sabrina Andres, 18, attends grade 12 at the Gymnasium. She has asked for an appointment at the career counselling centre. She makes the following comments during the counselling session:

- "I would actually like to leave school after grade 12 with a UAS qualification. I've pretty much decided to do that".
- "But my father in particular thinks I should do the full A-levels after all because I'm so good at maths and science subjects".
- "I mean, if I leave school now, I can study at a UAS and continue later".
- "I have also considered another path; namely, training as a pharmaceutical technical assistant, preferably in a local company. I read an advertisement about a career in this area".
- "After that, I can still study, which is what I intend to do—if possible, in the natural sciences area or in media".
- "I would actually like to know clearly from you today which of the options is the best for me. I haven't gathered that much information yet, besides, everyone says something different, and you can read everything out of the information material! There is no helpful weighting of alternatives from that!"

Exercise

1. Classification of the client's statements in the information structure schema.

Factual knowledge and alter-natives	Valuation knowl-edge Criteria	Process knowledge Prescrip-tions (heuristics)	Emotions

2. Determine the stages in the decision-making process and the deficits in the three types of information (if necessary, identify the relevant emotions).
3. Outline an approach for reducing information deficits.

Case Study 9

(Excerpts taken from Wegmann, 2005)

Andreas is 36 years old and studies art at a liberal arts college. The following statements were taken from the interview about his career so far:

1. On the first choice of profession
   (a) In the final year of secondary school, the students are supposed to do an internship. Andreas decided on carpentry because he likes working with wood and his best "buddy" also wants to learn carpentry. According to Andreas, he feels he has no other option.
   (b) The internship confirms his career aspirations, and the internship company offers Andreas an apprenticeship as a carpenter. This falls through for operational reasons shortly before the start of the training. At his parents' insistence, he is "persuaded" to learn electrical installation instead,

2. Professional development after the training
   (a) After Andreas fails his final exams twice, he decides to continue working in his training company (without a diploma) until he does his civilian service in order to earn money. He has not yet thought about further career options.
   (b) After a short time, there was a "row" with the boss and Andreas quit and took a few months off, gathering unemployment payments. When he needed money again, he got a job in a building material testing company through the intercession of his brother. Andreas felt that he had no other alternatives at that time.
   (c) After his civilian service, Andreas leased a restaurant with a friend.
   (d) He now characterises this decision as an ill-considered decision under the influence of alcohol. As he does not want to leave his friend in the lurch, he only quits the restaurant business after a few exhausting years. He has been unemployed for some time.
   (e) As he cannot find a job through the employment agency, he accepts the next best offer from an acquaintance and works as a self-employed contractor in his landscape gardening business.
   (f) This venture ends due to a lack of orders and Andreas then establishes his own horticultural business.
   (g) After some time, Andreas can no longer continue working because of physical problems and gives up. At the employment agency he learns that he is not employable. He then begins his current art studies. Andreas says that unlike in the past, when he only thought about money, he made this latest career decision according to what he enjoys most.

Exercise

1. Classification of the statements according to the decision-making strategies (heuristics) listed in Sect. 5.1.6 (Multiple classifications are possible)
2. Elaboration of possible emotions that accompanied the outlined career decisions.

Solution Suggestions for Case Study 2:

Factual knowledge and alter-natives	Valuation knowledge Criteria	Process knowledge Prescriptions (heuristics)	Emotions
1, 5, 12, 13	2, 3, 4, 6, 7, 8, 9, 10	11, 14, 15, 16, 17	(10), (2), (17), 18 19

Analysis Tools for Counselling Interviews

I. Supervision and Analysis Sheet

The following supervision and analysis sheet (see Fig. 5.1) structures the professional information according to its respective function in the counselling interview (cf. Ertelt et al., 1997, p. 19). It contains (scaled down) exemplary categories of occupational knowledge. It can be used either for participatory observation (time-line display), for analysing recorded counselling interviews or for role plays and

Functions in the counselling interview / Information about occupation and work (cf. BerufeNET of BA)	Problem definition (clarification of concerns and contract)		Develop criteria (Valuative Premises)		Generate and weight alternatives		Preparation for realisation, conflicts and set backs, the post-decision	
	CL	CO	Cl	CO	CL	CO	CL	CO
Sense of the profession								
Tasks at work								
Training content								
Working time								
Social contacts								
Work equipment, tools and technology								
Working conditions								
Job-requirements								
Aptitudes, suitability (inclinations, competencies,								
work behaviour)								
Physical features								
Entrance requirements/training /experience (assessment, minimum age, etc.)								
Employment situation and -outloMC								
Which jobs can be considered for the profession (substitution potential)?								
Development and further training opportunities								
Opportunities for self-employment								
Earnings and income development								
Placement opportunities, vacancies								
Media for self-information								

Fig. 5.1 Supervision and analysis sheet (Client = CL; Counsellor = CO)

exercises. (The sheet is to be adapted to the respective counselling area in terms of professional knowledge.) The entries are not made in a fixed time cycle, but according to conversation episodes. It is important that these episodes are recorded and numbered separately for the client and counsellor. Only in this way can logical consequences, breaks, "islands", etc. be identified. The occupational codes of the official classification of occupations should be used for occupational designations.

II. Instrument for content analysis of career counselling interviews taking into account the ISM

The decision-making behaviour of guidance seekers in career choice and other career decision-making processes can be studied and analysed qualitatively (cf. Weber, 2013). The application of a qualitative content-analytical procedure is suitable for this (Kohlbacher, 2006; Mayring, 2000, 2014). The basis is developed from recorded counselling talks, e.g. through audio or video recordings. Observation and recording of the conversations are also applicable for data generation. The recordings must be converted into texts through transcription (Mayring, 2014, pp. 45–47).

In the next step, the analysis is based on a deductively developed category system (see Table 5.1). The Table contains main and subcategories on the central aspects of the study, especially on decision criteria and heuristics (Ertelt & Schulz, 2019). In addition, aspects such as the role of the counsellor or the involvement of the client can be included. An investigation of the heuristics introduced or applied by the advisor also seems useful.

The evaluation of the data can follow the "step model" described by Mayring (2000). Based on the formulated research question and the definition of the objects of study, the deductive category system is developed and described. Theory-based definitions and rules for coding are described for the defined main categories and subcategories and recorded in a "coding agenda" (see Table 5.1). Next, all transcripts are analyzed. Each text passage that corresponds to a code in terms of content is assigned. It is advisable to assign whole units of meaning to a code ("coding unit"). The aim is to be able to extract the text passages assigned to a code from all transcripts, to describe them descriptively and to interpret them. The focus here is initially on qualitative description and interpretation, but—if there are enough transcripts—a quantitative analysis is also possible. To facilitate coding and evaluation, software programmes can be used, e.g. Maxqda (https://www.maxqda.com/) or Atlasti (https://atlasti.com/) (Mayring, 2000). The researcher should consider the quality criteria for qualitative content analysis, particularly the inter-coder reliability (Mayring, 2014, p. 42) (Fig. 5.2).

Table 5.1 Coding agenda for the qualitative content analyzes of decision-criteria and heuristics category system (MC = Main categories; SC = Sub categories)

	Category name	Definition	Coding rule
MC 1	Information areas/ Decision-making premises	Relevant and decisive factors in the choice of profession/job	
SC 1.1	Factual knowledge/factual premises	Stock of knowledge about factual Information (working and professional world); includes information on possible alternatives, their "offers of satisfaction" and their Realisation paths and opportunities	Includes purely informal facts, e.g. competencies, skills, abilities, framework conditions, requirements
SC 1.2	Valuation knowledge/valuative premises	Includes criteria that are derived from ideas about themselves compared to the perceived have developed in the professional-social environment; e.g. interests, own competence, Self-efficacy beliefs, desires, values, Environmental influences	Self-assessments and self-positioning in comparison to the social environment
SC 1.3	Problem-solving strategies/prescriptive assumptions	Personal problem-solving strategies show the individual the way in which factual knowledge and value knowledge are to be combined to solve the problem.	(Previous or current) solution attempts and approaches; dealing with decision-making difficulties; individual decision-making rules (=prescriptive information).
SC 1.4	Emotions in context with the three cognitive Areas SC 1.1-1.3	Perceived conflicts, anxiety/ fear, sympathies, feelings of reactance or cognitive dissonance, positive emotions, hope, curiosity, trust, friendship, A sense of achievement	Statements indicative of those listed in column "Definition".
SCHON 1.5	Phase in the Decision-making process	Pre-decision	Statements on problem perception, criteria, possible solutions and weighing of alternatives (pre-decision)
		Resolution with commitment	Statements that refer to a final commitment to an alternative and its realisation (commitment)
		Post-decision	Statements indicating regret after a decision and cognitive dissonance

MC 2	Selected decision heuristics	Client	(cf. Tittel, 2019)
SC 2.1	Satisfaction-Heuristics	Client decides on the profession that first meets their criteria when searching for information	
SC 2.2	Incrementalism	Client decides on the next possible alternative that leads to an improvement of his/her current situation	Incrementalism: Opting for the alternative that improves the actual situation at least a little.
SC 2.3	Take-the-First Heuristic	Client makes a decision in favour of the alternative identified first	There is only one known alternative. A "coincidence" taken by a person can be classified in terms of this heuristic.
SC 2.4	Take-the-Best Heuristic	Client chooses the occupation or occupational alternative that meets the criterion that is most important to them	
SC 2.5	Recognition heuristic	Client chooses the profession or professional decision in which he/she recognises a familiar aspect.	e.g. prototypical professions or well-known companies are chosen.
SC 2.6	Social imitation	Client chooses the occupation or career decision that close caregivers advise or that was taken by them.	The decision of reference persons is imitated (e.g. the father's profession or profession advised by the mother is chosen).
SC 2.7	Sub-optimisation-Heuristics	Client carefully weighs all alternatives and decides on the profession/career alternative that best meets all criteria	
MC 3	Role of the adviser	The function that the counsellor has in the event	
SC 3.1	Information helper/Expert	Improving factual knowledge	Information about alternative courses of action, chances of realisation and their "offers of satisfaction", expert knowledge about the education or labour market
SC 3.2	Corrective of the Valuation knowledge	Matching the client's subjective perception with "reality".	Counsellor gives corrective impulses to the client's factual and/or evaluative knowledge
SC 3.3	"Pedagogical role" of the adviser	Support the client's personal/ inner development (e.g. support for educational maturity)	Encourages the client to think about him/herself, to explore or reflect on him/herself.

MC 4	Motivation of the client	Personal initiative and participation in shaping the events or the counselling process	
SC 4.1	Passive search behaviour	Little engagement of the client with the career decision	Client shows little active involvement in career change/decision-making
SC 4.2	Active search behaviour	Client takes "initiative"	Client shows initiative
SC 4.3	Counselling context	Attending counselling voluntarily or involuntarily	The client has sought/requested the counselling himself/herself or has to participate in the offer
SC 4.4	Counselling topic	Reason for contacting the counsellor	Job placement, career counselling, business start-up, re-entry, retraining/qualification
SC 4.5	Intrapersonal influences	Processes within the person that have an influence on motivation	Emotions and emotional states that have an influence on the client's motivation
MC 5	Involvement of the clients	Subjective meaning(s) or importance of the future career choice and subjective importance the client attaches to the interview	
SC 5.1	Emotional involvement and activation	The client shows strong/weak emotional involvement and activity in relation to his/her professional development/decision making	e.g. problem-solving pressure, information stress, fear of irreversible wrong decisions due to incomplete information, doubts about chosen alternative
SC 5.2	Interest in support for the professional Development	The client shows little/much interest in the support from the counsellor/counselling during the conversation	e.g. participation in the conversation, interest in the ideas, suggestions of the counsellor.
MC 6	Heuristics of the counsellor		
SC 6.1	Consultant uses heuristics of the Clients on	Counsellor behaviour that corresponds to a reaction/influence on the heuristic of the person seeking advice.	In the interaction it becomes clear that the counsellor reacts to the counselee's heuristics and, if necessary, influences them, e.g. expands them.
SC 6.2	Consultant follows own heuristics	Counsellor behaviour that follows the counsellor's own heuristics in terms of his "subjective theory":	In the interaction, the counsellor brings his heuristics to the decision, e.g. by suggesting them to the client or offering them as a model.

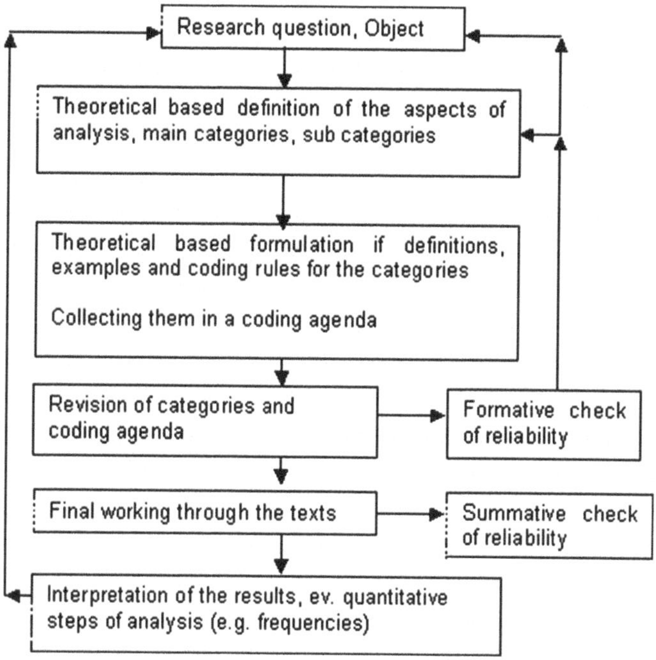

Fig. 5.2 Step model of deductive category application (Mayring, 2000)

References

Baldamus, P. (2018). *Differenzierung junger Arbeitssuchender nach Berufsinteressen, überfachlichen Kompetenzen, Coping-Strategien und Entscheidungsverhalten als Hilfe zur Optimierung des Instrumentariums der Vermittlungsberatung der Bundesagentur für Arbeit* [Differentiation of young jobseekers according to occupational interests, generic competences, copipng strategies and decision-making behaviour as an aid to optimising the instruments of placement counselling of the Federal Employment Agency]. Mannheim: Hochschule der Bundesagentur für Arbeit (HdBA).

Bamberg, E., Schmidt, J., & Hänel, K. (Hrsg.) (2006). *Beratung, Counseling, Consulting (Innovatives Management)* [Advice, counseling, consulting (innovative management)]. Hogrefe.

Braun, F., & Benz, P. (2015). *Genese natürlicher Entscheidungsprozesse und Determinanten kluger Entscheidungen. Theoretische und empirische Reflexion im Spannungsfeld zwischen analytisch-bewusstem und intuitivem Entscheiden* [Genesis of natural decision processes and determinants of wise decision. Theoretical and empirical reflections on the tension between analytical-conscious and intuitive decision-making]. Springer Gabler.

Brown, D. (2012). *Career information, career counselling, and career development* (10th ed.). Pearson Education.

Brown, D., Brooks, L., & Associates (Eds.). (1990). *Career choice and development: Applying contemporary theories to practice* (2nd ed.). Jossey-Bass.

Brown, D., Brooks, L., & Associates. (1996). *Career choice and development* (3rd ed.). Jossey-Bass.

Brown, D., Brooks, L., et al. (1994). *Karriere-Entwicklung* [Original title: Career choice and development, 1990]. Klett-Cotta.

Bundesagentur für Arbeit (BA). BERUFENET. *Informationssystem zu Berufen im Internet* [Information system on occupations on the internet]. https://www.berufenet.arbeitsagentur.de
Corey, G. (2013). *Theory and practice of counselling and psychotherapy* (9th ed.). Brooks/Cole.
Crites, J. O. (1981). *Career counselling—Models, methods and materials*. McGraw-Hill.
Dauwalder, J. P. (2007). Beratung: Herausforderung für eine nachhaltige Entwicklung [Guidance: A challenge for sustainable development]. *Ztschr Report, 1*, 9–19.
Dieckmann, A., & Krauss, S. (2005). Wenn weniger Wissen mehr sein kann: Einfache Heuristiken zur psychologische Entscheidungsindung [When less knowledge can be more: Simple heuristics for psychological decision making]. *Ztschr Für Erziehungswissenschaft, 8*, 187–201.
Ertelt, B.-J. (1975). *Microcounseling – Erfahrungsbericht und Ausbaumöglichkeiten* [Microcounselling—Experience report and possibilities for expansion] (p. 2). Heft: Zeitschrift Arbeit und Beruf.
Ertelt, B. -J. (1982). Lernbedingungen für einen entscheidungsorientierten Berufswahlunterricht [Learning conditions for decision-oriented career choice instruction]. In G. S. Seidel (Hrsg.). *Orientierungen zum pädagogischen Handeln* [Orientations for pedagogical action] (S. 72–97). Göttingen: Hogrefe.
Ertelt, B.-J. (1992). Entscheidungsverhalten und Berufswahl [Decision-making behaviour and career choice]. In B.A. (Hrsg.), *Handbuch zur Berufswahlvorbereitung* [Handbook on career choice preparation] (S. 90–105). Bundesanstalt für Arbeit (BA).
Ertelt, B. -J. (2001). *Informationsmanagement in der Beratung. Information für die Beratungs- und Vermittlungsdiente der Bundesanstalt für Arbeit* [Information management in guidance. Information for the counselling and placement services of the Federal Employment Service] (ibv 21/01), 23 May 2001 (Nürnberg BA), pp. 1385–1396.
Ertelt, B.-J. (2000). *Materialien zur Qualifizierung von Fachkräften für Berufsberatung im europäischen Kontext* [Materials for the qualification of career guidance specialists in the European context]. *ibv, 45*, Nürnberg BA, pp. 4715–4737.
Ertelt, B.-J., & Hesse, H. G. (1999). *Umfrage bei Arbeitsmarktkunden der Arbeitsvermittlung und Arbeitsberatung in Bezug auf Medienausstattung und Selbst-Information im LAA Baden-Württemberg* [Survey of labour market clients of employment mediation and job counselling with regard to media equipment and self-information in the LAA Baden-Württemberg]. Frankfurt a.M.
Ertelt, B.-J., & Feckler, K. (1979). Aspekte einer Intensivierung und Erweiterung von Informationsaktivitäten der Arbeitsvermittlung und Arbeitsberatung [Aspects of an intensification and expansion of information activities of job placement and job counselling]. *ibv – Doku, 5*.
Ertelt, B.-J., & Frey, A. (2013). Interessendiagnostik [Interest diagnostics]. In A. Frey, U. Lissmann, & B. Schwarz (Eds.), *Handbuch Berufspädagogische Diagnostik* (pp. 276–297). Beltz.
Ertelt, B.-J., & Frey, A. (2019). Die Berufsausbildung im dualen System aus Sicht ausgewählter Theorien der Berufswahl und Berufsentwicklung – eine Lücke, die es zu schließen gilt? [Vocational training in the dual system from the perspective of selected theories of career choice and career development – A gap that needs to be closed?]. In J. Seifried, K. Beck, B.-J. Ertelt, & A. Frey (Hrsg.), *Beruf, Beruflichkeit, Employability* (Profession, professionalism, employability]. wbv.
Ertelt, B.-J., & Muswieck, W. (2000). Berufsberatung und Europa-Evaluierung des Netztwerkes der Europäischen Berufsberatungszentren (EBZ) [Vocational guidance and Europe-evaluation of the network of European Vocational Guidance Centres (EBZ)]. *ibv, 40*, 4213–4232.
Ertelt, B.-J., & Ruppert, J.-J. (2011). Heuristic theory of decision making: Evidence and implications for career guidance. In S. Kraatz & B. J. Ertelt (Eds.), *Professionalisation of career guidance: European mobility—Chance and challenge* (pp. 192–206). dgvt.
Ertelt, B.-J., & Schulz, W. E. (1985). Microcounseling für beraterische Hilfen bei beruflichen Entscheidungsproblemen [Microcounseling for counselling assistance with vocational decision problems]. In A. E. Ivey & J. Authier (Eds.), *Microcounseling, Neue Wege im*

Kommunikationstraining [New directions in communication training] (2. Aufl., S. 169–179). Bratt.

Ertelt, B. -J., & Schulz, W. E. (1997). *Beratung in Bildung und Beruf* [Guidance in education and occupation]. Rosenberger.

Ertelt, B. -J., Möller, U., Schade, H. J., & Seidel, G. (1997). *Ausbildunngs- und Arbeitsmarktdaten im Beratungsgespräch* [Training and labour market data in the guidance interview] (p. 10/1997). IAB Werkstattbericht Nr.

Ertelt, B. -J., Hesse, H. G., & Weimer, M. (2004). *Online-Befragung zum Internet-Angebot des Instituts für Arbeitsmarkt- und Berufsforschung (IAB)* [Online survey on the internet services of the Institute for Employment Research]. Unveröffentlichter Abschlussbericht. Mannheim.

Ertelt, B.-J., Frey, A., & Kugelmeier, C. (Hrsg.). (2012). *HR zwischen Anpassung und Emanzipation - Beiträge zur Entwicklung einer eigenständigen Berufspersönlichkeit* [HR between adaptation and emancipation—Contributions to the development of an independent professional personality]. Lang.

Ertelt, B. -J., Bleckmann, H., & Röser, T. (2017). Subjektivierung des Qualitätsmanagements in der beruflichen Beratung – Wirksamkeit von Beratung aus Sicht der Beratenden [Subjectivisation of quality management in vocational guidance—Effectiveness of guidance from the counsellors' perspective]. In K. Schober & J. Langner (Hrsg.), *Wirksamkeit der Beratung in Bildung, Beruf und Beschäftigung* [Effectiveness of guidance in education, career and employment] (S. 119–131). Bertelsmann.

Ertelt, B.-J., Röser, T., & Bleckmann, H. (2015). Wirksamkeit der Beratung aus Sicht der Beratenden – Projektbericht des Forschungsforums des dvb [Effectiveness of guidance from the counsellors' perspective—Project report of the dvb research forum]. *dvb Forum, 1*, 4–8.

Ertelt, B. J., & Schulz, W. E. (2019). *Handbuch Beratungskompetenz* [A handbook of counselling competencies] (S. 199–266).). Springer Gabler.

European Commission. (2017). *Esco handbook. European skills, competences, qualifications and occupations.* https://ec.europa.eu/esco/portal/document/en/0a89839c-098d- 4e34-846c-54 cbd5684d24

Flederman, P., & Watts, A. G. (2014). Career helplines: A resource for career development. In G. Arulmani, A. J. Bakshi, F. T. L. Leong, & A. G. Watts (Eds.), *Handbook of career development* (pp. 481–493). Springer.

Frey, A., & Balzer, L. (2007). *Beurteilungsbogen zu sozialen und methodischen Kompetenzen* [Assessment sheet on social and methodical competencies]. smk-Reihe. http://www.kompetenzscreening.de/Beurteilungsbogen_smk_FreyBalzer_Description%202007.pdf

Frey, A., Ertelt, B.-J., & Ruppert, J.-J. (2016). *Berufsbiografien im Vergleich—Studienbrief im Modul 07 "Berufsbiografien im Vergleich" des Masterstudiengangs "Arbeitsmarktorientierte Beratung" (M.A.) der Hochschule der Bundesagentur für Arbeit (HdBA).* HdBA.

Gallhofer, I. N., & Saris, W. E. (1989). Three methods for analysing decision making using written documents. In H. Montgomery & O. Svenson (Eds.), *Process and structure in human decision making* (pp. 99–123). Wiley.

Gati, I., & Tal, S. (2008). Decision-making models and career guidance. In J. A. Athanasou & R. van Esbroeck (Eds.), *International handbook of career guidance* (pp. 157–185). Springer Science + Business Media B.V.

Gati, I., Levin, N., & Landman-Tal, S. (2019). Decision-making models and career guidance. In J. A. Athanasou & H. N. Perera (Eds.), *International handbook of career guidance* (2nd ed., pp. 115–145). Springer.

Gibson, R. L., & Mitchell, M. H. (1990). *Introduction to counselling and guidance* (3rd ed.). Macmillan.

Gigerenzer, G. (2004). Fast and frugal heuristics: The tools of bounded rationality. In D. J. Koehler & N. Harvey (Eds.), *Blackwell handbook of judgment and decision making* (pp. 62–88). University of Waterloo.

Gigerenzer, G., & Selten, R., (Eds.). (2002). The adaptive toolbox *Bounded rationality—The adaptive toolbox* (pp. 37–50). Cambridge: MIT Press.

Gigerenzer, G., & Todd, P. M. (1999). Fast and frugal heuristics: The adaptive toolbox. In G. Gigerenzer & P. M. Todd (Eds.), *Simple heuristics that make us smart* (pp. 3–34). Oxford University Press.

Gore, P. A., Leuwerke, W. C., & Kelley, A. R. (2013). The structure, sources, and uses of occupational information. In S. D. Brown & R. W. Lent (Eds.), *Career development and counseling—Putting theory and research to work* (2nd ed., pp. 507–535). Wiley.

Guichard, J., & Huteau, M. (2001). *Psychologie de l'orientation*. Dunod.

Hanna, A., Gregory, C., Lewis, P. M., & Rounds, J. (2019). International career assessment using the occupational information network (O*Net). In J. A. Athanasou & H. N. Perera (Eds.), *International handbook of career guidance* (2nd ed., pp. 581–612). Springer.

Harris-Bowlsbey, J. (2013). Computer-assisted career guidance systems: A part of NCDA history. https://doi.org/10.1002/j.2161-0045.2013.00047.x

Hellberg, B. M. (2005). *Entscheidungsfindung bei der Berufswahl – Prozessmodell der Emotionen und* Kognitionen [Decision-making in career choice – Process model of emotions and cognitions]. Deutscher Universitäts-Verlag.

Herr, E. L., Cramer, S. H., & Niles, S. G. (2004). *Career guidance and counseling through the lifespan* (6th ed.). Pearson.

Hick, A. (1992). *Entwicklung und Erprobung eines Kategoriensystems zur Erfassung von inhaltsbezogenen entscheidungsrelevanten Variablen* [Development and testing of a category system for recording content-related decision-relevant variables]. Lehrstuhl für Erziehungswissenschaft II, Universität Mannheim: Diplomarbeit.

Hofer, M., & Papastefanou, C. (1996). Theoriebestände für pädagogisch-psychologisches Beratungshandeln [Theories for educational-psychological counselling]. In M. Hofer, E. Wild, & B. Pikowsky (Eds.), *Pädagogisch-psychologische Berufsfelder* (pp. 25–55). Huber.

Hofstedt, P. & Löffler, S. (2021). Constraints. In G. Görz, U. Schmid & T. Braun (Hrsg.) *Handbuch der künstlichen Intelligenz* (6. Aufl.). Berlin/Boston: Walter de Gruyter GmbH.

Holder, L. (2016). *Der Zusammenhang von Berufsinteressen, überfachlichen Kompetenzen und Entscheidungsheuristiken während der Berufswahl von Schülerinnen und Schülern der Sekundarstufe II - Eine empirische Studie* [The relationship between career interests, generic competences and decision-making heuristics during the career choice of upper secondary school students—An empirical study]. Universität Mannheim.

Holland, J. L. (1997). *Making vocational choices—A theory of vocational personalities and work environments* (3rd ed.). Odessa PAR.

Holling, H., Lüken, K. H., Preckel, F., & Stotz, M. (2000). *Berufliche Entscheidungsfindung* [Vocational decision-making], BeitrAB 236. Bundesanstalt für Arbeit.

Horan, J. J. (1979). *Counseling for effective decision making*. Duxbury.

Ivey, A. E. (1983). *Intentional interviewing and counseling*. Brooks/Cole.

Ivey, A. E. (1998). *Führung durch Kommunikation* [Leadership through communication]. Rosenberger.

Ivey, A. E., & Authier, J. (1983). Microcounselling – Neue Wege im Kommunikationstraining [Microcounseling—New directions in communication training]. *In B. J. Ertelt und W. E. Schulz (Hrsg.), Microcounselling – Neue Wege im Kommunikationstraining*. Bratt.

Ivey, A. E., & Authier, J. (1985). *Microcounselling - Neue Wege im Kommunikationstraining Ing* [Microcounseling—New directions in communication training] (2nd ed.). Bratt.

Janis, J. L., & Mann, L. (1977). *Decision making: A psychological analysis of the conflict, choice and commitment*. The Free Press.

Kahnemann, D. (2012). *Schnelles Denken, langsames Denken* [Fast thinking, slow thinking]. München: Siedler.

Keller, N., & Katsikopoulos, K. V. (2015). On the role of psychological heuristics in operational research; and a demonstration in military stability operations. *European Journal of Operational Research, 2015*. https://doi.org/10.1016/j.ejor2015.07.023

Kirsch, W. (1977). *Einführung in die Theorie der Entscheidungsprozesse* [Introduction to the theory of decision processes] (2nd ed.). Wiesbaden: Gabler.

Klein, G. (2002). The fiction of optimization. In G. Gigerenzer & R. Selten (Eds.), *Bounded rationality: The adaptive toolbox* (pp. 103–121). MIT Press.

Klevenow, G. -H., & Weber, L. (2016). Ausbildungs- und Studiengangswechsel – Eine explorative Studie zur Veränderung von Entscheidungsstrategien und -kriterien [Training and study programme changes—An exploratory study on changes in decision-making strategies and criteria]. In A. Bienfait & A. Frey (Hrsg.), Ausbildungs- und Studienabbrüche - Empirische Befunde, Ursachen und Möglichkeiten der Prävention [Training and study drop-outs – Empirical findings, causes and possibilities for prevention] (S. 475–498). Verlag Empirische Pädagogik.

Kohlbacher, F. (2006). The use of qualitative content analysis in case study research. In *Forum Qualitative Sozialforschung* [Forum: Qualitative social research (Vol. 7, No. 1, pp. 1–30)]. https://epub.wu.ac.at/5315/1/75-195-1-PB.pdf

Krumboltz, J. D. (2003). Creating and capitalizing on happenstance in educational and vocational guidance, In SVB/ASOSP, International AIOSP Congress, Final Report Bern 2003. www.svb-asosp.ch/Kongress/Start.htm.

Krumboltz, J. D., & Lewin, A. S. (2004). *Luck is no accident: Making the most of happenstance in your life and career*. Impact Publishers.

Mayring, P. (2000). Qualitative content analysis: Demarcation, varieties, developments. In *Forum Qualitative Sozialforschung/Forum:Qualitative Social Research* (Vol. 20, No. 3). https://www.qualitative-research.net/index.php/fqs/article/download/3343/4445

Mayring, P. (2014). *Qualitative content analysis: Theoretical foundation, basic procedures and software solution*. https://www.ssoar.info/ssoar/bitstream/handle/document/39517/ssoar-2014-mayring-Qualitative_content_analysis_theoretical_foundation.pdf

Mauch, W. (1986). *Typen von Ratsuchenden nach ihren Informationsstrukturen in Entscheidungsberatungen der Arbeitsberatung und der Berufsberatung* [Types of guidance seekers according to their information structures in decision guidance in employment counselling and career guidance]. Diplom-Arbeit, Lehrstuhl Erziehungswissenschaften: Universität Mannheim.

Mellers, B. A., et al. (2002). Group report: Effects of emotions and social processes on bounded rationality. In G. Gigerenzer & R. Selten (Eds.), *Bounded rationality: The adaptive toolbox* (pp. 263–279). MIT Press.

Metzler-Burren, C. (2001). *Grundlagen der Untersuchung der beruflichen Telefonberatung* [Foundations for the study of professional telephone counselling]. Universitäten Bern, Freiburg. Zürich NABB-5: Diplom-Arbeit.

Mitchell, L. K., & Krumboltz, J. D. (1996). Krumboltz's learning theory of career choice and counseling. In I. D. Brown, L. Brooks, & Ass. (Eds.), *Career choice and development* (3rd ed., pp. 233–280). Jossey-Bass.

Mitchell, K. E., Levin, A. S., & Krumboltz, J. D. (1999). Planned happenstance: Constructing unexpected career opportunities. *Journal of Counseling and Development, 77*, 115–124.

Muswieck, W. (2001). *Distance Counselling—Planung und Koordinierung eines Pilot-Projekts im Rahmen des EU Programmes LEONARDO DA VINCI (Arbeitspapier)* [Planning and coordination of a pilot project within the EU programme LEONARDO DA VINCI. (Working paper)]. Unit: International Labour Market Relations, etc. Federal Labour Office.

Nationales Forum Beratung in Bildung, Beruf und Beschäftigung (nfb)/Forschungsgruppe Beratungsqualität am Institut für Bildungswissenschaften der Universität Heidelberg. (2014). *Professionell beraten: Qualitätsstandards für die Beratung in Bildung, Beruf und Beschäftigung* [Professional counselling: Quality standards for guidance in education, career and employment]. Bielefeld: Bertelsmann.

Nestmann, F., Sickendiek, U., & Engel, F. (2007). Die Zukunft der Beratung in Bildung, Beruf und Beschäftigung [The future of guidance in education, career and employment]. In U. Sickendiek, F. Nestmann, F. Engel, & V. Bamler, (Hrsg.), *Beratung in Bildung Beruf und Beschäftigung* [Guidance in education, career and employment] (S. 13–51). dgvt.

Nestmann, F., Engel, F., & Sickendiek, U. (Hrsg.). (2013). *Das Handbuch der Beratung* [The counselling handbook]. (Band 1-3). dgvt.

Noworol, C. (2013). *Miasteczko Zainteresowań Zawodowych (MZZ)* (The location of professional interests). NFDK.

Offer, M., Sampson, J. P., & Watts, A. G. (2001). *Careers services: Technology and the future*. The Higher Education Careers Services Unit (CSU).

Osborn, D. S. (2019). Innovating career development through technology via cognitive information processing theory lens. In J. G. Maree (Ed.), *Handbook of innovative career Counseling* (pp. 733–744). Springer.

Peavy, R. V. (1981). *Counselling adults for decision-making*. Guidance Centre, University of Toronto.

Peterson, G. W., Sampson, J. P., Jr., Reardon, R. C., & Lenz, J. G. (1996). A cognitive information processing approach to career problem solving and decision making. In D. Brown, L. Brooks, & Ass (Eds.), *Career choice and development* 3rd ed. pp. 423–475). Jossey-Bass.

Peterson, G. W., Sampson, J. P., Lenz, J. G., & Reardon, R. C. (2002). A cognitive information processing approach to career problem solving and decision making. In D. Brown & Ass (Eds.), *Career choice and development* 4th ed. pp. 312–369). Jossey-Bass.

Petty, R. E., & Cacioppo, J. T. (1986). The elaboration likelihood model of persuasion. In L. Berkowitz (Ed.), *Advances in experimental social psychology* (Vol. 19, pp. 123–205). Academic Press.

Rogers, C. R. (1972). *Die nicht direktive* Beratung [The non-directive counselling]. Counselling and Psychotherapy, Boston 1942. Kindler Studienausgabe.

Rosenberger, W. (2002). *Führungskräfteberatung* [Executive counselling]. Rosenberger.

Rübner, M., & Sprengard, B. (2010). *Handbuch für Berufsberaterinnen und Berufsberater – Beratungskonzeption der Bundeagentur für Arbeit (Bd.1)* [Handbook for career guidance counsellors—Guidance concept of the Federal Employment Agency (Vol. 1)]. Bundesagentur für Arbeit.

Ruppert, J. J., & Ertelt, B.-J. (2007). *"They preach water and drink wine" or The unbearable lightness of rational decision-making models in career counselling*. AIOSP/IAEVG International Conference, Padova/Italy, Sept. 2007.

Sampson, J. P., Peterson, G. W., Lenz, J. G., Reardon, R. C., & Saunders, D. E. (1996). *Career thoughts inventory (CTI)*. PAR.

Sampson, J. P., Lenz, J. G., Reardon, R. C., & Peterson, G. W. (1999). A cognitive information processing approach to employment problem solving and decision making. *The Career Development Quarterly, 48*(1), 3–18.

Saunders, D. E., Peterson, G., Sampson, J., & Reardon, R. (2000). Relation of depression and dysfunctional career thinking to career indecision. *Journal of Vocational Behavior, 56*(2000), 288–298.

Schiersmann, C. (2007). Auf dem Weg zu einer Beratungswissenschaft für das Feld Bildung, Beruf und Beschäftigung [Towards a counselling science for the field of education, occupation, employment]. In U. Heuer & R. Siebers (Eds.), *Weiterbildung am Beginn des 21. Jahrhunderts* (pp. 150–160). Waxmann.

Schulz, W. E. (2000). *Counselling ethics casebook* (2nd ed.). Canadian Counselling Association.

Schulz, W. E. (2014). Convergence of career development theory into a comprehensive theory and process. In J. Górna & D. Kukla (Eds.), *Vocational counselling—Changes and challenges on the labour market* (pp. 73–83). Jan Dlugosz University (AJD).

Schulz, J. (2017). Berufsinteressen, überfachliche Kompetenzen, Stressbewältigungsstrategien und berufliches Entscheidungsverhalten bei jungen Arbeitslosen [Vocational interests, generic competences, stress management strategies and vocational decision-making behaviour among young unemployed people]. Deutscher Verband für Bildungs- und Berufsberatung e.V. *dvb, 57*(2), 64–69.

Seidel, G. (1995). *Evaluation der MatAB - Sonderserie "Ausbildungsberufe und Urteil der Betriebe", Abschlussbericht* [Evaluation of the MatAB – Special series "Training occupations and the judgement of companies"]. Final report. Frankfurt a.M.: Deutsches Institut für Internationale Pädagogische Forschung (DIPF).

Seidel, G. (1997). *Untersuchung zu Informationsbedarf und Mediennutzung bei Kunden und Mitarbeitern der Bundesanstalt für Arbeit* [Study on information needs and media use among clients and employees of the Federal Employment Service]. Frankfurt a. M: DIPF.

Selten, R. (2002). What is bounded rationality? In G. Gigerenzer & R. Selten (Eds.), *Bounded rationality: The adaptive toolbox* (pp. 13–36). MIT Press.

Seyffer, S. (2015). *Individuelle Migrationsentscheidungen - Ein Beitrag zu einer innovativen Mobilitätsberatung* [Individual migration decisions—A contribution to innovative mobility counselling]. Landau: Verlag Empirische Pädagogik.

Siebert, J. U., Kunz, R. E., & Rolf, P. (2020). Effects of proactive decision making on life satisfaction. *European Journal of Operational Research, 280*(2020), 1171–1187.

Tittel, C. (2019). *Erhebungsinstrument zum beruflichen Entscheidungsverhalten* [Survey instrument for professional decision-making behavior]. Beau Basse/Mauritius: AV Akademikerverlag.

Trinemeier, H. G., & Ertelt, B.-J. (1978). *Praxisnahe Übungen an der Fachhochschule der Bundesanstalt für Arbeit in Mannheim* [Practical exercises at the Fachhochschule der Bundesanstalt für Arbeit in Mannheim] (pp. 10). Heft: Arbeit und Beruf.

Trisoglio-Wanka, J. (2008). *Überprüfung neuerer Erkenntnisse der Entscheidungsforschung im beruflichen Kontext* [Review of recent findings in decision research in an occupational context] (Diplomarbeit, ed.). Universität.

Walsh, W. B. (1990). A summary and integration of career counselling approaches. In W. B. Walsh & S. H. Osipow (Eds.), *Career counseling—Contemporary topics in vocational psychology* (pp. 263–282). Erlbaum.

Weber, P. (2013). *Qualität in der arbeitsmarktlichen Beratung* [Quality in labor market advice]. Universität Heidelberg. http://www.nb.uni-heidelberg.de/archiv/15159

Wegmann, O. (2005). *Individuelle Entscheidungsstrategien in der beruflichen Laufbahn im Vergleich zu Modellvorstellungen der beruflichen Laufbahnberatung* [Individual decision-making strategies in vocational careers compared to model conceptions of vocational career counselling]. Diplomarbeit. Universität.

Wresch, A. (2008). *Von der Notwendigkeit einer Umstellung auf heuristische Modelle in der berufsbezogenen Beratung* [On the need for a shift to heuristic models in vocational guidance]. Diplomarbeit. Universität.

Chapter 6
Competence-Oriented Vocational and Career Counselling

6.1 Introduction

In recent years, technological changes in society, caused largely by the internet and social media platforms, have permanently changed the way people receive and process information, make professional and private contacts and network (Hekkert et al., 2007). In contrast, technological change in companies and in the labour market, (e.g. through automation, robotics and artificial intelligence), causes employees with low and medium qualifications to lose their jobs, while at the same time vocational training and specialisations or retraining remain unused (Benešová & Tupa, 2017; Hutter & Weber, 2020). Meanwhile, technological change, which permeates all occupations and companies, causes new occupational activities and job profiles to emerge that can be particularly attractive and desirable for young people and adults.

Social and economic change is complex, and the dynamics of how fast people's private and professional lives will develop in order to keep up with these transformation processes place new demands on the counselling profession (Frey et al., 2014; Frey & Ruppert, 2017). The aim of the profession must therefore be to prove its flexibility anew. Will counsellors be able to be true to themselves as human beings and still be able to gain both identity and social esteem into the digital transformation processes of society and the economy (Sailmann, 2018)?

In order for young people and adults to be able to accept and cope with the processes of change in society and the labour market, it will be increasingly important in vocational and career guidance to refer to the corrective function of competencies on the often-one-sided orientation of guidance towards vocational interests or motivations. Arulmani (2015, p. 620), for example, warns against an overly one-sided focus on career-related interests, because their manifestation or individual motivation, no matter how strong, are not sufficient for individuals to acquire such a pronounced competence that they can hold their own in professional competitions. Earlier, Ertelt and Frey (2013, p. 297) called for the intensification of

B.-J. Ertelt et al., *Counsellor Competencies*,
https://doi.org/10.1007/978-3-030-87413-1_6

research on the connection between vocational interests and transferable competencies in order to provide counselling assistance in assessing the prognostic validity of various probationary fields in training, study, further education and employment.

The competence-resource model by Le Boterf (1994) provides vocational and career guidance with a theoretical framework to link competencies, vocational interests and motives of young people and adults with the requirements of companies and the labour market.

The analysis of selected theories on career choice and career development, the so-called object theories, shows different forms of including competencies (the overview of the most important theories and their convergence as well as the approach of a "comprehensive theory" by Schulz, 2014 are helpful here).

The "trait-and-factor" models, and their best-known representative Holland, emphasise the importance of the optimal "fit" between personality type and work environment. It becomes critical when individuals lack clarity and stability of self-image with regard to their own interests, abilities, values and goals, or when there is a lack of sufficient knowledge about the professional reality, especially with regard to the required competencies. The latter, however, tend to be neglected in the personality typology approach compared to occupational interests. Holland (1997, p. 215) emphasises, however, that each of his six type clusters requires largely matching competencies and interests.

According to the "developmental approach", essentially coined by Super (1984), career success, career satisfaction and career stability result from a harmony of "professional identity" (a person's objectified view of his or her professional goals, interests and talents) and "professional self-concept" (subjective appreciation of perceived abilities, interests and values). Professional success depends on the individual willingness and ability to master this assignment of both constructs in the sense of the respective task, which is described by the dynamically understood term "professional maturity". Competence orientation in guidance means enabling self-assessment of professional and interdisciplinary competencies as a contribution to harmonising professional identity and professional self-concept.

In following through with this approach through "life-designing" (cf. Nota et al., 2020; Nota & Rossier, 2015; Savickas et al., 2009), the dynamic character in the sense of the self-construction of the career path by the individual is underlined. Lifelong counselling support focuses on interpreting the respective career development tasks, strengthening adaptability to new situations and assessing the appropriateness of the self-concept. The adaptability that is particularly emphasised in life-designing takes into account individual attitudes, namely future-oriented planning ("concern"), professional determination ("control"), confidence as a professional self-efficacy expectation ("confidence") and curiosity ("curiosity").

For Hirschi (2012), these are not sufficient as success components; therefore, he adds "human capital resources" (education and training, interdisciplinary competencies, professional knowledge, cognitive skills), "social resources" (networks and mentors), "psychological resources" (clarity of self-concept and one's own goals as well as congruence of goals) as influencing factors in his career resource model. In our context, the "human capital resources" are particularly important because they form the essential basis for "employability".

The theory of "social learning", according to Krumboltz (1996, p. 234), emphasises that, in addition to the genetic endowment, it is, above all, the learning experiences in the interaction of aptitude and social environment that are responsible for a successful professional career. This happens because these experiences determine the cognitive and practical abilities as well as the emotional prerequisites for coping with professional challenges.

In his "Social Cognitive Career Theory (SCCT)", Lent (2013, p. 115) emphasises that the successful handling of a certain (professional) challenge by the individual depends on the interaction of three cognitive variables: "Self-efficacy beliefs" and positive outcome expectations ("outcome expectations") are sources of interest, which in turn determine personal goals ("personal goals") as an important factor influencing the direction of action. The importance of the competence reference in vocational information and counselling is particularly evident here, because according to this approach, people will only be interested in a certain action (e.g. vocational training, study, career change, promotion) if they feel up to the required technical and interdisciplinary competencies and expect a positive outcome.

The interaction of person and work environment gains central importance for competence-oriented guidance in the "Theory of Work Adjustment-TWA" (cf. Dawis, 1996; Dawis et al., 1968). If the person meets the requirements at the training or workplace, positive reinforcement by the environment occurs, which leads to individual satisfaction and renewed positive assessment by superiors. However, if performance is no longer guaranteed due to deficits in professional and/or interdisciplinary competencies, negative feedback is given and even job loss can occur, if no timely adjustment is made. *Active adjustment* aims to change the work environment and its reinforcement mechanisms, while *reactive behaviour involves the* individual trying to change to meet the demands and social environment of the workplace.

Effective counselling support requires a professional analysis of the discrepancies between the requirement profile and the performance profile as well as the adaptation style—individual flexibility—and perseverance as interdisciplinary competencies.

With regard to counselling practice, it can be assumed that counsellors are guided only to a limited extent by a specific theory, but rather by their "subjective theory". This subjective theory can be flexibly adapted to the specific counselling case: "Most career counsellors claim not to operate from a specific career development theory. That is, there is a big gap between theory and practice" (Schulz, 2014, p. 73). And "Efficient counsellors usually do not apply theories strictly but refer to their 'intuition'. In fact, their "intuition" refers to a holistic understanding of complex dynamics, which may be different for each client" (Dauwalder, 2014, p. 246). It can therefore be assumed that in practice, especially if the counselling also includes placement in training or jobs, the assessment of competencies plays a central role.

In the following pages, the topic of competencies will be further elaborated and the possibilities of competence-oriented career guidance in connection with the competence-resource model will be described in more detail.

6.2 The Concept of Competence

As early as 2005, the OECD demanded that young people and adults can only accompany and shape the digital transformation in the economy and society if they have developed and can apply competencies that go beyond knowledge and cognitive skills. "It involves the ability to meet complex demands, by drawing on and mobilising psychosocial resources (including skills and attitudes) in a particular context. For example, the ability to communicate effectively can be a competence that may draw on an individual's knowledge of language, practical IT skills and attitudes towards those with whom he or she is communicating" (OECD, 2005, p. 6). OECD classifies these "key competencies" in three categories:

1. Young people and adults need to be able to use a wide range of different media, aids, or tools such as information technology or language efficiently, and to understand, adapt and use such tools interactively.
2. In an interdependent world, young people and adults need to be able to engage with people from different cultures and to interact in socially heterogeneous groups.
3. Young people and adults need to be able to take responsibility for themselves, to situate their lives in broader contexts, and to act autonomously (ibid., p. 7).

These three categories are interrelated and form a basis for identifying and mapping key competencies. The need to think and act reflectively is central to this conceptual framework of competencies. "Reflectiveness involves not just the ability to apply routinely a formula or method for confronting a situation, but also the ability to deal with change, learn from experience and think and act with a critical stance" (ibid., p. 7).

Weinert (2001) describes competence as "the cognitive abilities and skills existing within individuals or which can be learned by them to solve certain problems as well as the motivational, volitional, and social dispositions and abilities to be able to use problem solutions in variable situations successively and in a responsible way". He thus addresses the characteristics described earlier and adds additional aspects to the concept of competence. A young person's individually existing resources, i.e. their physical and psychological assets, form the basis for acting competently. Moreover, individuals have knowledge, abilities and attitudes that can be learned. This implies that competence includes the ability to further develop one's own resources (Frey et al., 2014). This self-organised application of the mentioned dispositions can be described as competent actions.

Individuals that are acting competently are those who "act consciously, willingly, and responsibly, in accordance with criteria that are socially respected, not in the sense of a technically satisfactory (poiesis), but also an ethically correct performance (praxis). That is why the competent subject enjoys professional, and in a more comprehensive sense, social authority" (Ghisla et al., 2008, p. 22). Responsibility means more than just being reliable. That which is presented to the world as a new creative/innovative solution must not only be functionally reliable; it is mandatory

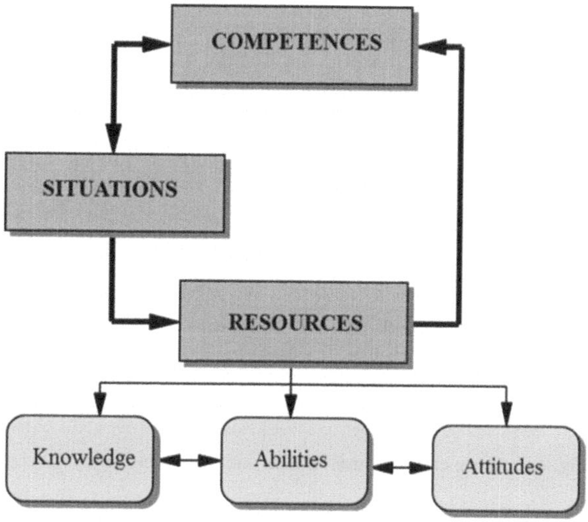

Fig. 6.1 Interaction of competences and resources in situations. Source: Kaiser (2008)

that it is also in tune with the basic values of a society and/or legitimate rather than just opportune. "Competence is therefore not simply rooted in the resources (knowledge, abilities, and attitude) from which it arises in the respective situation, nor in the sum of these, but acting in a creative and functional combination in order to mobilise these resources in concrete situations" (ibid., p. 23). Hence, what is important is that the three aspects of knowledge, abilities and attitudes in combination with responsible actions in different situations "coincide" with each other (Frey, 2008, p. 224). In this context, Ghisla et al. (2008) explain that a specific competence becomes apparent when a young person appropriately masters a specific class of situations and mobilises specific resources to do so (cf. Fig. 6.1).

The interaction of competencies and resources in situations, as illustrated in Fig. 6.1, can be described as follows: A professional situation defines which competencies are required to master the situation. For this, every competence needs a pool of resources (knowledge, abilities, attitudes) which young persons developed or further developed in their vocational training. A specified professional situation, therefore, allows the identification of the resources which are developed and must be pooled and connected to form different competencies.

Since several professional situations characterise an occupation, the young person needs as many different (action) competence constellations. These competencies derive from different resources and can be accessed as required and demanded by the situation (cf. Fig. 6.2).

The constellations in Fig. 6.2 show that to process Situation 1, you require Action Competence 1 consisting of Resources 1, 2, 4, and 5. To process Situation 2, you require Action Competence 2 consisting of Resources 1, 3, 5, and 6. This means that there is an ideal competence constellation for every situation, which in turn derives from different resources to solve the respective situation. At the same time, the figure

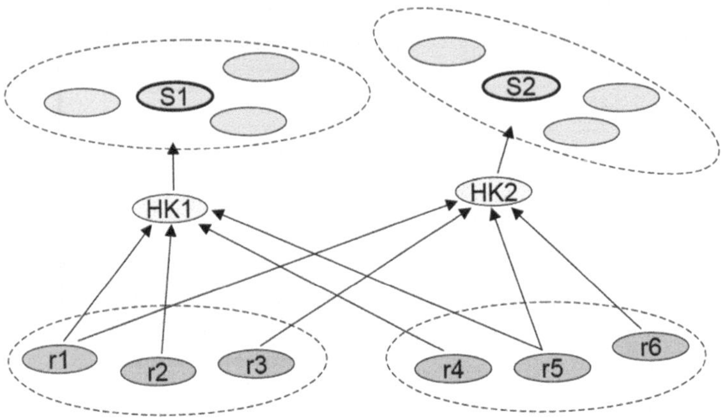

Fig. 6.2 Competence constellations and resources. Source: Scharnhorst (2009)

shows that Resources 1 and 5 must be important knowledge, abilities, and attitudes, as they are accessed by two competence constellations.

Nägele (2013) assumes that competencies are situation related. This means that acting competently becomes apparent when a young person is able to assess the exterior framework conditions of a situation and apply the existing situational (circumstantial) resources combined with the personal resources for their intentions (p. 291). Not only can competencies be applied in specific professional action situations, but they are also used to act appropriately in personal situations. Thus, they can be applied in various ways across several contexts.

According to Frey et al. (2014), competence can be described as follows: Those who have competence are able to act and hence able to access, according to the specific situation, these resources from the ones they have developed (knowledge, abilities, attitudes) which are required to solve the task at hand in a target-oriented and responsible way; thereby assessing a solution, and further developing their own competence constellations. The competence constellations can be divided into four sub-classes: the technical competence class on the one hand and, on the other hand, the methodical, social, and personal competence classes. The three latter are also summarised under the term "interdisciplinary competencies" and/or "key competence". The four competence classes are composed of different knowledge, abilities, and attitudes which again can be divided into different skills (Frey, 2008, p. 57 et seq.). All competence classes and the respective knowledge, abilities, and attitudes are interconnected and interdependent. Together, they form professional action competence.

Technical competence includes knowledge and abilities which are geared towards the discipline and/or occupation and are subject to change; thus, requiring constant further training. These technical ability areas constitute the purely technical specific basic knowledge required for a given occupation. Without technical skills, working in any occupation is nearly impossible, since the technical skills provide a person's skill set.

Social competence means, according to the situation and task at hand, the behaviour required to solve responsibly a task autonomously or in cooperation with others (Frey et al., 2014). If more than one person contributes to a problem-solving process, even in part, then the client is confronted with more behavioural dispositions. These are components of the ability to deal with conflict and to communicate, but also indicators of leadership ability and situation-appropriate behaviour. In detail, this includes the following abilities:

1. The *ability to cooperate* means the ability to cooperate with others. Cooperation is a work behaviour of at least two persons who work towards achieving a common goal in a conscious, organised, coordinated way and that complements each person. Therefore, cooperation always refers to a network of persons who are working or learning together.
2. *Social responsibility* describes the ability to act responsibly and autonomously, and to consider values and standards and the effects that can be anticipated for oneself, others, and specific situations, and also to accept the resulting consequences.
3. The *ability to deal with conflict* means the ability to engage in a confrontation with someone else or a group and to persist until a compromise can be reached or the problem is solved. The prerequisite for this is that a person can react to criticism appropriately, even calmly, and to accept and voice constructive criticism.
4. The *ability to communicate* means having the ability to assume different functions in a communicative feedback loop. On the one hand, this includes abilities such as expressing oneself clearly and precisely and presenting complicated facts comprehensibly and, on the other hand, abilities such as listening to others and letting them finish, as well as including others in a conversation.
5. In general, *leadership ability* means influencing the attitudes and behaviour of individuals and the interaction of persons in and between groups with the purpose of achieving certain goals together. Leadership is a trend-setting and steering influence on the behaviour of others to achieve a goal; it frequently includes utilising material resources. An essential characteristic of successful leadership in particular is its dynamic process in which responsibility is assigned and self-responsibility is motivated. Those being led are deliberately informed about the goals and the kind of influence. Successful leadership behaviour seeks to maintain and promote the motivation of those being lead, in spite of different interests. Furthermore, the promotion requirements of individuals and appropriate promotion measures are identified and offered in this process.
6. *Situation-appropriate behaviour* means having the ability to apply good manners and behaving and acting confidently in different situations as well as being impartial towards others.

Methodical competence means having the ability to think and act within a defined subject field (Frey et al., 2014). This includes the abilities to handle tools in a competent and reflective way, to structure work processes, to acquire knowledge and expertise about tools, and to understand working conditions. These abilities need to be applied in varying work environments and may also need to be expanded and modified (Nägele, 2013). Methodical competence frequently includes abilities assigned to various areas: autonomy, ability to analyse, flexibility, target-oriented behaviour, working techniques, digital ability and reflectiveness.

1. *Autonomy* means to take the initiative in social situations, set goals, and select and apply methods to reach these goals independently. Additionally, this includes abilities such as managing projects autonomously and acting confidently. Autonomy furthermore includes showing socially accepted and development-appropriate performances under existing sociocultural circumstances.
2. The *ability to analyse* means having the ability to analyse a situation systematically. The ability to analyse is very closely linked to solving problems. An improving ability to analyse is achieved through synthesis and evaluation of cognitive goals.
3. *Flexibility* means having the ability to react and adapt to changing circumstances in a straightforward way and adjusting to them, as well as work on different tasks at the same time. It can be quite complex helping individuals approach one or several problems using different solutions. This behaviour also includes the ability to question old facts and to try new approaches.
4. *Target-oriented behaviour* means having the ability to solve a problem, to get insights, or reach a target and by utilising specific action methods, application techniques, and cognitive strategies. Characteristic features are abilities like working systematically, differentiating important from unimportant matters, prioritising, and setting realistic goals. Solving problems leads to an increase in insight and allows independently finding ways of coping, even with new situations in the future. Tasks are mastered and problems are solved by combining the various learned rules.
5. *Working techniques* means having the ability to learn and internalise numerous treatment techniques and to have these methods available at any time in order to achieve a specific goal. Working techniques thus refer to having many regulated and planned approaches available to gain different insights and to achieve goals in general.
6. *Digital ability* means having the ability to use applications and programmes on a wide range of devices (computer, touchpad, smartphone, ticket machines, etc.) and to use them to retrieve, modify and/or create content.
7. *Reflectiveness* is the ability to assess one's own actions and oneself critically; this is important for the quality and efficiency of one's own work. Reflective behaviour means evaluating one's own past or current actions and structures in a rational, objective and authentic way. Reflection, for instance, begins when actions become problematic, when the desired success does not ensue, undesired side effects occur, or when certain situations are unclear. The reflection on practical actions and situations when problems arise can lead to better, more acceptable actions.

Personal competence includes ability concepts, attitudes, actions, or characteristics required to act in a self-responsible and motivated manner (Frey & Ruppert,

2013). The ethical ability is of significant importance here; insights gained which have become "guidelines for life" for the respective individual are reflected in virtues which can also be described as ethical attitudes. Personal competence is all about acting based on self-reflection paired with moments of solitude. That is, a solitary decision is when an idea, belief, or conviction forces decisions which need to be made alone and which no one else can make for you (Roth, 1971).

1. *Helpfulness and empathy* entails behaviour such as making others happy, being reliable and tolerant, and being considerate of others. This also includes friendly, honest, and trustful behaviour towards others.
2. *Composure and patience* means happy, patient, and composed behaviour. In addition, composed behaviour can be understood as fair thinking and acting.
3. *Sense of duty* can be described as showing self-discipline, keeping order, and fulfilling one's duties. Additionally, this factor includes being on time, being hard-working, and making sensible decisions.
4. *Love of freedom* implies loving life, being cheerful and free, and striving for happiness in general.
5. *Curiosity* describes behavioural aspects such as being creative and continuing to learn and explore. Additionally, curiosity also includes abilities such as being able to evaluate and being critical.
6. *Performance orientation* refers to a behaviour such as not avoiding difficult tasks, and seeking new tasks, challenges, and problem situations.

On the whole, the technical, social, methodological, and personal competence categories are not facts of competence independent of each other but must rather be seen as linked and/or interconnected units which, when brought together, reflect a person's professional action competence (Frey & Ruppert, 2013). The setup and synthesis of these competence units can over time and across different areas of activity and employment, lead to the development of comprehensive action competence (Nägele, 2013).

The Classification of European Skills, Competences, Qualifications and Occupations—ESCO (2020) describes competencies as the tested ability to use knowledge, skills, personal, social and/or methodological competencies in work, education, and in professional and personal development. Four levels of application of competencies are identified according to their degree of specification:

The transversal level refers to a broad range of occupations and sectors. The cross-sectoral level refers to occupations in different sectors of the economy. Sector-specific knowledge, skills and competences are relevant to a subset of occupations within a sector. The highest level of differentiation is found in occupation-specific competencies, where an occupation can contain several jobs.

6.3 Measurement and Development of Competence in Vocational and Career Guidance

Measuring competencies is a very demanding task for counsellors if they hope to reflect the independence and actual behaviour of their clients. This is also reflected in the fact that despite a large number of psychological instruments for measuring competencies, there is a remarkable discrepancy between the number of publications and their scientific quality (Frey, 2008; Frey & Ruppert, 2017). Moreover, many classical test procedures based on the measurement of personality, intelligence, etc. do not meet the requirements of a developmental competence assessment, even though personality tests or intelligence tests are often used in practice to measure competence (see Frey, 2008 for details).

The recording of competencies can best be achieved via self-assessments and interviews. From a methodical perspective, self-assessments using questionnaires is advantageous because they can be completed by many young people and adults in little time. Furthermore, the prevailing opinion in quantitative self-assessment procedures is that the concerned people themselves are best suited to provide information regarding professional competencies or professional behavioural dispositions (Rentzsch & Schütz, 2009). However, assessing competences requires that the respective individuals know themselves well, are able to observe and assess themselves realistically in retrospect, do not consciously want to rate themselves better or worse than they are, and, in addition, that they do not unconsciously base their assessment on social desirability or acquiescence. Even if an individual's self-assessment was objectively incorrect, this self-assessment would be subjectively more conducive to action and thus definitely of central importance for the description of behaviour (Nägele, 2013). Moreover, teachers, trainers, lecturers, managers, personnel development managers, or other HR representatives desiring information about the competence levels of individuals or groups, must make sure that the evaluations of such self-assessments have no negative consequences on an individual or group, but are instead processed in the sense of pedagogical diagnostics and that they help locate competence deficits and initiate promotion measures.

As compared to subjective self-assessments, measuring methods allowing for direct observing and recording of competences or attitudes in on-the-job situations have an advantage: Assessment centres, for instance, allow interviewing, watching, and assessing people in the context of social interaction situations. This means the assessor in concrete can ask or present further or deepening questions, tasks, or roles (Rentzsch & Schütz, 2009). In this process, displayed behaviour leads to conclusions about personal characteristics. Since most of the times this behaviour is more complex than this is the case in self-assessments, the expectation is that observation methods have a higher *prognostic validity* (Rentzsch & Schütz, 2009).

However, Oser (1997) points out that the objective identification of competencies (so-called professional standards) entails significant timely and financial expenses. Additionally, this observation method frequently underestimates the intelligence of the persons to be observed. In addition, observation errors can occur. Often the construct validity is problematic, as it generally turns out that the observers differentiate very little between individual characteristics, but instead have their evaluations influenced by their overall impression.

Objective measuring methods for determining emotional or social intelligence, for example, use tests that only have right or wrong answers. From these answers a total value is derived for handling problems in various situations. However, these tests for measuring abilities in social situations did not prevail, since the underlying abstract and decontextualised items had little or nothing to do with what constitutes the current competence of a person in a professional situation.

Subjective self-assessments are preferred to observation methods Intelligence tests are rejected out of hand, because you cannot require right or wrong behaviour within social, methodological and personal ability concepts. Instead, the focus of the investigation should rest on the degree to which the individual or group manifests social, methodical, and personal competencies with other individuals or groups.

Lang-von Wins and Triebel (2006) see a significant future trend in competence research as a clear interweaving of diagnosis, guidance, competence development and decision-making.

With competence-oriented vocational and career counselling, counsellors are able to identify not only competencies, interests and motives, but also competence potential. The interdisciplinary competences that are particularly important for counselling can usually only be developed from a combination of self-assessment and the client's biography. This development is made possible by the special emphasis on situational contexts, where each competence is measured for different contexts (school, studies, internship, leisure time, profession, ideal activity, etc.). This results in positive differences between different contexts, which are a good starting point for further competence development and career planning. For example, competencies shown in the context of internship (e.g. organisational skills in the company) can be made transparent and usable for counselling. Furthermore, in competence counselling—building on these identified competences and the positive differences between different contexts—these competencies can be reviewed and further developed in follow-up interviews and simulated with training and study opportunities, occupations, professional activities, or further education strategies. The identified competencies, the positive differences within the respective competence, the positive differences between different contexts as well as professional interests and motives, serve as a basis.

6.4 Assessment Sheet Social and Methodological Competencies (SOMECO)

The diagnostic instrument SOMECO developed by Frey and Balzer (2017) is based on the three competence classes by Frey and Balzer (2003) and Frey (2008). The conclusions made with this measurement procedure in career counselling are very

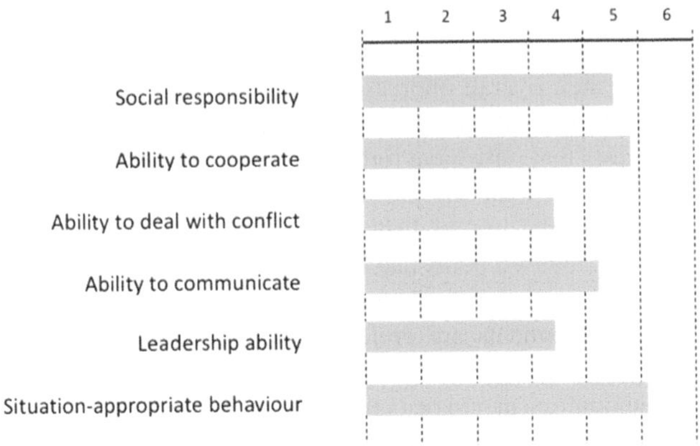

Fig. 6.3 Results of the 6 ability concepts of the social competence class

promising. The competence-oriented approach seems to be particularly well suited for vocational and career guidance, competence development and decision-making.

The current version of SOMECO measures the social, methodical, and personal competence classes distributed over 19 ability concepts:

1. The social competence class is divided into the six ability concepts *Social responsibility* (SV), *Ability to cooperate* (KO), *Ability to deal with conflict* (KF), *Ability to communicate* (KM), *Leadership ability* (FÜ), and *Situation-appropriate behaviour* (SA). The associated statements (e.g. "*Cooperating with others*") are rated along a six-level scale of 1 ("Does not apply at all") through 6 ("Fully applies").
2. The methodical competence class includes the six ability concepts *Ability to analyse* (ANA), *Flexibility* (FLE), *Target-oriented behaviour* (ZIE), *Working techniques* (ARB), *Digital ability* (DIA), *Reflectiveness* (REF), and *Autonomy* (SE). The associated statements (e.g. "*Reflecting on your own knowledge and skills*") are rated along a six-level scale of 1 ("Does not apply at all") through 6 ("Fully applies").
3. The personal competence class includes the six ability concepts *Love of freedom* (FRL), *Composure and patience* (GG), *Helpfulness and empathy* (HE), *Curiosity* (NEU), *Sense of duty* (PFB), and *Performance orientation* (PER). The associated statements (e.g. *"Being tolerant"*) are rated along a six-level scale of 1 ("Does not apply at all") through 6 ("Fully applies").

Figures 6.3, 6.4 and 6.5 show examples of the results of the 19 ability concepts of the self-assessment of a young person or adult:

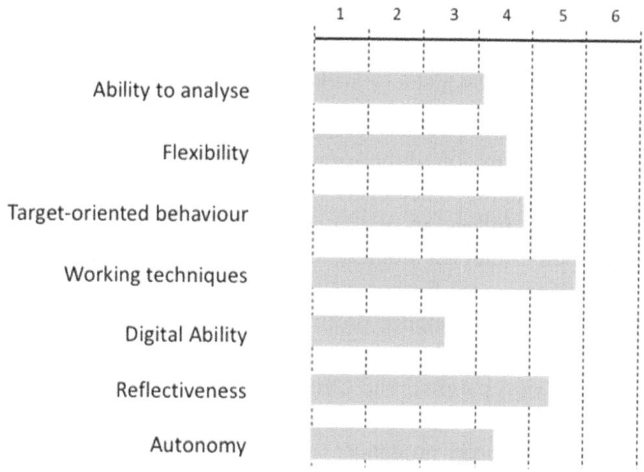

Fig. 6.4 Results of the 7 ability concepts of the methodical competence class

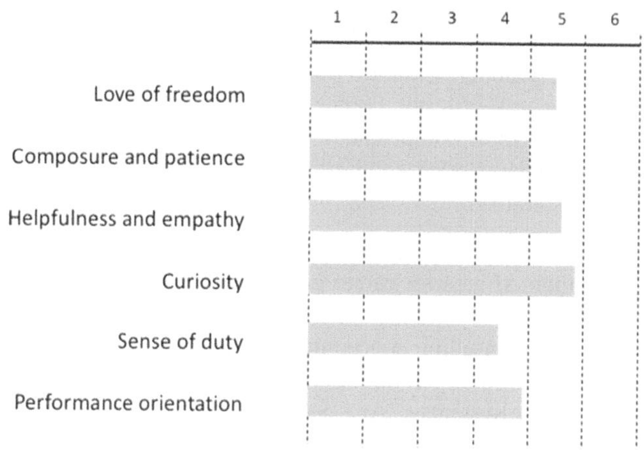

Fig. 6.5 Results of the 6 ability concepts of the personal competence class

6.5 Implementation of Competence Orientation in Vocational and Career Guidance

After clarifying the counselling goal, the young people and adults fill out the self-assessment questionnaire. A resource-oriented evaluation with a focus on positive connotations as a basis for the counselling interview, which consists of seven phases:

1. Review and concretisation of the counselling goal
2. Explanation and exploration of the three competence classes
3. Carrying out the competence diagnostics
4. Discussion of the competence profiles

5. Suggestions for further competence development
6. Derivation of realistic educational, occupational and career goals
7. Determination of concrete steps to achieve the goal

An essential part of competence-oriented career guidance is the fourth phase; namely, the in-depth discussion of the competence profiles. This phase is carried out separately for all three competence classes and usually proceeds as follows:

The counsellor asks follow-up questions about the three competence classes in the most vocationally relevant context (e.g. internship, training, study, further education, employment) until further concrete information is available. The focus here is on matching the competence profile with the additional information within this context. The aim is to use the competencies and additional information to derive realistic educational, occupational and career goals.

Four major challenges arise regarding the further development of competence-oriented vocational and career guidance:

1. Profiling the professional and interdisciplinary competences for specific occupations.
2. Comparison of self-assessed professional and transferable competences with the objective requirements of the workplace.
3. Interaction of personality variables such as occupational interests, decision-making behaviour, self-efficacy, coping strategies, involvement with other professional and transferable competences.
4. Development of AI-supported counselling procedures for the joint construction of viable career solutions.

Particularly regarding the last-mentioned research area, counsellor expect an innovative push in the AI area for career guidance and counselling in the next few years.

For AI supported counselling procedures to succeed, the inclusion of existing career education and guidance information services as well as mainstream computer-assisted career guidance systems (CACGS) will be needed. According to Gati et al. (2019, p. 137), most CACGSs do not support the professional career counsellor, but rather the counselling process typified through face-to-face encounters. Research has also shown that these systems are most effective when used in conjunction with a counsellor rather than as a self-help tool.

When involving intelligence systems in guidance and counselling, the question arises as to the desired degree of autonomy among the interaction partners; namely, "... in what form are humans involved in the decision-making processes of the respective system and to what extent does the system carry out autonomous actions beyond decisions" (Ebers et al., 2020, p. 63).

From our point of view, the systems for data analysis and visualisation, as well as the systems for algorithmic decision support through suggestions for decisions based on them, are in the foreground. The central condition for the development of AI systems, that are closest to counselling, is machine learning (ML); namely, the ability to "learn" knowledge independently from data on a specific problem and to generate transferable models for the analysis of new data. These functions of ML and the "machine thinking" (MT) that is based on it can be assigned to "weak" AI, as explained by Otte (2019, p. 35).

MT is considered the "engine of AI" (Ebers et al., 2020, p. 45) and represents an extremely important instrument in applying career counselling. MT is very helpful for recording the "subjective theories" of the counsellors in knowledge management. For this application process, both the counsellor's approach and the decision-making behaviour of clients must be processed by content analysis and entered into the MT system. To do this properly, counsellors will need increased professionalism and education.

On this basis, the AI system can generate case-related solution forms (heuristics) and the resulting selection, weighting and linking of information, and offering them to the interaction partners for counselling use. It must remain the responsibility of the counsellor how this decision support is implemented in counselling, taking into account object-theoretical and operational-theoretical aspects. Special attention must be paid to the interdependence of the personality variables outlined above and the occupational as well as labour market factors. It is precisely the linking of client variables and counsellor interventions to construct viable solution spaces that reflect the heuristics of the interaction partners. This linkage can also be depicted graphically during counselling.

A critical aspect is the transferability of the categories for describing competence requirements in occupations and professional activities. In an earlier study on the "characteristics" and "skills" required by companies in training occupations, a discriminant-analytical procedure was developed for this purpose, with which at least occupations in the same occupational field can be graphically represented with their specific characteristics (cf. Ertelt et al., 2018, p. 293). This approach could easily be transferred to AI-supported systems, provided that relevant data pools are available.

The use of AI-supported procedures enables the systematic recording of competence descriptions of occupational alternatives tailored to the client by the counsellor through ML. At the same time, it is possible to record how the counsellor translates the client's competence-related ideas and self-assessments into counselling categories. Solution spaces are therefore nothing more than "experience spaces" whereby the counsellor enables clients to experience tentatively matching processes between requirement profiles and their own performance and interest profiles. Particularly in the case of first career choices or career reorientations, clients can usually only assess their competences to a limited extent due to a lack of direct experience. AI systems can provide adapted scenarios for this purpose. However, it is crucial that these scenarios are not guided by models of rational decision-making (with their potential for 'information overload') and constraint systems with finite domains (Hofstedt & Löffler, 2021, p. 715). These scenarios should be guided by the respective state of heuristic problem-solving.

In view of the increasing importance of transferable competences, AI-supported systems offer the opportunity to precisely map the various reference levels of occupational aptitude. This can be roughly differentiated into suitability for job application, suitability for training, general occupational suitability, suitability for the workplace and suitability in the sense of employability. Korulczyk and Korulczyk (2018, p. 73) take an even more differentiated view of the relationship between person and work environment from the perspective of the "fit theories": (1) person–environment fit, (2) person–job fit, (3) person–career fit, (4) person–occupation fit, (5) person–organisation fit, (6) person–supervisor fit, (7) person–workplace fit, (8) person–group fit, (9) person–role fit, (10) person–person fit.

6.6 Exercises

The following exercises related to competence serve as research-based learning and knowledge management in counselling practice.

Exercise 1
Choose a profession of your choice and carry out a competence analysis. For the purpose of this exercise, check to what extent the social, methodological and personal competence classes (outlined earlier with their underlying 19 ability concepts) need to be developed in training or studies. Then check which professional competences are important to learn for this occupation. The following sources can be used:

(a) National job descriptions
(e.g. Germany: BerufeNet;
USA: O*Net (Hanna et al., 2019)
(b) European Skills, Competences, Qualifications and Occupations (ESCO)
Ask a recruiter (HR) in the company and a vocational counsellor about the connection between technical and transversal competences in the selected occupation and clarify which competencies will have to be increasingly used by employees in the future.

Exercise 2
For the profession selected in Exercise 1, analyse the relationship between the required professional and transversal competencies and their characteristics (using a scale of 6) on the basis of job advertisements.

Ask an expert for recruitment (HR) and an expert for job placement regarding concrete requirements for professional and transferable competences at a concrete workplace (job).

Exercise 3
What is of importance for you in today's career and vocational education, research studies, further education or employment of the professional and transversal competences? Relate this importance to other personality variables, such as interests, motives or desires?

Think of the 19 ability concepts of social, methodological and personal competence classes described earlier: Which are particularly important for you?

References

Arulmani, G. (2015). Assessment of interest and aptitude: A methodologically integrated approach. In G. Arulmani, A. J. Bakshi, F. T. L. Leong, & A. G. Watts (Eds.), *Handbook of career development – International perspectives* (pp. 609–629). Springer.

Benešová, A., & Tupa, J. (2017). Requirements for education and qualification of people in industry 4.0. *Procedia Manufacturing, 11*, 2195–2202.

BERUFENET—Berufsinformationen einfach finden [Vocational information easy to find] https://www.berufenet.arbeitsagentur.de

Dauwalder, J.-P. (2014). From heuristics to life designing new tools for coping with complex situations. In J. Górna & D. Kukla (Eds.), *Voacational counselling – Changes and challenges on labour market* (pp. 239–248). UJD.

Dawis, R. V. (1996). The theory of work adjustment and person – Environment – Correspondence counselling. In D. Brown & Ass. (2002). *Career choice and development* (4th ed., pp. 75–120). Jossey-Bass.

Dawis, R. V., Lofquist, L. H., & Weiss, D. J. (1968). *A theory of work adjustment (A revision).* Minnesota studies in vocational rehabilitation Nr. XXIII. University of Minnesota.

Ebers, M., Heinze, C., Krügel, T., & Steinrötter, B. (2020). *Künstliche Intelligenz und Robotik – Rechtshandbuch* [Artificial intelligence and robotics – Legal handbook]. C.H.Beck oHG.

Ertelt, B.-J., & Frey, A. (2013). Interessen- und Motivationsdiagnostik in beruflichen Zusammenhängen [Interest and motivation diagnostics in vocational contexts]. In A. Frey, U. Lissmann, & B. Schwarz (Hrsg.), *Handbuch Berufspädagogische Diagnostik* [Handbook of vocational diagnostics] (S. 276–297). Beltz.

Ertelt, B.-J., Noworol, C., & Seidel, G. (2018). Job differentiation in career counseling. In A. Biela (Ed.), *European questionnaire for job analysis (EQJA) – Theoretical and methodological basis* (pp. 293–303). Peter Lang.

Europäische Kommission (2020). *European skills, competences, qualifications and occupations: ESCO annual report 2019.* Publications Office, https://data.europa.eu/doi/10.2767/740371 ESCO

Frey, A. (2008). *Kompetenzstrukturen von Studierenden in der ersten und zweiten Phase der Lehrerbildung* [Competence structures of students in the first and second phase of teacher education]. Verlag Empirische Pädagogik (VEP).

Frey, A., & Balzer, L. (2003). Soziale und methodische Kompetenzen - der Beurteilungsbogen smk: Ein Messverfahren für die Diagnose von sozialen und methodischen Kompetenzen [Social and methodological competencies – The SMK assessment sheet: A measurement procedure for the diagnosis of social and methodological competences]. *Zeitschrift Empirische Pädagogik, 17* (2), 148–175.

Frey, A., & Balzer, L. (2017). *Assessment sheet on social and methodological competences - SOMECO.* University.

Frey, A., & Ruppert, J. J. (2013). Structuring and detecting competence. In K. Beck & O. Zlatkin-Troitschanskaia (Eds.), *From diagnostics to learning success* (pp. 185–198). Sense Publishers.

Frey, A., & Ruppert, J. J. (2017). Diagnosis of transferable competences of young people in the dual vocational education – A German perspective. *Psychology, 8*(10), 1546–1569. https://doi.org/10.4236/psych.2017.810103

Frey, A., Balzer, L., & Ruppert, J. J. (2014). Transferable competences of young people with a high dropout risk in vocational training in Germany. *International Journal for Educational and Vocational Guidance, 14*, 119–134. https://doi.org/10.1007/s10775-013-9257-8

Gati, I., Levin, N., & Landman-Tal, S. (2019). Decision-making models and career guidance. In J. A. Athanasou & H. N. Perera (Eds.), *International handbook of career guidance* (2nd ed.). Springer.

Ghisla, G., Bausch, L., & Boldrini, E. (2008). CoRe – Kompetenzen-Ressourcen: Ein Modell der Curriculumentwicklung für die Berufsbildung [CoRe – Competences resources: A model of

curriculum development for vocational education and training]. *Zeitschrift für Berufs- und Wirtschaftspädagogik, 104*(3), 431–466.
Hanna, A., Gregory, C., Lewis, P. M., & Rounds, J. (2019). International career assessment using the occupational information network (O*NET). Chapter 27. In J. A. Athanasou & H. N. Perera (Eds.), *International handbook of career guidance* (2nd ed.). Springer.
Hekkert, M. P., Suurs, R. A., Negro, S. O., Kuhlmann, S., & Smits, R. E. (2007). Functions of innovation systems: A new approach for analysing technological change. *Technological Forecasting and Social Change, 74*(4), 413–432.
Hirschi, A. (2012). The career resources model: An integrative framework for career counsellors. *British Journal of Guidance & Counselling, 40*(4), 369–383. https://doi.org/10.1080/03069885.2012.700506
Hofstedt, P., & Löffler, S. (2021). Constraints. In G. Görz, U. Schmid, & T. Braun (Hrsg.), *Handbuch der Künstlichen Intelligenz* (6. Aufl.) (S. 713–754). Walter de Gruyter.
Holland, J. L. (1997). *Making vocational choices – A theory of vocational personalities and work environments* (3rd ed.). PAR.
Hutter, C., & Weber, E. (2020). Corona-Krise: die transformative Rezession [Corona crisis: Transformative recession]. *Wirtschaftsdienst, 100*, 429–431. https://doi.org/10.1007/s10273-020-2676-5
Kaiser, H. (2008). *Berufliche Handlungssituationen machen Schule* [Vocational action situations make school]. Zürich: SMB.
Korulczyk, T., & Korulczyk, N. (2018). The role of fit theories in job analysis. In A. Biela (Ed.), *European questionnaire for job analysis (EQJA) – Theoretical and methodological bases* (pp. 65–85). Peter Lang.
Krumboltz, J. D. (1996). A learning theory of career counseling. In M. Savickas & B. Walsh (Eds.), *Integrating career theory and practice* (pp. 313–360). CPP Books.
Lang-von Wins, T., & Triebel, C. (2006). *Kompetenzorientierte Laufbahnberatung* [Competence-oriented career guidance]. Springer.
Le Boterf, G. (1994). *De la Compétence. Essai sur un attracteur étrange* [On competence. An essay on a strange attractor]. Eyrolles.
Lent, R. W. (2013). Social cognitive career theory. In. St. D. Brown & R. W. Lent (Eds.), *Career development and counseling. Putting theory and research to work* (2nd ed., Chapter 5, pp. 115–146). Wiley.
Nägele, C. (2013). Arbeits- und Tätigkeitsdiagnostik [Work and activity diagnostics]. In A. Frey, U. Lissmann, & B. Schwarz (Hrsg.), *Handbuch Berufspädagogische Diagnostik* [Handbook of vocational diagnostics] (S. 384–396). Beltz.
Nota, L., & Rossier, J. (Eds.). (2015). *Handbook of life design – From practice to theory and from theory to practice*. Hogrefe Publishing.
Nota, L., Soresi, S., Di Maggio, I., Santilli, S., & Ginevra, M. C. (2020). *Sustainable development, career counselling and career education*. Springer.
OECD. (2005). *Definition and selection of competencies: Theoretical and conceptual foundations (DeSeCo). Summary of the final report "key competencies for a successful life and a well-functioning society"*. OECD Publications.
Oser, F. (1997). Standards in der Lehrerbildung [Standards in teacher education]. *Beiträge zur Lehrerbildung, 15*(2), 210–228.
Otte, R. (2019). *Künstliche Intelligenz für dummies*. Wiley-VCH.
Rentzsch, K., & Schütz, A. (2009). *Psychologische Diagnostik. Grundlagen und Anwendungsperspektiven* [Psychological diagnostics. Fundamentals and application perspectives]. Kohlhammer.
Roth, H. (1971). *Entwicklung und Erziehung: Grundlagen einer Entwicklungspädagogik* [Development and education: Foundations of developmental pedagogy]. Schroedel.
Sailmann, G. (2018). *Der Beruf. Eine Begriffsgeschichte* [The profession. A conceptual history]. Transcript Verlag.

Savickas, M. L., Nota, L., Rossier, J., Dauwalder, J.-P., Eduarda Duarte, M., Guichard, J., Soresi, S., Van Esbroeck, R., & van Vianen, A. E. M. (2009). Life designing: A paradigm for career construction in the 21st century. *Journal of Vocational Behavior, 75*(3), 239–250.

Scharnhorst, U. (2009). *Kompetenzorientierte Bildungsverordnungen* [Competency-based educational regulations]. Bundesinstitut für Berufsbildung (BIBB).

Schulz, W. E. (2014). Convergence of career development theory into a comprehensive theory and process. In J. Górna & D. Kukla (Eds.), *Voacational counselling – Changes and challenges on labour market* (pp. 73–96). UJD.

Super, D. E. (1984). Career and life development. In D. Brown & L. Brooks (Eds.), *Career choice and development* (pp. 192–234). Jossey-Bass.

Weinert, F. E. (2001). Concept of competence: A conceptual clarification. In D. S. Rychen & L. H. Salganik (Eds.), *Defining and selecting key competencies* (pp. 45–65). Hogrefe and Huber Publishers.

The manufacturer's authorised representative in the EU is Springer Nature Customer Service Centre GmbH, Europaplatz 3, 69115 Heidelberg, Germany. If you have any concerns regarding our products, please contact ProductSafety@springernature.com

Printed and bound by CPI Group (UK) Ltd, Croydon, CR0 4YY
22/09/2026
02220982-0009